DON'T FIGHT THE FLOW

following your organic path

DON'T FIGHT THE FLOW

following your organic path

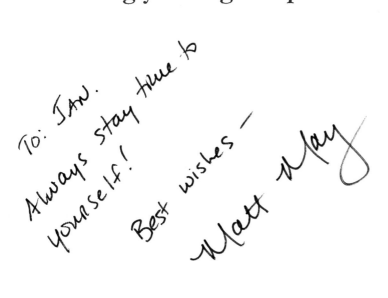

To: IAN.
Always stay true to
yourself!

Best wishes –
Matt May

MATT MAY

Printed in the United States of America

Published by Verve Central Productions

First printing 2023

For bookings, permissions, or questions, contact the author at PremierTeamBuilding.com.

Print ISBN: 9798868356704

KUDOS & SPECIAL THANKS

For designing a brilliant cover, thanks to . . .

Billy Mitchell

For proofreading, editing, & opining, thanks to . . .

Alana Graber	Mom	Rita Wells
Janis Tepper		Ladybug

For candidly sharing their stories and for willing participating in this book, thanks to the amazing interviewees . . .

Brian Curl	Daphne Herrin	Steve Paladie
Lisa Enochs	Heather Holloway	Victoria Reid
Chris Groom	Donna Horkey	Jesus Reyna
Sabrina Gore	Wei Huey	Michael Sweeney
	Gabriel Mizrahi	

For permission to reprint content under their ownership, thanks to . . .

John Breglio	Jordan Harbinger	Peter Pileski

For all those who assisted me in following my organic path, whether by offering opportunities, talking me off a ledge, supporting me in my decisions, or other, thank you!

For supporting me as I attempt to follow my organic path, thanks to . . .

Mom (Kathie May)	Dad (Mike May)	Brother (Tim May)

CONTENTS

Prologue

Chapter 1:   The Subjects

Chapter 2:   What Do You Do?

Chapter 3:   When I Grow Up

Chapter 4:   Hello, Ten-Year Old

Chapter 5:   Early Plans

Chapter 6:   Unexpected Career Moments

Chapter 7:   Unexpected Life Moments

Chapter 8:   But I Want It . . . I Think

Chapter 9:   Re-Do

Chapter 10:   Compared To My Other Half

Chapter 11:   Compared To My Parents

Chapter 12:   Success!

Chapter 13:   Separation Of Powers

Chapter 14:   If I Only Had A Heart . . . A Brain . . .

Chapter 15:   Money

Chapter 16:   Earning A Living On Your Organic Path

Chapter 17:   Don't Fight The Flow

Chapter 18:   Outside Of The Box

Chapter 19:   We're Not The Only Ones

Chapter 20:   Final Words Of Wisdom

Epilogue

PROLOGUE

I'm Type-A. I admit it. I'm a planner. I admit it. I like things organized, structured, laid out, and well-planned. When they're not, oh boy! Flexibility and patience are not my strongest suits, but I try to work on them daily. I like to think that the older I've gotten, the better I am at letting (some) things roll off my back, and not sweating the small stuff. It's still a challenge. I admit it. So, going with the natural flow is something that was not easy, but I like to think, in looking back, worth it.

My mother and father were born in the suburbs of Rochester, New York. They both worked jobs in high school: he was a lifeguard at a public pool and she, like many teenagers, was a babysitter and worked at a local bakery. They both worked their way through college, in various summer jobs, as many do. Mom became a second grade teacher at a brand-new elementary school, where my brother and I would eventually attend, and was there for ten years before I was born. While teaching, she earned her master's degree in education.

Dad's first job out of college was at a bank, where he lasted for three years. Over the next six years, he worked for four different companies, in various sales and marketing roles. Ultimately, in the final job, he grew tired of busting his butt for a company where, on top of sales, he was doing all of his own administration work, while the boss's wife, who was the shared administrative assistant, focused her energies only on her husband's sales. Having had enough, he followed his organic path and started his own advertising specialty company, alongside my mother. For the next twenty-five years, my parents operated a successful company, employing a number of family members, including my brother and I, as well as others. It was by watching their business thrive that I not only inherently developed my entrepreneurial nature, but also learned basic professional skills and concepts such as taking a proper telephone message (yeah, with pen and paper, while holding a phone between my ear and neck), and returning telephone calls within twenty-four hours. In 2001, they sold

1

the company. For five years, Dad served as a freelance salesman for the company that bought his, until the contract expired, at which point he moved to a competing company. He still writes orders today. I don't think he'll ever stop and fully "retire."

My maternal grandfather was a professional photographer for the majority of his life, a job he performed as part of the United States Marine Corps during World War II. My maternal grandmother was a waitress until she married, at which point she became a housewife and stay-at-home mom. When my mother left for college, my grandmother took a job in the cafeteria of my mother's alma mater high school.

My dad's father started out traveling the country, paying farmers to put signs for Pinkerton Tobacco Company on the sides of their barns, before starting a job selling life, health, and disability insurance with Metropolitan Life, from where he'd retire some thirty-five to forty years later. His mother worked as a secretary, commonplace for women of her time, until her first son, my uncle, was born, at which point she too became a full-time housewife and mother.

One or two "main" or "substantial" jobs within a lifetime seems crazy to me, but that's the way it was for my parents' generation, and certainly, for their parents' generation. It's different for my generation, and the ones that followed. Is company loyalty a thing anymore? Is employee loyalty? We don't stick with one company for our entire careers these days; we may even change career paths entirely. As I reflect back upon my journey to today, I see my career as a "mashup" if you will. If someone asks me in what industry I work, my usual reply is "events and entertainment," though, truth be told, if I look at the entire spectrum, it encompasses events, entertainment, education, and hospitality. That sure is a far cry from the definitiveness of "insurance salesman."

As a Type-A planner, it hasn't been easy to accept that I am not on a traditional path, and more often than I'd like to admit, I've found myself comparing where I was in my professional life, as well as what tangible items I had, with others. By the time they were age twenty-eight and thirty-two, respectively, my father and mother were married, owned a house, owned a summer cottage, had started a business, and had their first child. I had achieved none of that at either twenty-eight or thirty-two, and I compared myself to them. The comparisons continued, and I suppose still do . . . I'm in my late forties at the time of this writing. But, comparing myself to my parents, and others, is fighting the flow and not celebrating my organic path, so enough of that!

There's a quote early on in the musical *Kinky Boots,* where the protagonist is at a crossroads in his young life. His childhood friend tells him that if he is on the wrong road, he should turn back. I can't help but feel it's a profound statement, and the following anecdotes illustrate how taking the paths that life organically encourages you to take are, indeed, the "right roads."

I'm a musical theatre nerd. There aren't many musicals I don't enjoy. Two of my favorites, *Miss Saigon* and *Sunset Boulevard,* were choreographed by Bob Avian. For the longest time, I knew his work, but I didn't know "who he was."

All that changed in 2008 when I saw *Every Little Step.* I had just started my graduate work in interdisciplinary arts at Nova Southeastern University and that film had a significant impact on me. It still does, to this day. For a few years, I was an adjunct professor at Broward College and used that film in my Theatre Appreciation class, as it is such a fantastic illustration of how long it takes for a Broadway show to go up, and the struggles that actors and dancers face, daily. Immediately after my first viewing of that film, I had a huge appreciation for Bob, researching all of his work, and being embarrassed that I had known so much of it, previously, without "knowing him." From that moment forward, my admiration and adoration of him was in full force. I might've even had a little celebrity crush on him. So, you can imagine my giddiness when I had the great pleasure of meeting him, albeit briefly, in 2017. Not only was he an incredible theatrical talent, but he was ever the gentleman.

Bob passed away, suddenly, in January 2021, but fortunately, his autobiography, *Dancing Man*, was published in 2020. Now, I'm not a reader. I can usually count on one hand the number of books I read in a year. But, every once in a while, I'll come across a non-fiction book written by a professional whose work I admire and yup, I end up buying it (or asking Santa Claus for it). Such was the case with Bob's autobiography. He wraps up his book in a manner that is so fitting for what I had hoped to accomplish with this book, when he says:

> . . . and remain open to any and all influences and opportunities. When you see an open door, walk through it — find out what's on the other side.

And his final line:

> Take it from a certified late bloomer: you never know what door will open next.

Thanks, Bob!

I originally intended to write this book as a memoir, of sorts. I'm not a famous celebrity and I'm not a "guru" in any particular industry. Even if I were, I'd like to believe that I'm not nearly presumptuous enough to suppose that anyone, including my mother, wants to read a book where I tell stories from my life. I certainly don't have any interest in reliving them in my head, in order to write them. And yet, I'd like to think that maybe . . . just perhaps . . . sharing some of the stories that illustrate how I didn't fight the flow, and followed an organic, if unconventional, path might be a teensy bit useful to a reader or two. Then it hit me . . . find others who are willing to share their far-more-interesting stories!

I reached out to a number of individuals, sharing much of what you've just read, and told them how I felt somewhat like Michael Bennett, when he interviewed everyone for *A Chorus Line* . . .

> I want to tape it because what I want to do is really like an interview. It's really about examining a group of people in this society. I think that we're all pretty interesting and that all of you are pretty interesting. And I think that maybe there's a show (book) in that, somewhere, which would be called (*Don't Fight The Flow: Following Your Organic Path*).

The thirteen fantastic individuals included in this book agreed to be interviewed and asked for nothing in return. They range in age from twenty-seven to sixty-four, at the times of their interviews, and have a variety of backgrounds, upbringings, educations, career fields, and more. I asked all of them the same questions and allowed them to interpret the questions on their own. If ever I was asked for clarification, my usual response was to throw my hands up in an "I don't know" pose.

On some occasions, the interviewees started to answer a question, either in full, or in part, that I had planned to ask further along in our chat. Generally, I still asked them later on in order to get clear answers to every question.

None of the interviewees were provided with the questions in advance. Some answers were short, and some were longer. While some sentiments align strongly with others, there really are a wide variety of thoughts, opinions, and answers provided. All answers are, from my perspective, honest and sincere thoughts provided organically (pun intended), and while I don't agree with all of them, believe that they all hold great value and are worth pondering.

Sometimes the interviewees went off on what could be perceived as tangents. For the most part, I have included those thoughts as they are what came to mind at the time of the interview, have value, and bring different perspectives to the overall discussion.

Sometimes, if I felt it warranted, I asked follow-up questions. I've included them in this book. These follow-up questions should, in no way, suggest that I endorse certain interviewees more than others, or certain answers more than others. It just felt right to ask a follow-up question at the time.

Once I had all of the interviews completed, it was clear that the best way to share these interviewees' stories was to simply put their words in print. Therefore, their responses to the questions I posed are, for the most part, exactly as I received them, with the removal of vocalized thought pauses and filler words, the addition of some tense agreement here and there, and minor "cleaning" to make them read as well as they sounded, originally. I've also intentionally left their replies in a casual, speaking tone, as they said them. This sometimes results in incomplete and/or grammatically incorrect sentences, which normally would be like nails on a chalkboard to me. For the purpose of this book, I'm allowing it, in order to keep a friendly feel. They have each seen their final answers and take ownership of what you're about to read. So, truly these are their words of wisdom.

Before diving into what they have to say, please meet the baker's dozen of incredibly wonderful individuals who said "Yes," without any hesitation, and were open books (pun intended) with all of their answers, thoughts, and opinions. These biographies are as of the printing of this book. For simplicity's sake, they are showcased, as are their answers, in alphabetical order, by their last names.

CHAPTER 1: THE SUBJECTS

Brian Curl

Brian Curl is a professional performer, team-builder, teaching artist, and event host residing in Philadelphia, PA. As a multi-hyphenate, Brian found a natural fit in the world of events. His skill set includes creatively guiding event participants out of their comfort zone without them even being aware.

In late 2019, he founded daily8count.com, an online choreography education tool for theatre classrooms where he teaches *Confidence Through Choreography.* Additionally, Brian is a proud founding member of the TeachingArtistAlliance.com.

Brian never passes up an opportunity to learn new skills . . . and he never passes up the opportunity to make a dad joke!

Brian currently serves on the governing board of the Pennsylvania Thespians and he recently served as a member of the governing board of the international Educational Theatre Association.

As a lover of travel, he has been to all fifty states, across Canada, Mexico, the Caribbean, and most of western Europe.

Lisa Enochs

A *magna cum laude* graduate of UC Santa Barbara, with a double major in French Literature and Theatre, Lisa has been excelling in training, corporate entertainment, and team building for over twenty-five years.

With a strong background in performance, she is fantastic in front of a crowd and great at motivating people.

Lisa is a voice-over artist, a singer/musician, and actress who studied at The Groundlings in Los Angeles. Additionally, she studied at the University of Bordeaux for a year as an exchange student, where she sang with the regional choir, L'Ensemble d'Aquitaine.

She is a Certified Trainer in DISC and Emotional Intelligence, and enjoys creating a safe atmosphere for groups to learn new, more effective ways to communicate with one another and learn about themselves.

Lisa has designed and led workshops and events all over the world, and she especially enjoys programs that give back to the community. Her experience includes creating and delivering programs in English and French to groups ranging from eight to two thousand five hundred people. In addition to face-to-face programs, Lisa has created multiple online learning platforms for training and education.

Sabrina Lynn Gore

Sabrina Lynn Gore is an award-winning actress, singer, and director, located in South Florida. A two-time Carbonell Award nominee (*Next To Normal* and *Head Over Heels*) and a Silver Palm Award recipient (*Next To Normal*), she trained for her craft in Michigan and New York. Some of her favorite performance credits include *Othello, Diego & Drew Say I Do, Lizzie: The Musical, Precious Little, 9 To 5, Murder Ballad,* and *Much Ado About Nothing.*

As a director, she has helmed critically-acclaimed productions of *Fun Home, Hedwig And The Angry Inch, Peter And The Starcatcher,* and *Sweat.*

An Army brat, Sabrina has also consistently held down a "civilian" job, working as an Operations Manager and Executive Administrative Assistant for Fortune 500 companies and small businesses. These skills helped her start her own business, ActressesWhoCook, in 2020, which she continues to nurture and grow. Additionally, Sabrina has a passion for fitness and nutrition and is a certified NASM Nutrition Coach. She is also an ordained minister, a proud dog mom to her Aussie mix, Biscuit, a forever Pat Benatar fan, and was a former Guardian Ad Litem for Palm Beach County, Florida.

Sabrina believes in leading by example and always with humor, humility, and empathy, and believes that no job is too small no matter how "big" you get.

Chris Groom

Chris Groom is a working actor, personal trainer, screenwriter, marathon runner, teacher, voice-over artist, and author.

She worked as a public-school teacher for ten years before leaving that profession to become an actor. She has performed in various regional theatres throughout South Florida, has been seen on several television shows and short films, created a web series, and toured the country performing children's theatre.

A three-time Carbonell Award nominee (Supporting Actress in a Play for *Have I Got A Girl For You* and *Perfect Arrangement*, and as a member of the Ensemble for *Gideon's Knot*), Groom received a Silver Palm Award for her work in *Have I Got A Girl For You* and *Gideon's Knot*.

Chris started her own personal training business and taught virtual fitness classes while writing her first novel, which she published independently. That novel, *The Sword and the Spark*, received a Five Star Readers' Favorite Award, an IndieBrag B.R.A.G. Medallion, and was named an IAN Book of the Year Finalist for 2022 in both the Fantasy and First Novel Over Eighty Thousand Words Categories.

Currently, she is working on finishing her second novel and recording the audiobook for the first, while continuing to work steadily in cartoons and voice-over dubbing.

Daphne Herrin

Daphne joined the hospitality industry over thirty years ago and has enjoyed every step of her journey. She began working on the supplier side of the industry in hotels, convention centers, and a convention & visitors bureau.

Daphne is most proud of her career path as a planner as she feels this is the role she was always meant to have. She has been a one-person department where she had to work with internal non-planning team members in efforts to collaborate and successfully execute large franchise conventions. Daphne worked as a team member of a large corporation where she broadened her scope and gained undeniable knowledge from others; and most recently led a department within a corporate franchise organization where she was responsible for not only executing international meetings of all sizes, but managing, developing, and training a team of planners.

After commuting between two states for five years, she started her own meeting planning company – Herrin Hospitality. Daphne now has the pleasure of consulting with clients as an extension of their meeting planning teams where she can share her diverse industry skill set as well as her contagious passion and enthusiasm for coordinating the intricate aspects of meetings and events.

She currently resides in Atlanta with her husband and dogs.

Heather Holloway

Heather Holloway is a dynamic public speaker, voice-over artist, founder of Holloway Media Services, and host of the *Social Media Success For Professionals* podcast.

Heather has a unique energy that shines through in her work, helping entrepreneurs increase their influence and impact online.

A graduate of one of the world's premier entertainment business schools and with over two decades of experience in radio, television, and digital media, Heather leads her team of masterful content creators to produce high-performing organic social media marketing campaigns.

When not absorbed in a personal growth or marketing book, Heather seeks fun and thrills! She loves traveling, meeting new people, and gaining new perspectives. She once jumped out of an airplane, willingly, and was a contestant on *Ellen's Game Of Games*.

Heather hopes to one day host a baking championship series on the Food Network if she can stop binge-watching them first. She lives in Pennsylvania with her wife and their dog, Miley.

Donna Horkey

Donna Horkey has an extensive background in the areas of training and people development. She began her career as Director of Personnel for a Fortune 100 insurance company, and in 1988 started her company, Missing Link Consultants, Inc., having had clients from California to Maryland and everywhere in between, in both the public and private sectors. Through Missing Link Consultants, she has provided management training, organizational development, expert witness and defense litigation support, and one-on-one executive coaching services for organizations such as American Express, MTV Latin America, Sara Lee Corporation, Slim Fast Foods, Seminole Tribe of Florida, Johnson Controls, and Yamaha Motors.

She has an undergraduate degree in psychology and a master's in HR. Donna has been accredited since 1987 by the HR Certification Institute, is a certified management coach, is recognized by the State of Florida courts as an expert in Title VII, and is an award-winning HR professional.

She loves delivering interactive "toolbox" training that enables people to be more effective as soon as they get back to work!

Wei Huey

Wei Huey is proficient in cyber security and exemplifies the unstoppability of curiosity combined with willpower. From an early age, his parents, teachers, and mentors nurtured his inquisitive nature and desire to understand the whys of the world. Once combined with a college need for computer literacy, it was natural to tinker his way from his modest career beginnings in desktop support. Wei has almost 30 years of information technology experience and currently serves as a United States Department of Defense employee. He has a proven history of distilling challenges into manageable components, connecting stakeholders, and integrating processes and products to innovate solutions.

Wei loves to share his accumulated experiences. Activities such as mentoring work colleagues, organizing activities for a military-themed youth development program, and sharing vehicle repair skills with friends all feed his school-age desire to teach.

As a Washington, DC geo-bachelor, Wei enjoys flying home to St Petersburg, Florida to be with his husband, where they enjoy traveling, spending time outdoors, dining with friends, watching sunsets on the beach, and exploring spiritualities. When online, he shares his love for Florida by connecting people with people/events/resources in one of Tampa Bay's largest LGBTQ-focused social media groups.

Gabriel Mizrahi

Gabriel Mizrahi is a filmmaker and podcaster based in Los Angeles.

He has written and set up several film and TV projects over the years, including the romantic comedy *Give Or Take*, with Suzanne Farwell directing and Michelle Pfeiffer attached to star. His latest romantic comedy, *Otherwise Engaged*, is also in development at Resonate Entertainment, with Colin Firth and Jack Whitehall attached to star.

He's also the co-creator of *Accelerator*, a TV drama about the start-up world developed with CBS Studios, which led to a Google-Black List Computer Science Fellowship. *Beside Ourselves*, a romantic drama, was a Top Ten finalist in the 2018 Academy Nicholl Fellowships.

Gabriel has also been hired to rewrite and consult on several projects, including *Roo!*, based on the true story of the first mixed-breed dog to win in agility at Westminster, which is currently in development at Netflix.

In addition to filmmaking, Gabriel co-hosts the Top Ten Apple Podcast *The Jordan Harbinger Show*, voted Apple's Best of 2018 with over fifteen million downloads per month.

Before Gabriel began writing, he worked as a management consultant at Deloitte and Cirque du Soleil®. He graduated from UCLA with a B.A. in Philosophy and a minor in English.

Steve Paladie

Steve Paladie is a Las Vegas designer, artist, manager, and business owner.

As Creative Director and Scenic Designer for his company, Louder Than Silence Productions, he has worked on projects for every major Las Vegas Strip property. Recently engaged as Scenic Designer for the Usher Residency's Immersive Experience at the Colosseum at Caesars Palace, he had the pleasure of working directly with Usher to realize this groundbreaking theatrical experience. Additionally, directly involved in the creative and design process for Las Vegas residency announcements for Gwen, Britney, and Mariah, and event activations for Post Malone's *Posty Fest*, his design portfolio is wide-ranging in concept and scope.

Working as Creative Director with local Vegas producers, and Lead Designer for Sin City Scenic fabrication and design shop, clients have included Insomniac/EDC, Adele, Cirque du Soleil®, TikTok®, Caesars Entertainment®, MGM Resorts, and LVCVA.

Traditional theatrical scenic design credits include the 20th Anniversary production and national tour of *Smokey Joe's Café* for the Gateway Playhouse in New York, numerous local productions, and several cruise ship productions, including the international debut of *Liverpool Knights* for Celebrity Cruises.

Victoria Reid

Victoria Reid has been planning major events for corporations, entrepreneurs, and organizations for more than twenty years. She was named "Meeting Planner of the Year" by the Kentucky Bluegrass Chapter of Meeting Professionals International in 2022.

She has led events including small events, conferences, city-wide events, galas, trade shows, rallies, and community festivals for thousands of attendees.

A certified yoga instructor, after experiencing her own extreme burnout, she started to see the event world through a different lens that focused on wellness. Focusing on her career, she developed a passion for her personal well-being and those around her. Spending hours observing, researching, learning, and implementing changes gives her the edge to design events for the well-being of the individual, not the masses. As a result, she formed EventWell Consulting® in 2021.

Victoria has a vision for events that includes movement, takes into consideration how people consume and digest information, and acknowledges the differences of individuals. By acknowledging the uniqueness of each individual participating in an event, from dietary requirements to religious observances, her company, EventWell Consulting® allows all event participants to leave feeling seen, heard, and happy.

Jesus Reyna

Jesus Reyna was born in Madrid, Spain after his family fled communist Cuba. At the age of two, they moved to South Florida where he was raised and still lives today.

Jesus is a filmmaker and actor. He's produced two successful award-winning shorts with his filmmaking partner Deana Williams. "Tracks" was featured in over twenty film festivals around the world and "Torn" has won best short in Miami and garnered them an award for best new filmmakers in Tampa.

He has also appeared on several South Florida stages in productions of *Bent* (Captain), *Porgy & Bess* (Detective), and *Diego & Drew Say I Do* (Chauncey).

Jesus is also the creator of the successfully-funded movie trivia game, *Name Dropping: The Frustratingly Fun Movie Card Game*. In the fall of 2023, an online game show version of the game, featuring teams of two, competing for cash and prizes, is scheduled to be released.

Michael Sweeney

A native of Enfield, Connecticut, Michael Sweeney learned the game of golf from his father, with whom he played at the local nine-hole course. An all-state selection his senior year of high school, he continued to play annually, each summer.

Not one for the college scene, Michael worked at a bowling alley during the winter months, perfecting his game with the pins, while golfing during the summer. Additionally, he worked part-time at an equestrian club. For four years, post-high school, this was his routine.

In 2018, Michael left the Northeast and its limited golf season, and moved to Florida to pursue his dream of being a professional golfer.

Additionally, he performed as a rapper, using the stage name MikeyD860. Along with fellow rapper MackleMusic860, he has multiple songs on Spotify.

CHAPTER 2: WHAT DO YOU DO?

When I posed this question, I posed it exactly as written, below. I will preface this with the fact that I provided all of the interviewees with the prologue of this book, more or less as it stands now, so their minds likely were in a "when it comes to work" mode. Nonetheless, every one of them answered this first question in regard to their careers or work. When I brought this up to Lisa, after she answered, her reply was that we inherently answer that way and that "for work" is implied in the question. Jesus brought up this implication on his own, and it prompted a longer "identity" discussion. I find it interesting that so many of us automatically "go there" when asked the question, and yet, I'd like to believe that our work, no matter how much we enjoy it, flourish from it, and relish in it, is hardly the definition of "what we do." It's something to ponder, I suppose. With that . . .

When people ask you what you do, how do you respond?

Brian
Generally with a long pause where I ask, which route do we want to go? I always talk about the fact that my degree is in musical theatre. Right out of college, I performed on the road for four years as an actor. I did the whole New York thing for seventeen years and then realized that I was good at the educational circuit, so I got more involved teaching at conferences, schools, and doing masterclasses. But I think at the end of the day, I'm a professional networker. I'm a professional "let's figure it out as we go" guy. If you want to give me a chance, I'm going to follow through. I circle back, usually to the whole R. Erin Craig (a theatrical producer) situation and how I was an actor in the show, and I befriended Erin in a producer-actor relationship, and then she realized that there was more to me than simply performing, and that there was a lot that I could bring to the table as the educational director of *Austen's Pride: A New Musical*. But, I think the best way now to answer that question is that I am a director, choreographer, producer, caterer, waiter, dog walker, nanny . . .

welcome to the world of having a degree in musical theatre. I also own my own small business and I am a professional uncle to the best nieces and nephews out there.

You didn't say facilitator and M.C. for teambuilding.

Well, see, again, there are so many different routes that I could take with this question. Yes, that is something else I do as well. I think that a lot of times when I am asked this question, I have to compartmentalize it dependent on who the person is, because I don't want to get into a situation where I'm giving out every answer in my life and they're thinking, "Oh, so you have no idea what you want to do," even though I know exactly what I want to do. What I want to do is figure it out day by day. What I want to do is make money doing things where I don't have to sit behind a desk. What I want to do is be able to explore the world and get paid and have a good time. And honestly, I think at the end of the day, I don't want to work either in a company, or with somebody, that I don't enjoy. And what I came to realize very quickly when it comes to work is . . . one of my very first jobs was developing photos at the one-hour photo mat at Eckerd Drugs in Medford, New Jersey. I worked there for two days because it was a terrible job with zero training. There I was at sixteen years old, ruining all of these people's photos because nobody had really trained me on how to do the thing with the actual film. Yes, I'm older than you think I am. I thought "I don't want to do this." And if I don't want to do it, I'm not going to do it. There you go. There's your sound bite.

Lisa
That's a great question, because up until recently, I would have responded, "I do corporate training and team building all over the world," even though there are so many other things that I do. Now I lead with, "I work for a seasonal ice rink company, and I also do professional development and team building."

21

Sabrina
It varies depending on who I'm talking to and why they're asking me. If I'm talking to someone outside of theatre, I talk about my day job, probably. And then I mention the theatre and nutrition certification as things that I do in addition to my day job. But if I'm talking to someone involved in theatre, I'll probably focus more on the fact that I'm a director, and an actor, and a singer. And I used to be a producer. And then I'll talk about my day job or my nutrition thing, or if I'm talking to someone in the fitness industry, I'll talk about the nutrition thing first. I think it really depends on who I'm talking to and what arena I'm talking to them in. Because nine times out of ten, if somebody is asking you what you do, it's usually a pretty casual conversation . . . they're trying to get to know you. So I just kind of cater my answer based on where I am and what the topic of normal conversation might be. But I usually talk about all of the things that I do and then let the conversation go from there.

Chris
Oh, wow. Okay. The usual answer I give is, "I'm an actor, personal trainer, and author." That's my answer.

Daphne
I typically start off by saying that I'm a meeting planner, which . . . ironically people automatically think, "Oh, you do parties," or, "You do weddings," and I have to clarify and say, "I'm a *meeting planner*, not an *event planner.*" And I say that specifically because I plan meetings to their fullest. I work from the beginning to the end with outlining the strategy, the budget, and the agenda for *meetings*, and then plan all the details that support that for the audience, and for the stakeholder's experience, and I then execute accordingly. I also do incentive meetings, but I still think of that in the meeting realm versus event planning or wedding planning.

Heather
That's exactly how I respond. "What do I do?" Okay, so as a money-

generating business, I am a social media marketing agency owner. That is my primary area of business. And what that entails is social media marketing for businesses. So we create content, publish content management, manage content, run campaigns, and manage ad campaigns.

Okay, but what do I do? It's not only that. I mean, yes, I do marketing, but I'm also a transitional coach or a life coach. Pure joy and enthusiasm . . . I bring that to the table. And just recently, I became a voice-over artist. So I guess when people ask me that question, a fair answer would be, "I'm a multi-passionate entrepreneur who happens to run a social media marketing agency, who loves helping people unlock their true potential, who loves to read out loud."

Donna
Well, the practiced elevator speech is that I have a management consulting business. My background is all HR. I do standard things like management and leadership development training and I'm a certified executive coach. But my true bailiwick is that I have an expertise in sexual harassment and employment discrimination and I have extensive credentials that most HR consultants don't have in that area. And under that umbrella, I do investigations, training, behavioral counseling, and expert witness work. That's my elevator speech.

Do you have anything that you would add to that if it were a certain setting, or with certain individuals?

Yes. If I were trying to promote that last piece of business, the harassment and discrimination work, which quite honestly, is the most lucrative chunk of my business . . . I charge more for those services because it requires a much higher level of skill and expertise than training and general HR consulting. So that's the piece I promote the most, because that's where I can make the most money. And it's way more fun! It's the most fun because it's the juicy, interesting stuff that people like to hear about. So if I were in front of people who could potentially hire me to do that, I would elaborate on that and explain that the investigation work is not just being able to ask questions. In fact, that's the least of it. It's about reading the people who are answering the questions: what they say, what they don't say, how they say it. And really my job in that setting is to gather information, separate the facts from the fiction, the facts from the opinion, and drill down to exactly what happened, determine if something happened that was inappropriate or unlawful, and then make recommendations about how to resolve it going forward.

And then, of course, the classroom training . . . that's pretty straightforward. The behavioral counseling, because I have a psych background also, I do one-on-one behavioral counseling with people who have been accused of bad behavior at work. Sometimes we call it the "come to Jesus" meeting. So my job is to help them understand the error of their ways and help them replace those bad behaviors with more acceptable behaviors in the workplace. And at the same time, I'm assessing whether I think they get it and they'll walk the straight and narrow, or if they're just a pig dog and given another opportunity, they'll do it again. And then I provide a professional opinion letter that says either this person doesn't want to lose his or her job, she gets it, she's going to do what she needs to do, or this guy's a pig dog and he knew exactly what he was doing, and he knew it was wrong, and he'll do it again, and you should cut your losses now.

And then there's the expert witness work on the back end, where I'm looking at depositions and trying to poke holes in other people's testimony and such. So I would elaborate in that way about that work.

And I can do the same about the value of coaching . . . the fact that I'm a certified executive coach, that I've been doing that for literally thirty years this year. I got certified in 1993, so I can talk about that.

I also do a lot of performance management work helping organizations overhaul their performance appraisal tools, coming up with a whole performance management system that includes training the supervisors and managers on how to give constructive feedback in a meaningful way, how to document performance issues so that when they've had enough of someone and they go to HR and say, "You have to let me fire this person," HR will say "Okay" because they've handed in the stack of documentation necessary to justify it.

I would focus on the piece of business that I think the person in front of me would be most interested in hearing about, or that they've identified for me. I learned a long time ago not to tell the whole story in one sitting because then you just bore people and they tune you out. So I try to do what I call sinking the hook . . . sink the hook and get them interested and then down the road, get the opportunity to tell them about all the other things you do when the time is right. And that timing is really important.

Wei

The first thing I say is that I work in cybersecurity. I basically work to secure our information systems across the entire United States. What that usually entails is asking the system owners a bunch of questions, figuring out what it is their systems do, how they're resourced to handle the information, or the processes that they're charged with, and work with them to find a happy medium for what's secure versus what still needs work in order to meet the requirements that they have.

There's a common perception that in order to be secure, it must be absolutely locked down, by the book. The reality is that most of us who have been working in this field for a long time realize that if you do that, you actually can't use the system. So, it's just finding that middle ground where it's secure enough and it's still usable.

Gabriel

I've been asking myself that same question recently. What do I put on my Instagram bio? I guess I would say filmmaker and podcaster, but it's taken me quite a while to just say those two things and mean them honestly.

Steve

That is generally a hard thing to define or answer. I usually start by saying, "Well, currently I'm a scenic designer and a theatrical production manager." And that usually is enough to have people say, "Oh, okay," and move on from there. I don't do any one thing, so I always find myself kind of stepping over myself trying to answer that.

Victoria

Oh, wow. That's a loaded question, to be honest with you, because I do so many things. Over my lifetime I've evolved into several people. So honestly, I am a twenty-five-year event professional. I have planned events for corporations, motorcycle rallies, church festivals, citywide events, you name it. I have done it all. I am also a passionate person when it comes to individuals' wellbeing. So with that being said, after I left my corporate job, I became a registered yoga instructor and have now combined those two roles into a company called Eventwell Consulting®.

Jesus

The easy response is to say, "Oh, I work at a museum and I work at the gift shop, but I'm also a docent." And then I go into describing what I actually do at the museum and how I got the job. But then I'll say, "I'm also a filmmaker and an actor." That's where they say "Oh, that's your hobby, right? Your job is the museum, and your hobby's that thing." That's a hard question for me to answer. To pay the bills, I work at a museum, to facilitate what I really want to do. The museum allows me to have a roof over my head, food in my mouth, clothes on my back. It gives me resources that then allow me to do the things that I'm truly passionate about. I don't want to complicate things for people, so that's why I don't say a filmmaker or actor, because then it ultimately leads back to, "Oh, how do you make money as a working actor, and how much money do you make, and do you have health insurance?" I'm not Meryl Streep over here making a movie every year for a million dollars. So, I will answer by saying that I work at a museum, I'm a docent, and I work in the gift shop, but my goal, ultimately, is to make a living as a filmmaker or as a creative.

And then the filmmaker answer gets me questions like, "Oh, are you a director? Are you an actor? Are you a writer?" I say, "Well, I'm mostly an actor. I don't know that I'd be a very good director, and I don't think I'm a very good writer because I don't have the training for that." So then they'll say, "Well, what do you mean by creative?" I'm an idea person. I remember a friend told me this a long time ago. He said, "You're an idea guy. You have a million ideas. And most of them are really good. It's just you don't have the training to know how to take these ideas and turn them into something." So when I elaborate on being a creative, I say, "I invented a movie trivia game" and they'll reply, "Oh, wait a minute. So you are also an inventor?" And I reply, "Well, I'm not Thomas Edison, not like that, but I made a movie game." The best way to answer that question, I think now that we're talking about this, is when people ask me what I do, is to just say, "I'm a creative," . . . however you define that . . . or however I define it.

Michael

I tell them I am a professional golfer and then they usually respond with something like, "Are you playing on the PGA Tour?" I reply, "No," and then I kind of give them the whole breakdown. I usually use the comparison to minor league baseball, where they have Single-A, Double-A, Triple-A, and where I stand in relation to that, in the PGA. Then people usually respond with, "OK, how do you afford to do all that?" I give them different sorts of answers, depending on how I'm affording to do it at that given time.

How did you answer that five or ten years ago?

Brian

Ten years ago, I said "I'm an actor slash bartender slash waiter slash caterer - all of the things that only focus on the life of being an actor." And I like to think I was pretty successful. No, I didn't do Broadway, but I did off-Broadway, off-off-Broadway, regional theatre, dinner theatre, and performed in forty-nine of the fifty states. I did it pretty successfully. I would also bide my time teaching at conferences once in a while.

Five years ago, I said "I am a professional workshop facilitator slash masterclass presenter slash dabbler in acting, getting more heavily involved in choreography." I kind of transitioned more from the actor side to the creative team side, which I thoroughly enjoy. There are pluses and minuses to both sides, but where I am in my life and in my career, I love being on the creative side more because I get to guide the fun. I get to direct the fun. I get to choreograph the fun. I like having fun.

You get to tell people "No" and not be told "No."

Well, I think I'm told "No" a lot, but I think part of it is not even telling people "No," but it's guiding people to discover other options. I work a lot in the high school circuit and working with high school kids . . . they think there's only one way to do it and that's it. When I choreograph and I give them something to do and it doesn't work, that's on me. But if I ask them to help come up with something, create something, they look at me like I'm crazy because that fear of failure takes over. And probably ten years ago, yes, that was also true for me . . . fear of failure prevented me from actually doing anything. And then a very good friend of mine, her name is Jeni Incontro, she got her degree in musical theatre, and she's very smart, so she ended up going to the Wharton Business School and now has her M.B.A. in Business. And as I was trying to develop my business, the daily8count.com, she said, "Just launch something. Just do something, create something. Stop sitting there worrying that it's not perfect, because you could spend all this time and energy and money developing the "perfect thing" that never becomes the perfect thing, and you've wasted research and development time. The best stage of research and development is to launch something, figure out what works, or doesn't work, and pivot right away, as opposed to having to develop and insert time and money and energy for years and months and days." So I was happy I did that. That was good advice that I needed to get kicked in the head with.

Lisa

Five years ago, I had a lot more going on . . . disparate jobs, so I would have said, "I do corporate training and team building, I do murder mystery dinner theatre, and I have a trio that I perform music with." Ten years ago, I would have said "I'm a performer and corporate trainer," as I was doing a lot of voice-over work back then, a lot of animé work, that was so much fun, and the murder mystery dinner theatre. It was about that time that I started doing the corporate training. So, that would have been new for me, but probably training and team building and performing corporate improv shows. I don't think I was doing musical theatre at that point, anymore. So that would probably be what I would have said.

Sabrina

Five years ago, I said I was an actor because that's all I was doing at the time . . . that and I had my day job. But I didn't really talk about my day job because I didn't really like it that much. It was kind of boring. So I was an actor five years ago.

Chris

Five years ago, I was an actor. That was it.

How do you feel about the change in your answer over five years?

I'm doing things I never thought that I would be doing. Five years ago, I never imagined that I'd be a personal trainer. And I certainly did not think that I would have a published book out in circulation. So those are two huge steps for me. The personal training is a huge responsibility in terms of the clients and how I'm helping them. And then the authorship is really just . . . I've been writing since I was eight. So to finally actually have made the step of taking that hobby and turning it into something that I've actually shared with complete and total strangers is something that I would never have expected in my life. So it's just added to the acting, which has decreased in the amount of work that I'm doing. I'm primarily focused on voice-over acting. I'm not doing stage work. I'm doing occasional commercial work. So it's just been this interesting shift in the balance.

Daphne

Five years ago would have been the same answer for me. I've always been in the meeting planning arena. I have never ventured or detoured from knowing that I wanted to be a meeting planner and knowing that I enjoyed every aspect of meeting planning to its fullest. So I've been pretty targeted with my role, my position, my preference or what I like to do. Now, I have accumulated a few different niches that have determined the portions of meeting planning I prefer the most.

In my past world, more than ten years ago, I led a department, so I had to be all-encompassing with meeting planning. But I've always focused on meeting planning. I've dabbled in wedding planning, and I've never done events because I just don't enjoy them. I don't do golf tournaments. I don't do awards dinners. It's never been my area of excitement or enjoyment.

So when you said in your past world, more than ten years ago, you led a team, was that at a company?

Yes. In my last corporate job I led a team of meeting planners. I was the head of the meeting planning department and we did several different types of meetings and events. It's different when you're an independent planner than when you work for a company. I had to do whatever I had to do as a meeting planner, whatever that meant. Sometimes the requirements were more of a social nature, or a fundraiser, or hosting events at the CEO's home. It was a little bit over-encompassing of everything you can think of in the hospitality realm of meeting planning. But I still always categorized myself as a meeting planner, pretty specifically.

What prompted you to leave the company and go off on your own?

Oh, that's a good one. I loved corporate America. I always worked in corporate America. I started off in the hotel world, worked for a convention and visitors bureau for a time, a convention center, and then I moved towards the meeting planning side, which I did intentionally. I knew I wanted to be a meeting planner when I worked in hotels. I think I enjoyed the stability of corporations. I enjoyed the fact that while you may work more hours than you were getting paid for in your mind, or even on paper, it was the stability of "I had a job, I did what I had to do, I knew who I was doing it for." I worked for a company and I enjoyed that.

I'd never had an entrepreneurial spirit. That's just not my thing. I didn't grow up with a lot of people in my world that were entrepreneurs, so it was nothing I was very familiar with, as a person, to know the woes, the goals, the greatness, the negatives, the pros and cons of being an entrepreneur. However, when I left my last corporation, I did it out of a personal desire. I did it because at that time I was commuting. I lived in Atlanta, but I was working in Louisville, Kentucky, and I made that choice. That was a personal choice.

Let me back up. When I lived in Nashville, I got a corporate job at Home Depot in Atlanta, which moved my husband and I there. Great . . . perfect timing . . . great next step for me, and purposely I looked for work in Atlanta, because I wanted to be closer to family. My family, and my husband's family, are all in the southeast. So that worked out for us. Then following that, I got laid off in the 2008 timeframe, when the world just tanked, financially. So for about five months, I created and worked my LLC with the idea of, "Okay, maybe I'll do some work on my own." And I was blessed to get something quickly, and went to my next corporate job within five months, and that one was in Louisville, Kentucky. So that's where the next opportunity was. It was the perfect opportunity because that was the opportunity to lead a team at an international company . . . all the things that I thought were great for my next path. My husband and I had just moved to Atlanta two years prior, loved where we lived . . . new home, the dogs were settled, everything was good, and we were not moving again. So I made the decision . . . we made the decision . . . for me to go back and forth and to commute. So I got a place in Louisville, and I had my home in Atlanta. For five years I went back and forth and it worked. It allowed me to put all of my energy when I was in Louisville into that corporation and do that work. But then came the time where I was exhausted, and tired of going back and forth, and after five years I made the choice to resign. I had to figure out what was next.

So fast forward, I looked for another corporate job, and then I just realized that I had this LLC that I created when I didn't know what I was doing. I decided to talk to my ten friends who do things on their own . . . find out how they did it, what they did, what they said, and I just started working it. I've always been in sales. I'm a natural salesperson. I have the drive. Well, I hate sales, but I know how to do it. So it was easy enough for me to anticipate or think through how to sell myself. And that's what I worked towards doing in this entrepreneur fashion . . . to figure out how to find people that would want to work with me and that I could work with. That's how it all morphed into me now doing it on my own. It's nine years now that I've been independent and I love it. I would never turn back. It's been hard. It's been a challenge, but it's what's meant for me in my life.

Heather
Well, my agency just turned five, so five years ago, I was exiting a role as a public speaker. I got to use my voice. I loved it. It was my jam. I thought it would be the last company I would ever work for because I thought it was that. It turned out the ownership wasn't so hot. So five

years ago, what did I do? I would've said "I'm a social media marketing agency owner." The funny part is that girl, versus today's social media marketing agency owner, is totally different.

Do you want to elaborate on how you're totally different or just leave it at that?

Well, when I first got into it five years ago, and people asked what I did, I said, "I'm a social media marketing agency owner." What that consisted of was really a content creator. I came from television and radio, so I knew how to write advertising copy and either put a picture in front of it or a video in front of it. And I thought that was all social media was . . . just doing that over and over again. Well, I didn't realize really what the marketing aspect of it was. Before, when I was an employee, it was dictated . . . this is what we need to sell. And the strategy was handed to us. When you're the agency owner, you don't have a director over top of you telling you what to do. So the marketing and the strategy piece sort of was missing. Now, fast forward five years . . . I've trained, I'm now training people, I have skin in the game. I have the experience you need to really give yourself that expert title and that marketer title. So two very different places in my business.

Donna

Same answer. The scope of my work has not changed, and I will tell you that I think that one of the reasons I have survived in the consulting business for so long, and been successful in it for so long, is because I don't try to be everything to everybody. And that's a very common mistake that I see others make who say "I'm going into consulting," and three or five years later they're back in a corporate HR job because they couldn't make it. You can't charge a lot of money because you know a little about a lot of things. You only can charge big money when you know a lot about a couple of things. That's what makes you an expert. So no, I haven't changed the scope of my practice in a really long time.

Wei
Five years ago I was in cybersecurity. Ten years ago, it was different. I was more on the system admin side of things. I wasn't in cybersecurity then.

I actually worked my way up from a help desk to where I am today. Back in my help desk days, being a person with a literature background, it was pretty hard to actually break into I.T. Yes, my educational background is in literature. The challenge of breaking into I.T. really didn't stop until about ten years ago. When interviewing for work in the I.T. field, typically, the first question I would be asked was, "What makes you think you can actually do I.T. work?"

So being somebody who was more of an I.T. hobbyist, without really having boundaries, I was able to explore the I.T. field, computer systems, operating systems, and applications on my own, unrestricted, though still bound by laws, and that actually provided a very healthy learning environment for me to grow and to get to where I am today. I was afforded a lot of opportunities by really good mentors, and really good bosses who recognized my analytic background and my ability to distill problems and processes into smaller pieces for ingestion, and to figure out what actually made sense.

So, from there, I went into system administration where I'm literally the person who's taking this piece of hardware, and this application, and merging it into something that an end user is actually interfacing with. I think that really helped mold me, combined with the help desk experience, into the service-oriented person I am. And yet, having grown in I.T. as a career really helped give me that insight to go from soup to nuts, building something good, securing it, and moving forward.

Gabriel
Five years ago I would have said "screenwriter," and gotten very sweaty about it.

Why would you have gotten sweaty?

Because screenwriting for me has been a slow, long road, and even though I've been paid for my writing, and I've set up a couple of movies, and I got hired to rewrite a movie . . . it was more than just a dream, in terms of the identity, or how you identify yourself in the world as "this is my job." Screenwriting is a very theoretical role. You're writing a blueprint for a movie. You're not actually making the movie. So, I was definitely a screenwriter, but I had no produced credits and everything felt so abstract and theoretical that it always came with a little bit of, "Am I really doing that thing, or is that just the word for the thing I hope to be doing?" I guess it was somewhere in the middle, but that's why I would get a little uncomfortable. Anyway, now it's easier because I've made something. I guess I'm a podcaster too, so I guess I can say that now.

Steve
Well, ten years ago, I would have said that I was a theatrical company manager, and that was probably a little more definable in terms of what my day-to-day job was, at the time. And, maybe that actually goes back even further than ten years. It's probably been ten or fifteen years that I've been in this morphing kind of career path.

Do you have any feelings about having been a "manager" and now being a "designer"?

There was a moment in time where I kind of made a very conscious decision to get where I am today . . . not specifically as far as a job title is concerned, as the term has always been less important to me than what it is I'm doing. Everything that I've ever done has built up to what I'm currently doing.

Years ago, I had a really good friend who was a box office manager at the Minnesota Opera. I was on medical leave from my then job running a copy center in downtown Minneapolis, because I had back surgery, so I was out for a little while. He called one day and said,

"Hey, I've got season subscriptions coming in. Do you want to come in and help me sort these out?" I said, "Yeah, absolutely. That'll be fun." I didn't have an entertainment background, or theatrical background. I was in one musical when I was in high school. We did *Annie Get Your Gun* and I played Pawnee Bill. At one point early on in the rehearsal period, the director/teacher called me aside and said, "Hey, Steve, listen, I think we're going to go ahead and just have you speak your lines and not sing them." And I thought, "Oh, okay. So I guess acting and singing obviously aren't for me."

So I went with my buddy into the opera building, in the warehouse district in downtown Minneapolis, one morning. It was this brick building and it was just kind of cool. We walked in, and everyone there was in jeans, and had a casual attitude, and it was just an amazing environment. They had a cat who lived in the offices. I literally knew at that moment that this is what I wanted to do. This is what I wanted to do for the rest of my life. I had never had any kind of an epiphany like that. I tell that story because literally from that moment, everything that I've done professionally has been building on what that moment was. I didn't say, "Oh, I want to be a whatever the job title" was. It was just the environment that I wanted to be in. It fit and it felt right and it just . . . it settled.

So everything I've done has kind of piggybacked on what I've just finished. I never had any specific goal in mind. Again, like I said, I never thought, "Oh, I want to be a producer," or, "I want to be a scenic designer, a company manager or whatever." It's more a mindset of, "Oh, that's kind of cool. I enjoy doing this," or, "I learned something new." And so I kind of follow it that way without any preconceived expectations.

Victoria
I'm an event planner, and on the side, if somebody wanted to really get to know me, I'd say I do yoga here or there. I hike mountains here or there.

36

Jesus
I worked for a college. I worked in the equipment room for a film school. I was the assistant manager and I wasn't acting and making movies back then. I was just working at the school. For me, when people ask me, "What do you do," I just assume they mean work, what you get paid for, like, "Oh, I'm a therapist or I'm a teacher, I'm a so and so."

Why do you think people automatically go to that mindset for the question "what do you do?"

I don't know. I think it's a societal thing. I think, first of all, a lot of it is small talk. I don't know why anybody should care what anybody else does. Whenever I ask people that question, what I get is, "I'm a therapist," or, "I'm a model," or, "I work for a cigar company," or, "I work in a ministry of services," or whatever. So that's how I answer the question, because I think that's what they mean. I feel like if I was to say to them, "Oh, I'm an actor," they'll reply, "Oh, have I seen you in anything?"

Okay, here's an interesting story . . . years and years ago when I was working at the college in the equipment room at the film school, I remember this guy said something that was really hurtful. I was moving a lot of boxes. It was a lot of manual labor. And we were chatting and he asked me, "Well, what do you do?" I said, "I'm an actor." He said, "Oh, an actor who moves boxes?" And I thought, okay, all right, you're not wrong. At that point, I wasn't a paid actor. So he was making it seem like if you're a musician, then you can only call yourself a musician if you make a living as a musician. You can only call yourself an actor if you make a living as an actor. If you're not making a living as an actor, if you're not supporting yourself, then you can say, "I act," or, "I consider myself an actor," or, "I want to be an actor," but you can't really call yourself an actor because then what are you doing here, lugging boxes, if you're an actor? I kind of understood where he was coming from, but what I ended up saying to him was, "Yeah, but whether I'm moving boxes or whether I'm

37

working wherever, I'm still an actor at heart. That's what I want to do."

When I watch films, the main thing I focus on is the performances. I love theatre because I love performance. I love reading about actors' lives and the work that they do. But I kind of understood what he said. And I think that always stuck with me.

I just did a podcast recently where they were interviewing me. We were playing *Name Dropping*, the movie trivia game I created, during the podcast, and I remember the woman, who was the host, said, "Jesus, are you an actor?" And I said, "Oh, yes, I am." She said, "Oh, I saw you in *The Short and Short Of It* with my friend, Brooklyn." So, it was nice to be recognized, to know that somebody came to see a show, but I don't know . . . I don't know if there's shame or if I'm embarrassed because I feel like if I say, "Oh, I'm an actor, an inventor, and a filmmaker," people think "Okay, show me your work." "Well, I produced two short films. Here they are," and I can show them to people. And then they might say, "Oh yeah, but that was written and directed by your best friend. You just co-produced it. You were the producer. Oh, you acted in this other one, but it was a small part. I thought when you said actor you meant a big, known one." And no one's ever said that to me because even when I tell people I'm an actor, they say, "That's cool. What have you done?" And I tell them I did this show or I did this movie, and they reply, "Oh, that's awesome. Can you show it to me?" No one's judgmental in that way. It's just something in my own head. It's like that joke . . . "you're an actor? What restaurant do you work at?" That's how I feel. I don't know if that's shame that I have or if I still have that guy's comments in my head or what. I feel like I don't have the authority to say I'm an actor unless I'm making a living at it. Matthew McConaughey is an actor. Audra McDonald is an actor. I'm a guy who works at a museum who likes to act. I'm still an actor because that's what I'm doing, but in terms of work . . . yes, it's work, but it's not . . . now saying it, I feel kind of dumb because it's like, wait, if you're in a show and you're acting, aren't you an actor? Yes. So why would you say "No"? I guess it's my thought process that I'm not an actor the way someone is a therapist. If I ask someone what he does and he says, "Oh I'm a therapist. What do you do?" my reply is going to be, "Oh, I work at a museum," because from that I can show a paycheck. I can show the money that I make. I can show that it sustains me. I can show that I pay bills with that.

My family is from Cuba . . . my sisters, my parents, my uncles, my aunts. When my parents left Cuba, they went to Spain and I was born in Spain, and I came here to the States when I was two. So if you want to talk about identity . . . I grew up in a Cuban home, so the way that I speak Spanish is very Cuban. I have very Cuban idiosyncratic behaviors, but they're from forty or fifty years ago because they come from my parents. So an eighteen-year-old Cuban would look at me and say, "Oh, you're an old Cuban. You're like a Cuban from the 1940s and 1950s because we don't use those expressions anymore." So growing up, I would say "I'm Cuban." But then when I would meet actual Cubans from the island, that weren't my family or people that I knew growing up, they would say . . .

"Well, what part of Cuba are you from?"

And I'd say, "Oh, I wasn't actually born in Cuba."

"Oh, so you're not Cuban."

"Okay, well, then I'm American."

"Were you born here?"

"No."

"You're not American. Where were you born?"

"Well, I was born in Spain."

"Well, you're Spanish."

But then if I spoke to a Spanish person, they'd say, "Well, if you're Spanish, why do you sound Cuban?"

And then if I spoke to an American, they'd say, "Yes, yes, you're American, but your name is Jesus (pronounced hey, Zeus). So where are you from?"

I felt like I couldn't fit in anywhere. I couldn't fit in with the Cuban kids who didn't consider me Cuban, because you had to be born there, even if you left when you were six months old. Even then, at least you're Cuban.

Another conversation I had was when I asked . . .

"If you left when you were six months old and you were raised in Australia, aren't you Australian?"

"No, you are where you're born."

"But even if you left when you were really young and you had no influence from that birthplace culture?"

So I guess maybe that relates to the reply of acting where yes, I consider myself an actor, but if I were to talk to a real working actor, they would say, "Oh, honey, no, you're not an actor like me. You have to be born on the stage." So, I don't know. Maybe it's connected.

How do you feel about everything you just said? I'm bunching it all up, here . . . how do you feel about a reply of, "Oh, I work in arts and entertainment." Everything you said funnels into that. Between the museum to your stage work to your film work to creating the game and everything.

Mhm. Yeah. That is technically what I do. Yeah. That would be better if I said I worked in arts and entertainment.

It doesn't have to be better.

No, but it is. It does encompass everything. The game isn't acting, but it relates to acting in that it's about movies and actors' names and it's entertainment. So yeah, I could say I work in arts and entertainment. I work in the entertainment business, which I have. I've been a P.A. and I worked on film sets and such.

I don't know why I'm so hesitant to . . . sometimes I don't know if this even relates, but sometimes I just don't feel like I'm good enough. I'm not a good enough actor. I'm not a good enough writer. I'm not a good enough director. I don't know. It's weird. I should just say that I work in the entertainment business. I just don't know why I'm hesitant to say it.

Michael

Five years ago, that'd be 2018 . . . so that was just before I moved to Florida. At that point, I told people I worked at . . . in early 2018 I was still working at the bowling alley, back in Massachusetts, and then after that, I was working at a Subway in a gas station down here in Florida.

And did you tell them at that point that you were golfing or had you not really jumped into that yet?

I was always playing golf, but at that point, I wasn't really a professional golfer. I hadn't made that jump yet. So I guess I technically "turned professional" in 2018, but I wasn't really playing . . . I didn't have the financial ability to play golf. I didn't have the physical ability to play professional golf at that point. So, it was in my mind. I was still on that path, but I wouldn't say that was a career, yet, at that moment.

CHAPTER 3: WHEN I GROW UP

As a child, what did you want to be when you grew up?

Brian
Well, according to my eighth grade yearbook, I wanted to be an anesthesiologist because I had just recently had my tonsils out, and I thought that was the coolest thing ever. Although, sidebar . . . I had to have my mother pull over on the way home because I threw up everywhere, because that stuff in my system was just killing my body. So, for some reason I thought that was cool, but looking back on it, I guess . . . I'm a middle child, so I am an attention seeker. My mother is a middle child, so we are super tight. I was in my first musical theatre production at six years old and I continued to do the theatre thing, I think, because I craved the attention. So I knew that was partly what I wanted to do. I got to the big fish in a small pond point where I was the choir kid, I was the theatre kid . . . if there was a solo, I was probably going to have it. Not to pat myself on the back, but when you're the big fish in the small pond, you don't need a ton of talent to stand out. So I knew I wanted to do something in the world of the arts. And here we are forty-one years later . . . I guess I was six, so thirty-five years later . . . still doing something dabbling in the world of the arts, getting paid for it year after year.

Lisa
I wanted to be an archaeologist. I was obsessed with ancient Egypt. I got *Egyptology Magazine* when I was around eight years old. I was obsessed. I was told by my parents, "That would be a great hobby, honey. But that's not a career. So find something else."

When did you make that change and find something else?

I feel like I'm almost always adjusting and finding changes or making changes and finding something else, to be honest, because I like diversity and I like to be constantly learning and being challenged. So, just doing one thing might not have been enough for me. However, I feel like archaeology could have been that kind of career for me, where I would have been discovering new things and challenging myself and learning and growing. I still have quite an affinity with it.

Sabrina
I wanted to work in theatre . . . an actor, singer, etc. like I do now. A lawyer . . . I wanted to go to law school and I was "this close" actually . . . or weirdly enough, a cook or chef, all of those creative things.

You said you were "this close." Why did you not go to law school?

I just couldn't afford it, frankly, I didn't have money growing up, so college was something that was not something many of us did.

Do you have a four year degree?

I have an associate's degree from New York . . . specialization in film. I didn't get to finish. I didn't get my bachelor's degree. That's a whole different story of circumstances. I thought I had it. It turns out I was short on credits. When the school changed accreditations, it was a whole drama. So I went for years thinking I had my bachelor's degree and it turns out I still only have my associate's. I went further in my education than most of my family did, but not as far as I probably would have preferred, just because I ran out of money, to be honest.

Has not having that four-year degree prohibited you from anything you wish it hadn't?

I don't know, because I haven't pursued the things that a four-year degree probably would have helped me get, like a certain kind of job. So I don't really know. I bet if there were certain jobs that I was applying for, it probably would be problematic. But over the years, I've gained soft skills that college couldn't teach that have become far more valuable.

You mentioned that you went further in school than anyone in your family. Was that something you wanted to do or did it just happen? Why did it happen?

Most of my family members, with the exception of my grandmother on my mother's side, were high school dropouts due to various reasons. In my grandfather's generation, it was due to the fact that they had to enlist to go fight wars. In my mother's generation, it was because women were expected to get married and pop out kids.

My grandmother went to college, but she didn't really use her degree. She became a mom and popped out kids. That's what you were expected to do back then. My mother was a high school dropout because she got pregnant, I found out later in life. She just couldn't manage high school while also taking care of another family member, my cousin, whose mother, my sister's mom, abandoned. We have a whole history of that sort of thing going on in our family. But my mother did go back and get her GED. My father was in the military, so he didn't go to college. His father was in the military, so he didn't go to college. My grandmother on his side was one of those women that just got married and popped out kids. There was no expectation for her to go further. Plus, to be very frank, we were all extremely poverty stricken. We grew up extremely poor. So college was a pipe dream for most of us.

Where did you grow up?

All over. I was an Army brat, so we moved around a lot. I lived in Germany for the very first part of my life, until the second grade. Then we moved back to the States where we lived in Maryland up until about sixth or seventh grade. Then we moved to Georgia for my eighth grade year, stayed there until my sophomore year of high school, moved back to Michigan when my parents got divorced, and I stayed with my maternal grandparents, graduated high school there, and then I went to New York, right after high school.

With the intention of schooling or to try to "make it," initially?

Both. I had gotten a scholarship to film school and then I was trying to make it in the business on Broadway and in film.

Chris
Honestly, as a child, I wanted to be a paleontologist. I'm not even going to lie. When I was a kid, I wanted to be a paleontologist and then I decided that I wanted to be an archaeologist. And what's funny is that in the back of my head, I always wanted to be an actor, but I was focused on more "hands on" kinds of things and, as I got into my teenage years, I had this love/hate relationship with theatre and acting and performing. So I went to college for English because I decided that I wanted to be an English teacher. During my studies, I took a linguistics class and decided, "Oh my gosh, I'm coming full circle. I'm going to be an archeological linguist and study ancient languages." I actually took a couple of courses in that direction before I decided that I wanted to teach. So yeah, I did this weird full circle thing. That was an answer you didn't expect. I'm big on history. I'm a huge, huge history buff.

Daphne
I was first going to be a ballerina because I was in dance all of my young life. While growing up in New York City, I danced with a dance company, and actually minored in dance in college. So I really believed I was going to be a dancer. That was all I ever thought about until, when I was going to go to college, my father told me, "You may not make it as a dancer, so let's find a real profession that you can go to." So I did. I majored in journalism because I always loved to write. I never thought of writing as a career path. I didn't know that could be one, because I was going to be a dancer. But I love to write. So I took journalism and then I failed history, and I didn't know you had to know history to be a journalist. Who knew that? They didn't go together. So I went into public relations, which made sense for me

because I love to talk and I like talking to people. So I majored in communications, and all this time . . . as I said, growing up, all I ever wanted to be was a dancer, nothing else.

Once I started in college, I knew that I wanted to get into the hotel world due to the T.V. show *Hotel*, which is the old show with Connie Sellecca. *The Love Boat* people wanted to work on cruise ships because of that show, and I wanted to work at a hotel, because of *Hotel*. My school, at the time, did not have a hospitality program, so I continued on with my degree in communications, knowing that I wanted to work at hotels. And when I got out of college, I beelined it right towards the hotel world.

Heather
Oh, that's easy. I wanted to be on Nickelodeon. I wanted to be on TV. I grew up in the eighties and nineties. I wanted to be slimed, you know what I'm saying? I saw myself on *You Can't Do That on Television* on Nickelodeon. I was a Nickelodeon kid. *Double Dare*, baby . . . give it to me. I wanted to put my hand up the nose. And I had my opportunity, and passed it up, when I visited my wife in the Mall of America, where they have the nose. They have a *Double Dare* challenge there. So we have to go back up there and do that someday. But that's what I wanted to do. I wanted to be an entertainer on camera, on television, or movies.

Do you feel like you are fulfilling that as a podcast host?

No. But I do feel like I'm fulfilling that by entering into voice-over work and am ultimately seeking out how to get to Hollywood in some sort of capacity. I'm asking the universe right now to conspire on my behalf. I am ready to do it. So podcasting definitely scratches an itch because I get to be on the mic and I get to use my voice, but I'm not delivering the message I want right now. I don't mind delivering a marketing message, but that's not my true life's purpose.

Donna

Well, early on I wanted to be a teacher because I was always the teacher's pet. I loved school. By the time I went to college, I was sure that I wanted to be a psychologist with a private practice. When I went to college, I was a psych major, and by the end of my freshman year I added a second major: management. I did some peer counseling and I laid awake at night worrying about all these people I counseled. The next day, I would see them out with their friends, perfectly fine. Meanwhile, I'm worrying about their mental health. They sat and shed tears with me, but now they're out being normal. I'm more worried about them than they are. This is not going to work with my psyche over the long term. So I added the management major with the psychology major. The college I went to did not have a personnel management track back then. It was before they had the phrase HR, but I had a management professor who loved me and he basically helped me create the courses that would give me the personnel management pieces I needed. He let me create independent studies and do my own thing, which was phenomenal. So by the time I left college, I knew that HR, personnel management, was going to be my route.

At that point, my goal was to work my way up to Vice President of HR in a great company. That's what I thought I would do, where I thought I would end up. And it was only because, well, maybe not only, but it was largely because I had a boss who was such a sh*t . . . feel free to print that . . . I'll give you his name, even. He was such a terrible leader, I didn't think I could survive in a corporate setting . . . certainly not with him. And after I did my master's degree and got invited back to the university to teach in the graduate program . . . I really loved doing that . . . I realized if I could parlay that into a training gig, that would be really fun. So, I started marketing my training sessions and my first two clients were Renaissance Cruise Lines and American Express. Being able to trade on those names to get other clients . . . when you say, "Oh, I just did this training for American Express," people pay attention. So that was sort of the evolution of how I ended up in consulting. I had two years with small companies and then a little over six years with the Fortune 100 insurance company. And I started my consulting practice on a part-time basis, for two years, while I was with the insurance company, and then took it full-time. I started it in 1988. I took it full-time in 1990. So this year it was thirty-five years from the inception.

Wei

As a child, I honestly wanted to be in architecture, because that melded my like of pretty things. It merged art with math and literally, structures, or structure. I think it's an evolution from playing with Legos. You are literally building things with Legos. I kind of wanted to build with concrete, and steel, and glass. That didn't really pan out.

In high school, I was in an internship program with the city of New York. And what I learned from that is that it's a pretty cutthroat industry. Hindsight being twenty/twenty, it's like every single field out there. You have to start from the bottom, and when you're at the bottom, you do a lot of work for other, more seasoned folks. What I did not like about my internship is that I worked on a design. That design was incorporated into a building. And, when I finally saw the final blueprints and whatnot, nowhere on that list of contributors was my name. I thought, "Well, to hell with this. If this is how it's going to be, I don't want to be in this field." Naive little high school me was very much about giving credit where credit was due. I still am, to this day. But, as somebody who was under eighteen, looking back, there were probably legal reasons why I could not be part of the credit listing.

Gabriel

I think I wanted to be a lawyer or a politician, which is so funny because I don't want to be those things now, and I don't have the temperament or the skills to be either. In the back of my mind, I think I always thought, "Oh, one day I'll write a book or something, when I'm sixty." It's just turned out to be the thing I should actually do.

Steve
The two main things, I think were . . . I wanted to be a rock star. I wanted to be a guitarist. I took guitar lessons, and I wanted to be on electric guitar . . . a cool rocker. My parents got me an old acoustic, nylon-string classical guitar that I had to hold up here like this to play and . . . that never panned out, although I still play, and I still write. I also really, really wanted to be a truck driver . . . a big rig semi truck driver. And an artist. I drew a lot when I was a kid. I always drew semi trucks and big rigs and . . . when I was a kid, I think that was a relatively popular line of work. There were TV shows and . . . this was back in the 1970s . . . *B.J. and The Bear.*

Victoria
Oh, my gosh, I wanted to be an attorney and a mom. I always wanted to be a lawyer. My grandfather was a corporate lawyer. I never got to meet him, but he was supposedly pretty influential. And I always thought that's the route that I wanted to go down. I gave up on that dream and just wanted to be a mom. I loved being a mom. So yeah, that was my career. But then again, you have to understand, I was born in the 1950s, so that was the aspiration for women . . . to be married and have children.

Jesus
I wanted to be an actor, no question. I was constantly trying to escape my reality, growing up, on a daily basis. I wanted to be anybody else. So pretending was almost a form of survival for me, because I was really immensely shy. I hardly spoke. If I said ten words in the entire school day, it was a lot. I didn't have any friends. So whenever I had to do something, when I was forced to do something, for example, give a presentation in class or answer a question . . ..

I remember one time, I had read in one of those *Scholastic* . . . I don't know if you remember those *Scholastic* booklets that they would give you in school . . . how you could make friends. Oh God, this is so pathetic. It said in the article, "You should try going to the cafeteria, finding someone that you recognize, sit at their table, and then try to engage in conversation" or something to that effect. And I was so desperately lonely that I thought, "Okay, I'm going to try. I don't know how I'm going to do this, but I'm going to try it." I remember I had never eaten in the cafeteria before, so I grabbed my tray of food and I saw this girl that took the bus with me. I felt that girls were safer than boys, and I thought she would be less prone to make fun of me or beat me up or something like that. She was sitting with a group of friends at one of those long cafeteria tables. I remember sitting all the way at one end and they were sitting all the way at the other end, but I could hear what they were saying. I was too shy to actually introduce myself or say, "Hi, we take the same bus," or whatever, so I waited for her to make the first move to acknowledge me. And I thought, "Okay, you're not you right now. You have to take a deep breath and just think of a character from a TV show, whether it's Ricky Schroder on *Silver Spoons* or someone that you think is cool and try to emulate that person. Go in there with some kind of confidence." So I was constantly pretending.

I did that . . . I don't know for how long, let's say a week or something like that. And then I'm on the bus and I try to sit close to her hoping that she might turn and say, "Hey, you always sit at our table and you never talk. You should join us next time." She was talking to the really cute boy on the bus. Everybody had a crush on this boy. So, she's talking to him and another boy and the cute boy says, "That guy is always so quiet. He never talks." And then she said, "Ugh, do you know that he sits at our table and eavesdrops on our conversations?" I thought, "Oh, my God, she's so right." That is not the impression I was trying to give. I thought, "I'm so stupid." How could I have not figured out that that's exactly what that would look like? "You're so stupid. You're so dumb. This is why nobody likes you. Of course, it looks like you're eavesdropping." I remember at that point, the cute boy did something that it took me decades to learn how to do for myself. He said to her, "Why do you assume he's eavesdropping? Maybe he's sitting there and you guys are so loud he can hear you and maybe he enjoys the conversation. Why not just include him in it?" I remember thinking, "Oh, God, I feel so bad for her because she likes him and she was trying to impress him by putting me down." Granted, I don't condone that, but I know what that feels like. I was flattered that he did that. I was really touched by that, but I also felt bad for her.

Years later, we were taking driver's ed together and we had gotten to know each other a little bit. One day I was going to walk home and she said, "I can drive you home if you want." I said, "Oh, okay, thank you so much." We had a really nice moment together, and I'd like to think that was her way of saying, "Hey, I'm sorry I said that sh*tty thing about you." The point was that until I started doing community theatre, I was pretending so much.

I remember there was a neighbor who invited me to go to church because she thought I was gay and she thought I'd find Jesus and whatever. I was really nervous about going with her because her son had invited me, but then at the last minute, he pulled out. So then I was supposed to just go with her. I remember being behind the door and listening to her, conversing with my mother, and thinking, "I can't do this. Oh, yeah, you can. You're going to think of somebody cool. You're going to become somebody else . . . emulate certain behaviors." And I remember I jumped out from behind the door and said, "Hey, I'm ready to go to church," and she kind of looked at me with this face of "Who is this person? This is not the shy kid that I know." Then I was really talkative in the car and I wouldn't shut up, and that was me pretending.

I'd come home from school and I'd watch *Wonder Woman* and I would want to emulate her confidence. Or I'd watch Olivia Newton-John in *Grease*, and I thought, "Oh, I relate to her, the goody two-shoes . . . she doesn't curse, she doesn't drink." I would kind of emulate those behaviors in such a way as to try to manipulate people. If I knew that acting soft and demure made it so that a person wouldn't bully me, that's who I would be at that moment. If I thought that having confidence was what a person liked, and that would draw that person closer to me, then I would pretend to be that.

Often, people were kind of confused about me. "I don't know who he is. He's so weird. He's like multiple personalities." And then when I would watch performances, like seeing Whoopi Goldberg in *The Color Purple,* I thought, "God, I so relate to her." I would just cry and cry. I realized that acting is such a powerful thing because not only does it speak to the audience . . . you see a character and you think, "Wow, that character taught me something about myself or other people," but also in performing characters, or playing characters, and doing this pretend thing, you may figure out something about yourself. To this day that happens. For example, my husband will say, "Oh, let's go to the pride festival," and I'll say, "Okay, I'll go." And he'll say, "Oh, I want to get under the rainbow flag that they do at the end of the parade." I'm too shy to get under the flag, and I don't like to dance in public, and yet, if I'm home alone with him, I put on shows for him. So people sometimes are confused and ask me, "How do you get up on stage and perform and do all this stuff? How could you cry in front of strangers when you proposed to your husband on a stage, but in other large settings you just can't?"

So pretending and escaping reality was a thing that I think helped me survive. It was a coping mechanism. And because that's all acting is, pretending and convincing yourself that what is happening in this imaginary setting is real, it's kind of what I've always been doing. I would create these imaginary scenarios in my head and convince myself that the emotion I was trying to convey was real, to the point where my body didn't even know what was going on. In a very stupid kind of over-the-top way, I guess you could say that acting saved my life . . . and continues to.

I used to display a large Wonder Woman collection in my bedroom, and when I was single, guys would see it and look at me almost as if to ask, "Oh, are you an adolescent? It's like you're a kid." I remember telling one guy, "Oh, she's not a joke. She's not laughable to me." And he said, "Well, what do you mean by that?" I said, "Well, she taught me to love myself, so she's not a joke to me. Every time I look at her, I remind myself that I can do this, I can get through this. I'm strong enough. I can't deflect bullets, but I can deflect negativity. I can't force someone to tell me the truth through a magic lasso, but by being truthful myself, maybe I can inspire the truth in others. So she's not a joke to me."

And acting is not a joke to me. I take it very seriously. And that's why, when I feel I'm not doing a good job, or I feel like I'm disappointing the director, or the critics, or the audience, it affects me adversely.

Now I've gone to the other extreme. I know this is off topic, but when people ask, "You don't like to meet the audience?" No, I do not. "You don't want to be nominated for anything if you did a great job?" I don't. I don't like doing acting interviews. I don't like being asked about it. I just want to go in, do the performance, and go home, because I don't think anyone or anything is worthy of praise. I can take a simple compliment, but sometimes I'm embarrassed by it. I just like escaping reality, and for my whole life, that's what I've done. I played different people or facets of my own emotions and different scenarios to try to survive. "Okay, maybe I can get out of this without being beaten up or being made fun of," or, "How can I manipulate the situation to survive here?" It was a survival tactic. In fact, I remember telling my therapist at one point that I felt like a coward. She replied, "I don't think you're a coward. I think you were very smart." So yeah, I always wanted to be an actor.

Michael

For most of my childhood, I wanted to be a professional hockey player. Actually, I played hockey for seven or eight years growing up, and I really loved hockey. That was my main sport when I was younger. I'm not exactly sure when the switch to golf happened. Probably around twelve or thirteen years old is when I started to kind of get more into golf. But for most of my childhood . . . I remember in elementary school, they had us do the "What do you want to be when you grow up, yada, yada, yada" thing, and they had all of our answers posted on the wall. My answer was that I wanted to be a professional hockey player.

You said you don't really know when or what prompted that and changed that.

I don't think there was any one specific moment. My dad always played golf and he always brought me to the driving range with him. I had my own little set of clubs that he got me and whatnot. But as to why it started becoming kind of my main sport, I don't really know. I don't know exactly why, or when, it happened. It just happened.

CHAPTER 4: HELLO, TEN-YEAR OLD

If you could write a letter to your ten-year-old self, how would you describe your career trajectory thus far? Did it go "as planned"? Why or why not?

Most interviewees organically (do you see what I did there) changed this to the "advice" they would give to their ten-year-old selves.

Brian
I feel like that's such a loaded question because even in writing a letter to my thirty-eight-year-old self, the plan will change. The outline that you have made up in your brain is never going to look the same minute after minute, let alone decades later. But you're still in the career path that you are choosing. I knew when I did that first musical at age six that I loved performing. I loved being on stage. I loved entertaining. The amount of family reunions that I was "forced" to sing at . . . . Am I in the same world now? Yes. Am I doing the thing I thought I would be doing? Probably not.

I mean, the one-person production of *Les Miserable* that I did around the dining room table for my mother . . . that never took off. Every year between Christmas and New Year's Eve, my mother and I would sit in the dining room, around the table, and do a puzzle, and we would listen to some recording of whatever was hot-ish at the time. We had just seen the tour of *Les Miz* in Philly, and while we were listening, I literally played every role . . . every part, even the harmonies. So, yeah, you're still in the ballpark, kid. You're making money, you're paying your bills, you're enjoying your life, your frequent flier miles are through the roof, and your husband still likes you, on occasion.

Lisa
Whoo, doggy. So, let's see . . . if my ten-year-old self is still thinking she is going to be an archaeologist and own a hamster farm . . . I loved hamsters . . . I would say to that precious little soul, "Follow your

heart because it's going to lead you on a lot of amazing adventures, and don't get too attached to how you think things should turn out, because there's a lot of gold in the moments that surprise you."

Sabrina

Oh man, I would tell her to be patient because I have no patience, sometimes. I've gotten better as I've gotten older, but I think we all know this about me, that there are certain things for which I have no patience. I'm an A-type personality, but I think that's more from conditioning, because I was forced to grow up very quickly. It's not how I was born. But, I would tell my ten-year-old self to be patient, that you don't need everybody to like you, and it's okay if people don't like you. And no, my career trajectory did not go anywhere near where I thought it would go. But at this point in my life, I'm extremely grateful that it didn't because there were so many things that I wanted to do, or I thought I wanted to do, that in hindsight look very insignificant in my journey. So I would tell her to stop being a people-pleaser, to be patient, to hold on to her sense of self, and don't let anybody take that from her. And then when it came to my career trajectory, again, you know what, sometimes you have to say "Yes" to things you never thought you'd say "Yes" to, and learn from them.

Do you want to elaborate on any of that?

I never thought I would say "Yes" to one day running my own theatre company. It was never a dream of mine. And then there, I found myself. I kind of fell into it and it did not always go well, but holy crap, the lessons I learned from it made me a better actor, made me a better person in general, and taught me what I will not put up with in the business. So, saying "Yes" to something that I never thought I wanted brought me so much further to where I am now, and I think honestly enhanced my career a lot more.

Chris

Honestly, if I could tell my ten-year-old self anything about my trajectory, it would be to keep all doors open and not be guided by fear, because my path has meandered due to doubts and fears, rather than allowing my passions to drive me. And it's only in my forties that I've started to carve a path for myself instead of letting the current just take me.

Daphne

I'd tell my ten-year-old self to keep dancing and thriving and thinking about being a dancer, but also know that you have a different plan in place that is set for you, and you're going to love it. Just follow the path. I believe there are paths for all of us. Follow the path and enjoy every step of it and try not to detour too far from it, because if you stay on the path you're meant to be on, it'll be a wonderful life.

Heather

If I'm talking to ten-year-old Heather about her career trajectory that she's about to get into, the first thing I'd say is to have a plan. She didn't have a plan. She didn't know how to properly write out goals in her authentic voice. Back when we were kids in the eighties, and in the nineties, things were dictated. You were a doctor, you worked in the bank . . . especially in a small town. I grew up in a small town, so it wasn't like, "Heather, go to Hollywood. You could make it." It was, "Heather, you need a nine to five job. You need money. You need a retirement account. You need health benefits." Those were the perks . . . 401(k) and health benefits . . . not realizing your true potential or following your passion.

So I would tell ten-year-old Heather, "Start to document the things that light you up and don't worry about doing the grunt work. This is all according to plan. You are learning how to operate." I went into a creative field, thank goodness, but I was learning how to use all of the equipment, learning how to write the copy, learning how to use the cameras, learning how to make graphics, which has all propelled me towards where I am today. So I guess to answer that question best is to say, "All right, girl, you need some goals. You need to never forget the North Star . . . what you want to do. You can do it. Nobody needs to give you permission, and just enjoy the journey."

Donna

At the age of ten, I was already head of the girl gang at lunchtime. We used to chase the boys around and kiss them, if we caught them . . . in fourth grade . . . I was ten . . . that's what we did on the playground after lunch. So in that sense, I don't know if at that time I pictured myself as being in charge. I just was. I'm not sure that I psychologically thought about that or recognized the implications of that in my ten-year-old self. But if I could talk to that ten-year-old self, I would absolutely say keep doing what you're doing because whether I realized it intellectually or not, I was a take-charge person then, and I'm still a take-charge person now, fifty years later. And I think to be successful in a consulting business, you have to be that confident, ballsy, take-charge person. Frank, my husband, refers to me, and my friends, as having PBS . . . pushy broad syndrome. And that's why most people who go into the consulting businesses don't make it, because you have to have such a supreme level of confidence that nothing throws you, that no one throws you, and that you honestly believe you're the best at what you do.

I've said that to so many people who say, "Oh, can I pick your brain? I'm thinking of going into consulting." I say "Yes" to everyone who wants to have that conversation, and I answer their questions one hundred percent honestly. They can ask me anything. When I think about my personality when I was ten, I'm exactly the same person now. So, I would tell that ten-year-old self to keep doing what you're doing. Don't be afraid. Take charge. It's okay to piss people off because ten-year-olds still want everyone to like them. I didn't outgrow that until I was in my mid-twenties, when I realized that because of my PBS personality, I would never be able to make everyone like me. That was a hard lesson. It was a big blow because I want people to like me. But I realized that it was more important, certainly in a professional setting, to have people respect me than to have people like me. And if I can't have both, I'll take the respect over the like because I have lots of friends and I'm great at making friends. But in a professional setting, I don't care if you like me, although you do have to respect me. And that's a really hard lesson to learn. And that's not one that a little kid would know. But if I could have helped myself learn that sooner, that would have been nice.

Wei

If I could write a letter to my ten-year-old self, I would literally tell myself to just go with the flow, since honestly, nothing that I had planned actually went as planned. It's funny, one of the things that I've learned in the course of my career is that . . . actually in the course of my life . . . is that things that are really hard to come by may or may not be meant for you.

There have been times in my life . . . like applying for the Navy Reserves . . . I tried three separate times, and, for whatever reasons, didn't get in . . . just didn't go according to plan. Frankly, looking back, if I had been accepted and gotten my commission, my life would have been very different from what it is. The doors that could have been . . . or the doors that opened as a result of not being in the military would not have been there if I had gotten my commission.

And so, the lesson for my ten-year-old self is to basically just go with the flow, let it happen organically, and not worry about things that just don't go according to plan.

Gabriel

It did not go as planned. I would describe my career trajectory as a series of happy accidents and unexpected opportunities that showed me what I actually want to be doing, or where I could be most useful. There was very little strategy or planning involved.

Why do you think it happened that way?

I suspect that it probably happens that way for many people, or most people, if they let it. But I also think that I happened, maybe, to walk a more unconventional path. If you go to law school, you become a lawyer, and you work at a law firm, and you want to stick with the law. There might be a certain set of experiences or milestones that you follow, that are sort of prescribed, or circumscribed, because there are only so many things that you would be put in touch with. In my case, I have stumbled into multiple weird jobs.

I was hired to be an anchor for a startup YouTube news channel. That was incredibly fun and it was really exciting, but it was one of the most poorly-run operations I've ever been part of. It was a sweet group of people, but it was just kind of a mess, and I had no interest in being a broadcaster, or news anchor. Obviously, there's some connection between that and podcasting, but I wasn't trying to become a . . . I wasn't trying to be on Current TV, or trying to break into the cable news world or anything. I did it because, well, a) I really needed money at the time, and b) I had this policy which I developed at some point along the way, where I started just saying "Yes" to things, once. I could always say "No" later, but I try not to say "No" to weird opportunities, and the more random and unexpected they were, the more I felt inclined to say "Yes," because I felt that there was some weird divine logic at work that I should probably not argue with too much. I still have to remind myself of that sometimes, because sometimes my natural inclination is to say "No." But usually, when I say "Yes," something interesting comes of it. So that's how I've stumbled into these things that I couldn't have really planned. And each of those experiences showed me what I did or didn't want to do. Even if they were things that I didn't want to do, like that anchor job, I was developing cool skills, I was meeting interesting people, I was getting comfortable being in front of a camera, which was very uncomfortable for me. I was learning how to write in a new way. I was learning how to structure a story. Now I have a weird story about working at a startup YouTube channel. Who knows how that might play into a script one day or be part of some story?

I think that once I stepped off of the very traditional corporate career path that I was on, when I was in my mid-twenties, it was all kind of Wild West. I gave up all of the traditional metrics and milestones, and then I had this weird mix of skills and interests and they're not very well-defined. I'm still figuring out what they mean. So, I met this person and they wanted me to do this. I met this other person and blah, blah, blah. It was one accident after another. When I look back, it starts to make sense, but I was not really being very strategic or deliberate, and I'm not sure that I would have wanted to, because I kind of like doing it this way.

Steve
Oh, wow. Like I said, I didn't have a specific real job in mind, as in "this is what I want to be." I still think I would say something along the lines of, "Whatever you think you might want to do now, and whatever you think you might need to do to get there, go ahead and do it. But, whatever you think it is, it's not that." And again, I would never have, as a child, thought that I would be living in Las Vegas and working as a scenic designer. And I've done graphic design. I designed a logo for a show that ran for years. I would see that logo on cab toppers and think, "Holy crap, that's me." Millions of people have seen this now over the years, coming to Vegas. And you know, that was mine. I did that. And it never, never would have occurred to me, as a kid, that I would be doing what I'm doing. And especially not how I got here. The path that brought me to this seat talking to you right now is unfathomable.

Victoria
Wow, that's a good one. I really need to think about this one. I feel like I'm in a job interview.

"Dear Vicki: I know you love to twirl around in your ballerina costume and to tap dance in the garage . . .." Thinking back, now that I am where I am in my life, knowing what I know now, life did not come with an instruction manual. I really didn't have the support that I needed at home, in order to be who I am today. It was through a painful evolution and realization that I had to take my life into my own hands and create what I wanted. It didn't just happen. When I look at other people growing up, that went to wonderful schools, and had two parents at home, who sat down and set out their career paths with them, and worked with them on how to develop those individuals . . . . a sort of human resources department . . . or your boss, you really want somebody that can develop you and bring out the best in you. . . . I didn't have that.

So, "Dear Vicki: I think that we've done okay. We could have done better." I wish that I had another thirty years in my life. But if I'm good, I've got another twenty. Seriously, not to be morbid by any means, but it keeps me in check to make sure that I'm living the best life. So, "Dear Vicki: Think differently. Grab the bull by the horns early in life. Try to figure it out. Find all the support you need. Scream. Holler. Jump up and down. Try to find the people who will support you and guide you to a better life and future."

Jesus

I would tell my ten-year-old self, "Buckle up, kid. You're beautiful and I love you and you're perfect just the way you are. But, buckle up because you have no idea where you're going. You have no idea what you want to do. You have no idea how you're going to get it done, but you will figure it out along the way."

I had no plan. What I would tell him is to come up with a plan, because you have the intelligence, the charm, the personality, the talent . . . well, I don't believe there is such a thing as talent, but you are a hard worker and you will do good work. So come up with a plan, finish high school, go to college outside of Florida, pursue what you're passionate about, go to the places where that's happening. I can almost guarantee you you're going to be successful because you've got it, kid." But, if the kid were to ask me, "Well, how does it turn out? We can't change anything." "Kid, we go left, right, in circles, up, down, through it, above it, below it, behind it, in front of it, next to it. It's like trying to figure out a Rubik's Cube. You eventually figure it out, but you have no idea how you figured it out."

Do you feel like that's the same for most people?

No. There are people who do have a plan and who follow that plan. And I think a lot of that has to do with the way that they were raised. Does it happen for most people that they make a plan and then end up veering off a bit? Yeah, I think that probably happens to most people.

Let's say the plan is to be a therapist, and you're heading in that direction, and you've finished high school and you're in college and studying therapy, but then you fall in love with your philosophy courses. So you veer off to philosophy. And then you end up writing books on philosophy, and you didn't intend that, but it kind of ended in that direction. I think that happens for most people. Having a plan that I'm going to finish high school, go to college, and then have a career, and I'm going to get my car by a certain age, and I'm going to . . . those kinds of things, that plan was still happening, even though you veered off.

For me, I had absolutely no plan. I didn't think I would live past 25. When my mom passed away, I was nineteen years old. I hadn't even graduated from high school. I didn't have enough credits to graduate. So I got an empty booklet with no diploma. The ceremony was in June, and my mother died in October. It was quick. So my dad was looking at me asking if I was planning on going to college. "No. High school was traumatic. I'm not going to college. They're going to beat me up. They're going to bully me." I thought college would be just like high school. Then he asked, "Well, do you plan to get a job?" No, I was planning to live there for the rest of my life, and Mom would take care of me. I had absolutely no plan. Anything that happened to me was a surprise. Everything came by hard knocks. Nothing was easy.

My first job was working with my father because he thought I was going to kill myself. So he forced me to go to work with him. I was there the first week and I would go to sleep in the back of the warehouse. My father was a musician, but he worked in a warehouse. I would fall asleep in the back and then he would kick me, gently, and say, "Hey, wake up, we're working here." And I'd think, "Why am I even here? How long do I have to be here? I want to go home." I wouldn't say that, but I would think it. At the end of that first week, the boss gave me a check and I asked, "What is this?" He said, "It's for the work that you did. You're working here now." I wanted to kill my father. This man had seen me sleeping in his warehouse and I didn't know that I was working. Nobody told me I was hired. Nobody told me I was going to make any money. It was mortifying, and obviously the boss, who was a family friend, was thinking, "Well, he's falling asleep because he's depressed. He just lost his mom." That was the first job I had. I had no idea what I was doing. I had to learn everything as I went along. So, I don't know if that's true for most people. I'd be surprised if it is, but I don't think that's indicative of most people. That's why, when I watch *Stranger Things*, I envy those sixteen-year-olds that are working at the mall and saving up money to get a car . . . man, if I could go back and live my life again, that's exactly what I would do. But I had no idea. None. And I was too afraid. I never stood up for myself. If I went back, obviously I would.

Michael
Absolutely not. I'm in a much different spot than I ever thought I would be when I was ten. I definitely didn't think I would have been living in my car at any point when I was ten years old. And, obviously, as a ten-year-old, I don't even know if you can comprehend living in your car. I don't think a ten-year-old could understand what that does and what that means. And yeah, it's just a completely, completely different spot, a completely different location in life, a completely different path than anything I would have ever expected to be on.

I know you've told the story many times and it's been printed. Do you want to tell that story again now, about living in your car?

All right. Yeah. That's not a problem. So, let's see . . . the summer of 2021, I was an assistant pro at a golf course in Callicoon, New York, in the Catskills, called Villa Roma Country Club. I finished that job in mid-October, and headed back down to Florida, to play professional golf . . . to try to play tournaments, to try to ultimately reach the PGA Tour. That's the long-term goal. And I was looking at my finances from the summer and I had some money saved up, not a ton of money, but some. And I was looking at places to try to live, and I couldn't really afford to pay to play golf and to pay for a home. So I said, "Well, I moved to Florida to play golf. I moved away from all my family and friends to try to play golf, professionally. I'm going to put that as the priority." And I ended up living in my car for . . . I think it was for three or four months or so, just trying to play golf for a living, and chasing the dream and supporting the reason that I came to Florida.

When you were doing that, where was your car stationed and how, and where, did you bathe?

Yeah, so showers and all that stuff I did at the gym. That's a pretty standard option. As far as where I stayed, it changed around a little bit, depending on where I had to be the next morning. If I had a tournament down in the south part of Florida the next morning, I would go sleep somewhere down there. I stayed in a couple of rest stops, but I'd say the main spot was the Walmart parking lot in Port Saint Lucie, up there off of Saint Lucie West. That was the main spot where nobody would really bother me, I wouldn't get kicked out of there, etc. So that was kind of, I guess, the most "comfortable" spot, as far as a comfortable spot can be sleeping in your car at night.

When you drive past that Walmart today, do you have any thoughts or feelings . . . does anything flash through your head, or is it just a non-issue or . . .?

It's weird. It doesn't really bother me that much. Everybody . . . obviously, when I qualified for that Korn Ferry event, back in the spring, and the whole story blew up, everybody was making such a big deal out of it. For me, it was just . . . it felt like that was the right move at the time. And at this point, I still think it was the right move. So I guess it's not that weird to me. It's not out of the ordinary. It's just what it was and I'm OK with it. I think it's funny. It doesn't really strike me in any certain type of way or anything. It just is what it is. That's what my life has been.

CHAPTER 5: EARLY PLANS

Thinking back to your high school and/or college plans, if you had followed that planned path, where would you be? Did everything play out as expected? If not, what diverted your path? Why didn't you follow it?

Brian
In high school, I was a theatre kid. I hated high school. The reason that I survived high school, like many young theatre children, is because of theatre, because of the ragtag group of friends that are the most amazing people. And I wear that with a badge of honor every day. The plan did not fully work out because I did not star in the original company of *Rent* on Broadway. Trust me, I carried that *Rent* bible around forever and a day. This is shocking, but growing up in New Jersey, we didn't really go to New York all that often to see shows. We went to Philly to see shows. So, *Rent* was the first Broadway show that I got to see right after it opened. My mother and I went up and saw it and I thought that was the thing. I knew that I wanted to go to college for theatre. And while I was in college for theatre, I realized that I was not a rock vocalist and that was never going to happen. I am a classically-trained tenor if you can't tell by the speaking tone of my voice. So again, to not answer, but answer your question, the path did not work out exactly as it was in my brain, because I was as sure as day that my path was going to Broadway. And yes, I'm still in the ballpark of the entertainment, creative arts career field.

What diverted your path? Was there any one thing or a multitude of things? Was there a certain time that your path was diverted?

Sure. I got off the road from one of the tours that I had done, and our stage manager said, "Hey, I teach at these conferences and they're always looking for people to come and teach workshops. Do you want to go?" I was very quick to stop myself from saying "No," because usually, if it's something we don't feel comfortable with in this industry . . . this is an industry where we are told to show our strengths and hide our weaknesses. And if you don't know that something is a strength, you automatically hide that thing. I had not really taught, but I thought, "No, you know what? I'm gonna do this thing." So I went and I was pooping my pants walking in the room thinking, "They're going to hate me. I have no idea what I'm doing." And I got up there and I loved it. I had a bunch of teachers come up to me during that week of the conference saying, "Good, God, you're so good. The way you talk to kids, the way you . . .," and I'm thinking that the way I talk to kids is just the way I want somebody to talk to me. I'm treating them like the young professionals that they are. I'm not sugarcoating things. It's not my job to blow smoke at the industry.

Then I had a teacher that had come to my workshop who said, "Hey, I want to bring you down to choreograph my musical." At that time, I was thinking that I had never done that, and had no idea what that would entail. "Yes, let's do it." I think what diverted my path was me stopping myself and saying, "Try it, figure it out. You might not like it, and if you don't like it, don't do it again, but in the meantime, you don't know what you don't know until you know it." I totally credit my father, in life in general, saying, "Hey, look, your job is your job. Do it to the best of your ability, and then if you don't like it, get a new one. You can always do something for a year." That was his other famous quote. "Do it for a year, see if you want to continue doing it. If not, move on to the next thing." So I think him talking in one ear and my inner Jimminy Cricket talking in my other ear, saying, "Try it. Why not?" shaped me. My mantra in life is that I will always jump in the deep end and figure it out. I will plunge into the pool and then figure out how to tread water later, because that's so much easier and so much more fun for me than tiptoeing into the shallow end. There's a place for that. But that's not me. I don't need a bazillion spreadsheets. I want to jump in and figure it out.

Lisa

In high school, I was still sort of searching for what I wanted to do that fell within the parameters of what was laid out as acceptable and responsible. Performing was something I've always done. I mean, since I was eight years old, I've done it and I continue to do it, so that's always been a part of who I am. And I feel like I bring that into all the arenas that I'm working in now, which is kind of fun. But in high school, when I found out it was possible to study abroad in college, I decided that was for me. That was the thing I had to focus on. I had to go to one of the schools that would allow me to do that. I had to make that happen. I spent my junior year in France. And really, the goal at that point was to graduate from college and then move back home for about a year and start waiting tables . . . and then I ended up bartending too . . . but to start by waiting tables. I'd have some "flexible work" to do performing. I did pursue performing and got to certain levels of success with it in my twenties, but there was a little wrench that I look back on, and I think I could have made another choice.

When I was in France, there was a foreign language school, Département d'Études de Français Langue Étrangère, and if I had spent one more year in France, and continued to study there, I could have been certified to teach French anywhere in the world, except France. So that could have been a very different path for me and it also could have been a different potential revenue stream. However, I would not have graduated from UCSB because I would have had to stay in France, defer for a year, and then come back and finish, which at the time didn't feel like an option because my goal was to graduate in four years with my two majors. I graduated with high honors. I did it all. I spent my year in France, and got all of my requirements in. So I've had lots of micro goals that have sometimes prevented me from taking advantage of some of the opportunities that came my way.

Sabrina

I would probably still be in New York, either hustling like the actors do, or working regularly, because I work pretty steadily in Florida. I never would have moved to Florida had I not gotten married.

That was my next question. What diverted your path?

I did what you're told you're supposed to do as a woman. When a man proposes, you say "Yes" and you uproot your entire life and you make all the sacrifices for your marriage. That's what I did. So if I hadn't made that choice, which I don't regret in hindsight, I'd probably still be living in New York, either acting or going into directing like I am now. I don't think my career path actually would have deviated that much . . . it just went a different way, logistically.

Is there a reason you haven't "run back to New York?"

There are multiple reasons. The first, obviously, is money. It's far too expensive to move back to New York. Two, I built a life down here and I have roots here, whether I like to admit it or not. I have a lot of complaints about Florida, but I've kind of developed my own little community and my own little family down here, which is very hard to leave. Plus, I'm in a new relationship now that I'm very happy and very stable in. So we would have to decide to move together if I were to move again, which we are talking about. Oddly enough, I was thinking about moving back to New York before the pandemic, and before my current partner and I got very serious. I was debating whether or not I was going to go back to New York because I was flush with cash at the time, after the divorce, selling the house, making a lot of money working independent contracts. I was able to put a pretty good sum away, and then the pandemic hit and everything changed.

Would you say that not going back to New York was out of comfort or genuine contentment with where you were in your life in Florida at that point?

Oh, comfort for sure. I think I was way not ready to make the leap to go back yet. Definitely. I got comfortable.

Well, being in New York when you're twenty-two is heck of a lot different than when you're forty-two and you want some nice things.

Yeah. I would have had to accept a much smaller apartment, a much lower quality of living, and go back to living like I was in college again, which, when you get to a certain point in your life, you have to decide if it's something you want to do or not. I don't think I was ready for that, to be honest. I don't think I was ready to make the kind of sacrifices that I was willing to make in my twenties when I had nothing to lose.

Chris
I would still be a teacher. I decided that I wanted to be a teacher in high school. I chose my university partially based on the fact that it was highly rated as an educational school. Also, because my boyfriend was local at the time, and then we didn't even last six months into my freshman year of college. You know how that goes. But I had decided that I wanted to be a teacher. Again, I let myself explore and learn a lot in college and my ideas changed, but I came back to the idea of being a teacher and I did it for ten years.

There are two reasons I stopped. The first was, even at that time, I could already see the writing on the wall with the educational system, and I'm glad I got out when I did, but also because I hadn't been pursuing all of those other wonderful opportunities. I was saying "No" to things. Doors were opening and I was saying, "No, I can't. I'm a teacher." Finally, after some family trauma, I decided that you only live once. You can always come back to teaching. So I did follow that path for a decade before deciding to throw the cards up in the air and see how things go.

And what diverted your path at that point was the family trauma?

It was a combination of family trauma and me actually saying "No" to several acting projects . . . turning down paid acting gigs. One of them was a full-time job at Disney. What sucked is that after I quit teaching, I went back and that job never came back up. I got as far as the callback room many times after that, but I never got the offer.

Daphne

Right now I would be on Broadway. I'd be starving, of course, but I'd be there. I've always wanted to work for Alvin Ailey Dance Company because I love them and they were based in New York City, so I knew a lot about them. And as a black female, that just made sense to me.

I was never the body type, in all honesty, for dance. I loved dancing for the enjoyment of it. I loved everything about it except for the discipline. I learned, probably more than anything when I went to college, with dance as my minor, the discipline associated with dancing, and the fact that dancers in the professional world starve themselves, and exercise all the time, in addition to dancing. So, I do believe that taking a more stringent look at it, during college, diverted me.

In high school, I danced the entire time with a company, and on the dance team, but college was when I learned the discipline of it, and I realized that it's not for me. It would take away my joy by doing that. And there were other ways I later learned to keep the enjoyment of dancing and that love for it. I ended up, later in my life, teaching dance through the church that I was involved with when I was in Nashville. So I was a dance teacher, a dance leader, and it was my joy. I got to enjoy dance without the discipline.

And, I found joy in the meeting and hotel world. I will say that I've been fortunate with that, and I think everybody should feel this way. It doesn't always happen, but I do believe in it. You've got to find what you enjoy, because my dad always said, "If you enjoy what you do, you'll never work a day in your life." I really, truly believe that. With the hotel world, while it was work, I enjoyed it. I've always enjoyed what I've done. Yeah, there've been times I wanted to get out of something, but never changing professions, never on a different path.

Heather

I'll just give you the history, the actual factual things that happened. I was a senior in high school. I didn't want to be there. I almost failed because of attendance. And so to tell me that I needed to continue education just wasn't my bag, baby. And I didn't know what to do. I didn't have a college lined up. I had no plans. I really didn't. Counselors didn't help me. My parents did the best that they could to try and find solutions for me, but I literally, as I'm remembering it, had to forge my own way and I knew I "had to," and I'm going to put that in air quotes . . . at that time, you "had to" go to college or you "had to" work. The options were thin. So I thought, "What the heck am I going to do?" Because, as a five-year-old, I took apart my electronics and put them back together and they worked, I was told, "Oh, maybe you should go be an electrical engineer. If you become an electrician, you make a ton of money." Oh, okay. Well, I went to ITT technical training after high school to become an electrical engineer and there was a lot of math involved. There's no color, there's no excitement, there was nothing there happening for me. And I dropped out.

But the most fun that I had in ITT was when we were designing resistors. You can use a resistor to move current. That's about all I remember. All I wanted to do was make sculptures out of my resistors. I didn't want to use them to direct a flow of current. So I quickly got out of that and thank God for my mom . . . one of her friends told her about a college in Orlando that was about music and movies and video games. My cousin said, "Look, you're a musician, you love to sing. Why don't you go do something in that field?" And so my next path was to go to college at a private university in Florida, alone, having never been there, having no family down there, and I just kind of forged my own way, and I went. *And,* I received perfect attendance. This is after almost failing high school for not attending.

So, that started the creative services trajectory in my path. Once I had that Full Sail University degree, stuff opened up for me. I realized that when I went into Full Sail, I was going to become a sound effects technician. I was going to make sound effects, which would be really fun, but I didn't want to move out to California, so okay, what else am I going to do? Long story short, that's how I ended up in radio, because I went for a recording engineering degree. So I became a morning producer and that started me in communications . . . I didn't know I would ever, ever realize it, going into radio, but looking back at it, it makes total and complete sense. I wanted to be a radio DJ. I had my opportunity, but nobody gave me, again, air quotes, "permission" to do so. So, I thought I had to do production. And that's where I stayed until now.

Do you still feel you "need permission"?

Absolutely not. I don't need permission at all. I'll ask for forgiveness, but I don't need permission. In 2013, I started energy work. I started growing spiritually and really over the last four years, because I've doubled down on that, I realized that I am the answer and so I'm going for it. In 2013, I was unhappy as an employee. I was unhappy that I was tethered to a desk where somebody told me what I had to do, and where I had to be. I always wanted to be a business owner . . . always, always, always. But, I didn't have terms when I was younger. As I got older, I knew that I just wanted to be a business owner. And my transition in 2013, from being in production in television, to a public speaker, working from home all the way back in 2013 . . . I had autonomy and I got a taste of that. There's no turning back.

Donna

There were two big factors. The first job I had, where I was in personnel management, my boss loved me, but the company mistreated me in that they saw I was a workhorse and they kept piling more and more on me, with the promise of more money, that they never delivered. I kept going to my boss, saying, "You said that if I did this, I'd get that, so show me the money." And it never came. And when I gave my notice, they were in a state of shock. "I don't know why you're shocked. I've been telling you for six months that I'm happy to take on more responsibility, but I expect to be compensated. And for six months you've been lying to me and promising me something you didn't give me. And now I'm leaving. And you're surprised? Now you're asking what you can do to make me stay? Well, it's too little too late. I've been telling you that for six months." So I left. And within two weeks they were calling me, begging me to come back. And I asked, "Why would I come back? You already mistreated me once. Shame on you. If I come back and you do it again, shame on me for being so gullible. Why would I believe you?" When you're the kind of person who promises one hundred percent and delivers one hundred fifty percent, you expect people to treat you right. And when they don't, it's a letdown. It's a shock. It's a disappointment because you delivered on your part of the bargain, and they didn't.

So having had a couple of those experiences, it just seemed logical to pursue the opportunity to be my own boss, because I won't mistreat myself. I'm in charge. If I have an asshole client, I can say "I've completed this project for you, and oh gee, I'm really too busy to do that additional work for you," or, "Oh, sorry, I can't. I'm not available," and be done with them because I want to be treated with respect and appreciation. I'm good at what I do. And there's a certain level of respect that I expect to get. I can count on one hand, in thirty-five years, the number of clients that didn't treat me the way I felt they should treat me. So that, combined with the experience I had teaching at Nova University, and seeing the impact that I could have on people, those were really the two things that made me course correct when I was already on that track, that path.

When you taught at Nova, was it Nova Southeastern University, or was that before the merger?

It was way before the merger. It was still two buildings in the middle of a swamp! I taught in the executive M.B.A. program. Abe Fischler, who was the president at the time, was the pioneer of distance learning. Nova was way ahead of its time in having what they called "distance learning" and "remote sites." They did what they called "cluster training." I had a cluster up in Palm Beach. The executive program was Friday night and Saturday, every other weekend. That's how I did my degree and that was the program I taught in. I would drive to Palm Beach every other weekend, teach Friday night for 2 hours, stay overnight, and teach Saturday for 4 hours. I was teaching the advanced level HR classes, like management development, organizational development, stuff like that. It was before the university was accredited, so I went to the dean and said, "I really hate this syllabus. Can I make my own?" He said, "As long as you use the same textbook, that's fine." I literally threw out the whole syllabus and created the entire curriculum for each class that I was teaching, on my own. That curriculum became the basis for all the management training I do today, because it was in two and four-hour modules. So that's how I still sell it, thirty-five years later. I sell it as a training program that's flexible. If you want to do a three-day retreat with your executive team, we can do that. If you want to do six or eight half days, we can do that. If you want to do two-hour modules over sixteen weeks, we can do that. It gives clients the flexibility to pick and choose the delivery method and it lets me customize the content based on what their desired outcomes are. But, I'm still picking and choosing from these pieces that I started creating literally thirty five years ago. I market it as, "This is not Management 101. This is a master's level curriculum," because that is what it is. So it's a much higher level of sophistication and that, I think, is a huge selling point to HR people, because most HR people that I'm dealing with have master's degrees, so they understand what that means.

I think that the impact of having done that work at Nova and having been allowed to create my own curriculum and delivery system as a facilitator, rather than someone who droned on and on like a typical professor, totally created my training persona and my delivery style. It's still how I deliver it today, and how I market it as "This is not me standing up here talking at you for four hours. Only my husband gets the benefit of that. This is me facilitating learning and discussion within the group," and people love that.

Wei
Yeah. So, I think what was really fruitful was having opportunities in

high school, and in college, where I lived the career I was looking at, and it really gave me a sense of what I liked about that field, and what I didn't like about that field. And so as a result, I changed my career focus a bunch of times. Fortunately, I think that my working hours are far easier than if I had become an architect, like I had planned. With architecture, it can be a matter of feast and famine. Working as a government employee, my hours are a bit more predictable, I think. It is far more a nine to five job, even though there are days when I work longer, or days when I work shorter hours. But the advantage is that I actually have a work/life balance. And that's something that the U.S. Government prides itself on.

So as far as college, what was your planned path at that point?

Honestly, my path in college was to just get a piece of paper that says I am certifiable in something. It didn't matter what the paper was in. I just knew that I needed a piece of paper, from a four-year institution, that basically said, "Wei is capable of sticking to, and finishing, a curriculum." I think that was a lesson I learned in college . . . just get it done and figure it out later.

Gabriel
In high school and in college, I thought I was going to become a lawyer. I don't know why I thought that was what I wanted to do. I didn't really know many lawyers. I didn't have a particular passion for the law. It just seemed like . . . and I hear many people who go to law school feel this way . . . that it's a safe bet, or a decent foundation for other things you might want to do. I really was not being very thoughtful, although I guess I was sort of drawn to the philosophical aspect of the law, which I still think is really interesting.

Anyway, I went to UCLA and in my first quarter, I took this philosophy class, and I *really* liked it. I had a T.A. who was really cool, and we got to talking, or I don't know, maybe I opened up in a borderline inappropriate way about what my bigger plans were. I don't know why I was talking to this person about this, but I said, "I really want to go to law school." He said, "Well, if you want to go to law school, you should be majoring in philosophy or economics, because philosophy is one of the best backgrounds for the law, and it correlates very highly with a good LSAT score, apparently." I thought, "Oh, I've never heard of that, but that makes sense." I loved the class so much, and then the next quarter I took one or two more philosophy classes and thought, "Oh, this is great. This is totally what I want to be studying. I get to read, and think, and learn how to argue. This is great." So I guess I was on the law school path, but again, had zero plans . . . didn't even sign up for the LSAT, didn't do research on law schools . . . I don't know what I was thinking.

If I had followed that path, I guess I would have taken the LSAT and gone to law school and worked at a law firm. It's so hard for me to picture and I probably would have ended up having the same crisis I had, but in a different field, and I would have maybe transitioned or given it up, or . . . I don't know. It's hard to know. It's all abstract.

But, one day I was in class at UCLA, in my junior year, I think, and I was sitting next to this guy and he was studying some weird thing while the lecture was going on, and it was some business-y stuff that I had never really seen before. "Hey man, what is that?" He said, "Oh, this is a case interview." "What's a case interview?" "It's this type of interview they give you at consulting firms, where they come up with a business problem, or a case that they worked on, and then you have to work through the case with them. You simulate the case." I asked him "What's consulting?" I'd never even heard of it. He told me, and I thought that sounded interesting. I went home and I Googled it and thought "This is such a cool industry." I had no idea this existed . . . this world of people who just advise other companies. I was so intrigued that I was almost over-thinking . . . this is what I'm going to do, which was so funny because I was so ill-equipped for this. I'm a philosophy and English major with zero business experience, terrible at math, famously. I mean, I really was the worst candidate, but I did feel in my bones that I might have something to offer, or that I could develop certain skills and I would be good at it. Those skills were just that I can kind of speak in front of people, I like working with people, I am intrigued by the business world, and I loved reading the newspaper and figuring out what was going on, but I wasn't a hardcore nerd about it.

That day when I met that guy and he told me that, my whole life changed. The path just veered off this way and the next year . . . actually, it was less than a year . . . I probably had six months from that point forward to invent a whole new narrative for myself. And I did. I made up a whole story. I didn't entirely make it up, but I did a lot of work. I took classes I needed to take. I did all the things I needed to do to move forward, but I was also kind of learning how to tell a new story about myself, as a kid who had something to offer, and, "Just let me get in there and I'll figure it out." I managed to get an offer at a consulting firm and I'm so glad that happened because I think the other path would have been very frustrating. I don't know. You never know. It could have been cool in its own way, but this definitely felt like a more interesting one.

Steve

I wasn't particularly good in school, both at being *in* school and the school work, and I didn't have very high expectations of myself when I was in high school, nor do I think did those around me. This is the truth and honestly, this is not something that I've probably ever put into words or thought about in terms like this. I really didn't have high expectations. I didn't feel like I was college material. And I never really thought I was going to amount to much. So I didn't put a lot of effort or a lot of pressure on myself to do anything other than get through high school. Once I got through high school, I wanted to do something, so I signed up and went to the Minneapolis College of Art Design for a year . . . for actually a semester and a half. And I thought that I wanted to be an artist . . . a fine artist. I did that, and again, didn't really find my place, didn't feel like I fit in, and didn't like the teachers, the students . . . again, I just never felt like I fit in. So after a year and a half or so, I decided it wasn't for me and dropped out.

A couple of years later, I decided to try again and I went to the College of Saint Thomas in Saint Paul, where I took a couple of business classes and a couple of accounting classes. And again, why that? I have no idea, other than it seemed like that was what I should do . . . go into business and accounting. My dad, I think, was an office manager and did . . . inventory was a big thing that I remember when I was a kid. Exactly what that meant, I had no idea. But, inventory. And so I took these management and accounting classes and actually kind of enjoyed them. I felt like, "Oh, this is kind of something that maybe I'm not good at, but at least I have an interest." So I thought I would go into some sort of management . . . business management . . . accounting . . . those kinds of generic terms. I never really thought of myself doing something, specifically. I didn't see myself sitting at a desk, or running an office. So I took classes and I thought, "This is good. This is kind of a direction." Honestly, I kind of got bored with it and thought, "Well, maybe this isn't what I want to do, and I don't feel like myself doing this."

Then I got a job at Xerox and I was running a copy center . . . I was a younger guy and I had people who reported to me and I had duties as assigned and responsibilities. And, I had keys to the place and so on. I explained, earlier, kind of from there where things went. After Xerox, it was the Minnesota Opera.

Victoria
No, my high school and/or college plans did not play out as expected, because there was no expectation. The expectation was, back in the day, that if you got a job as a secretary, and it just makes me cringe to use that term, you were doing good. You had a good job if you were a secretary. Back to the earlier letter that I wrote to myself . . . there was no guidance there. There was no direction. I was just trying to figure it out as it happened. Now, keep in mind that I left college when I became pregnant with my daughter. So I was pretty young, and raised her, and then went back to college and earned my degree. I think I was fifty when I finished and finalized my degree in communications. So, no, it didn't go according to plan. I think that you need a network of

people to guide you along the way, which I didn't have.

Jesus
I'm convinced I'd be a working actor, no question. I would have gone to New York or L.A. and I would have gone to acting school, and I would have learned method acting back then, which is what everybody taught. Then I would have fixed my teeth and I would have worked out and I would have built myself up and I would have gone to auditions and I would have killed it and I would have been on a sitcom and then in movies. I'm convinced that's what would have happened. Why I didn't do it back then is because I didn't believe in myself. There was no way I was leaving Florida. I was scared to leave my house, much less the state of Florida. And if I went to college, I thought . . . first of all, my parents couldn't even afford that. I certainly couldn't. I had never held down a job. If I had worked at a place with someone barking orders at me, I would have been anxious, and stressed out, and nervous, and probably crying every day. And then if I went to college and someone was bullying me or hazing me or doing something, I might have ended up killing myself. I don't know. I wasn't prepared. I wasn't ready emotionally or psychologically. I was not ready for the world. My parents gave me absolutely no coping skills. They're great parents. I love my parents to death. But they absolutely gave me no coping skills. None.

Michael
I don't really think I had a planned path in high school, to be honest. I was just kind of living. When I was in high school . . . I didn't know . . . I always loved golf. I didn't know professional golf was a thing, or college golf was going to be an option, or . . . in Connecticut, the golf scene is obviously way different than it is in these southern states. It wasn't like if you're good at golf in Connecticut, you're guaranteed to go play golf somewhere. So I don't really know if I actually had a path in mind, or had any goals. I was just kind of living day to day and just enjoying life for the most part.

CHAPTER 6: UNEXPECTED CAREER MOMENTS

What unexpected career moments have brought you the most joy?

Brian

I'm generally not a person who likes unexpected things. I hate haunted houses, I hate scary movies, I hate things that I can't pseudo-plan for. With that, I was never expecting to get as involved in working as a choreographer and then a director.

Last year, I saw a job posting. They were looking for an assistant director for this immersive theatre *Alice In Wonderland* show that was coming here to Philadelphia. I almost didn't send in my credentials, and I thought, "No, you know what? What's the worst that is going to happen? I'm going to have an interview for it." I had an interview, and the guy I interviewed with was all, "Yeah, I really like you. I have a couple more people to interview, so I'll be in touch," and not twenty minutes later, he called me back and he said, "Clearly we had a good conversation. I'm going to hire you. Let's do this." And I now get to travel. I'm about to go to Austin, Texas, next week. I've been to Boston, Atlanta, and Tampa. I get to travel and create cocktail theatre, magic, fun. And it wasn't anything that had been on my radar, literally, even a year ago.

Lisa

I was doing murder mystery dinner theatre, and one of our stage managers . . . she did a lot of voice-over work and still does . . . she's phenomenal . . . one of the organizations she was working with was looking for younger voices. So, she just put it out to us: "Hey, anybody that wants to give this a try, they're having auditions. Go on down. It's for an advertising company." I went and auditioned for that and became the National Teen Spokesperson for John Robert Powers for two and a half years, and absolutely fell in love with voice-over work. It was such a blast. I would not get much sleep because I'd be closing the restaurant, or bar, at night, and getting up and doing voice-over work in the morning before I would go back to work at the restaurant. But it didn't matter because it was so much fun. And then that led to being the British Teen Spokesperson for John Robert Powers for about a year. Every single time I went in . . . I'd have to go in very early, because it would be 7 or 8 A.M. for us and it would be the end of the day in London . . . I thought, "They're going to tell me it's been fun, but really, honey, nobody's buying that." But it never happened. We kept it up for a year and it was so much fun. So I think voice-over work was an unexpected career joy because I had never considered that as a thing to do. I didn't have any experience with voice-over work. So that was a big happy surprise. After all of that, I had about seven years where I did a bunch of anime and I did a jingle for a commercial and I did some voice-overs for computer games . . . animated games, and had an absolute blast with that.

Sabrina

The most obvious one is when I got my first Carbonell Award nomination, and my Silver Palm Award, for *Next To Normal,* just because I feel like that was a decade's worth of work finally coming to fruition. It seems shallow in hindsight, but it really did. I was so proud of it. I would also say every time I direct a show . . . every opening night . . . I find so much joy and elation in that because that's, I think, where I'm at my best . . . when I'm directing, to be honest. I know that I'm a great performer. I will not ever stop being a performer at heart. But I know that I'm good at taking that and turning that into a storytelling experience on stage, and empowering other people to tell the story on stage. So the opening nights of shows I've directed are those career moments that are just like, "Mwah!" I couldn't ask for anything better.

Also, I would say with my other job . . . I just started, so I'm still kind of new . . . but my boss . . . I was super proud a couple of weeks ago when I reminded her that I had only been there a couple of months. Because I didn't know something, I asked her a question and she said, "Wait, why don't you know that?" I said, "Because I wasn't here when you did that." She replied, "Oh, oh my gosh, you're so good. I forgot that you've only been here four months. It feels like you've been here a year." It was a really proud moment for me. I thought, "Gosh, I'm really doing a good job here. Good for me."

And then summer camp, weirdly enough, summer camp in 2019 . . . I was working with these little biddies from the age of five to twelve . . . five to thirteen, something like that, in a neighborhood that does not really have a lot of arts or theatre . . . low income kids, kids who had never been exposed to theatre or that kind of music in their lives. There's a stereotype that goes with that, but it was a very, very diverse group of kids. I think my proudest moment was when we did two showcases that year, and both of those showcases were four weeks apart. And in every single one of those showcases, those kids were just absolute rock stars. And I knew that was because of what I had taught them. We had one kid who was extremely, extremely shy and just could not come out of his shell, and his mom wrote me the best letter saying, "The eight weeks with you has made him more alive than he's ever been as a kid." That's what I like to hear. He may never be a professional actor. He may never pursue it as a living, but he has learned some communication skills, in this summer camp, with his time with me, that he's going to take with him the rest of his life. I think those have been the more outstanding moments that stick out.

Chris

Number one would have to be being at Disney World for a week-long trip to celebrate my fortieth birthday. I was at Epcot, making my rounds through World Showcase, getting a little tipsy, and got a call right after doing a shot in Mexico, that I booked *Bloodline* and would actually have to drive back to Miami and shoot the episode on my actual birthday, while all of my friends, and my husband, were still celebrating my birthday in Orlando. I took the car, drove all the way down to the Florida Keys, and got to do a scene with Norbert Leo Butz. And that's how I celebrated my fortieth birthday. It was great. It was incredible. I wouldn't say it opened any doors, but it did give me the confidence to do a lot of other things. It was one of those . . . getting to act with him in those scenes, having a really fun moment.

They were setting up the lights for the scene. Then Butz started to ask about Orlando, Universal Studios, all that stuff. So I said, "Oh, I was just up there." We started talking about theme parks, rides, what's great for kids, the best hotels to stay at, where you can bring your pets, and I felt so great. You can be a good actor, but it doesn't matter if you have nothing else to offer. So that gave me a whole lot more confidence in everything else, because then I went, "Hey, you know what? Not only did I do my job on set to the point where they gave me two extra lines so my pay got bumped, but everything I did, everything I shot, the two extra lines, made it in the final cut. Plus, I actually got to have the conversation with an actor I respect, who was a lead on the show, and have this moment of two people connecting." It was great. That was a huge learning experience for me.

Daphne

My last corporate job, and it wasn't necessarily anything about the job, but as I mentioned before, I had a team. I developed this team and we did the Derby. I was in Louisville, Kentucky and the company I worked for was the main sponsor of the Kentucky Derby. I had never heard of Derby, and never knew what Derby was. I had no concept of how important it was to many people, but there I was. They spent gobbles and gobbles of millions of dollars and had hundreds of people come in who attended the Derby. But the enjoyment I had was the team of six of us executing the weekend. And while we hated it because we didn't get to participate . . . I never saw a horse run, never got to make a bet, and I didn't get to see much of the excitement, because it was such a massive, major part of what we did as a company, and our team got to execute it from the lineup of the A-Team limos caravanning our executives through the city of Louisville to the Derby, the amazing parties we put together, the gifts we ordered, the food & beverage, the decor, the entertainment . . . watching it all happen was the most thrilling and most gratifying thing for us as a team . . . to pull it off and pull it together for one weekend, one big day, or sometimes it was just for a moment.

When I resigned and left the company, my team members were all still there. It was a heartfelt goodbye. And we still, to this day, stay in touch. We do Zoom calls and we get together. We became family and friends and they will always be in my life..

I've been independent for nine years, but in the last five years, I pinch myself at least once a year and realize I work for myself and I'm successful. And that amazes me. And I always have to have that moment of, "Holy crap, I'm doing this and I'm doing this for myself in whatever way that means." I'm very overwhelmed and overjoyed at that realization that it's working, because I never had this plan. This is not part of my plan, and it's working.

Heather
When I worked in radio, I was asked to voice commercials and I was able to do it without training, and that was a "Huh, maybe I do have something here" moment. When I was a public speaker, and I was one of the top reps in my first year, I mean, I was one and two, one and two, one and two . . . because of how well I could present information, I didn't realize I was a public speaker. That was an "aha" moment. That was a turning point where I realized that I have a voice. I can use my voice. People are listening to me. I can make things happen. Most recently, I would say, and I believe it was last year that I had my first photoshoot for myself . . . not behind the camera. . . . now in front of a camera and I hired a stylist. Having a branding photographer and a stylist to help you realize what you feel on the inside, to help you realize it physically on the outside . . . huge turning point, big bolster in my confidence. And then recently, literally today, my colleague and I were being trained for voice-over acting, and our coach said, "Oh, I didn't realize you guys . . ." me, specifically, that I'm coming to the table with, "such expertise and professionalism and experience. I didn't realize that." Oh yeah, hey, this is what I wanted to do. So today is a big turning point in my life.

Donna

I got some work with a law firm that was based in Western New York. They have offices in Florida, D.C., New York City, all over the state of New York, and a few other states. They hired me to do harassment and discrimination training for their entire workforce of hundreds of attorneys, and all of the other personnel. I traveled to all of their offices on a regular basis for years and years doing that. At some point, the president of the firm . . . every few years they elected a new president . . . they had their first woman president and she was a ball buster. I loved her. So they hired me to do this harassment and discrimination training, and after I had delivered that for the whole organization, I met with her. I would go up to their main office for a week at a time and deliver training. So I was in her office, talking to her, and I said, "You know, during this time that I've been working with everybody, it seems like you guys make a really great effort to recruit women to become attorneys." She said, "Yes, we pride ourselves on recruiting a lot of women right out of law school. We have a mommy track and everything." And I said, "Well, you know, I've identified what you don't have for them, which is a mentoring program to help them get acclimated and hit the ground running quickly, and I wrote a book about that. I would love to talk to you about helping you create an in-house mentoring program." And she engaged me to do that. She put together a committee of women attorneys to work with me, and I facilitated the creation of a mentoring program for them.

About six months later, I was in her office again, and I talked to her about doing some executive coaching with some of the . . . in law firms, they have practice groups, like employment law, real estate, etc., and they have an attorney who's the "head" of that practice group, but they can't manage their way out of a paper bag. No one teaches lawyers how to manage. In fact, many of them suck at it and can come across as obnoxious. So I went to her and said, "You could really do with some coaching for some of these people who are managing other people, and don't know what the hell they're doing." She said, "Oh, that's a really great idea." So, she engaged me to do that. About a year later, I was in her office, and I was talking about something else and she started laughing and I said, "What's so funny?" She replied, "You are the best cross seller I have ever met." I said, "What do you mean?" She answered, "You know the exact right time to hit me up for the next big thing I didn't even know I needed." And I said, "That might be the nicest compliment I ever got. You just made me so happy." And she said, "And I meant it as a compliment, because I don't feel like you're trying to talk me into something I don't need. I see that you're talking me into something that I just didn't know I needed. And you're really good at it." And that stuck with me ever since.

There was a famous speaker named Bill Gove, when I belonged to the National Speakers Association, and he always said, "It's so much easier to go back to an audience you already know loves you, than to look for a new audience." So I recognize that one of my talents is fostering new business with clients who already love me. I have clients for years and years in many cases, because I'm able to parlay X into Y, and Z back into A, and all through the alphabet all over again. So that was a great moment of joy for me, at the law firm, because not only was it a nice compliment, but it helped shape my philosophy about my business model, and that what I was doing, without even realizing it, was a really good tool and exercise for me. That was making my business successful. I was able to put a framework around that and then think about, "How do I need to be doing that with other clients? Am I doing that? Am I missing any opportunities because I'm not always thinking about the next big thing I need to be doing for Client X?" So that was a true "aha" moment of joy.

Other moments of joy . . . well, signing really big engagement letters for a lot of money is very joyful! And I think that one of the reasons people fail in consulting businesses, which I guess is tied to the confidence factor too, is you have to be able to look someone in the eye and say, "My fee is X," with a one hundred percent straight face, with no doubt, no insecurity visible, like you're worth every penny of that, and then some. You have to really believe that. I think a lot of people don't have that confidence level in their deliverables, and you have to, in order to charge big bucks. You have to. And I've been in many situations where someone has said, especially on the harassment and discrimination work, and the training work, "Oh, well, I spoke to someone else and they only want this much for training," or, "They only want this much for an investigation," and I have a decision to make. Do I lower my rates to get the work, or do I stand firm and risk losing the work? We all go through those situations throughout our careers. Early on, I made exceptions. And when I got to the point where I felt like, "I'm not getting paid enough to put up with this stuff," that's when I knew, "Okay, no more exceptions." My husband, Frank, has this conversation with me all the time. "Well, why don't you just lower your rates if so-and-so is going to get the business?" I say, "Because so-and-so is worth what she gets paid and I'm worth what I get paid." So some of my moments of joy have been when someone has called me, heard my fee, and said, "Oh, well, that's a lot more than this person. That's a lot more than that person," and I explain why I'm worth more. And then I get the callback. I get the engagement letter. I get the work. Or, I've even had one better, where they go with the other person and then the next time they call me. So those are joyful moments too, because being in business for yourself doesn't mean that you don't still need validation. We want that validation, especially someone who does what I do for a living. It's all about people. Again, I separate being liked . . . that I reserve for my personal life, though certainly I'd rather do business with people I like, who like me . . . from being validated as a professional, and as an expert at what I do. That's more important. So, knowing that they're picking me, even though I'm more expensive, is a moment of joy.

I don't do what I do for free. I don't want to do what I do for free. I want to get paid. I want to make a lot of money, especially at this stage of my career. I want to rack up as much as I can because I have, what, ten years left to work, maybe? And Frank and I have both decided we want to work as long as it's still fun, and I'm having a ball, so I don't see an end in sight for me. I can certainly slow down as I get older, and don't want to work as hard. But that just means being pickier and choosier about what work I take. And I've really already started doing that. There are clients who are PITAs . . . pains in the ass . . . it's a technical HR term . . . I teach it to all my clients! So, I have the luxury of not having to work with clients who are PITAs anymore. I've had that luxury for a long time. When I come home and say, "That was just not worth the aggravation. I'm done with them," it's my one Donald Trump moment in life to say "you're fired" to a client because it's just not worth the aggravation.

And then separate from everything I just said, the best moments of joy are when I'm doing executive coaching and the person I'm working with has that light bulb click over the head, and has that epiphany, that "aha," and I see it happening. That is the most rewarding moment I have.

Wei

I think the most joy I get is in the unexpected bumping into people in hallways, talking to them, asking them how they're doing, which potentially just leads to impromptu discussions about either their life, or their careers, which evolve into mentorship opportunities. I think that's been the best part of things for me . . . being able to help them understand to not sweat the little things, or to adjust to any challenges that they're facing, and potentially make lemonade . . . to help them see the value in that conflict that they're experiencing and grow from it. More than anything, it really is about the people that we encounter. The work is always going to be work, but it's about the enduring relationships that we make. I think that really is the most rewarding for me.

Is there any specific example, or time, on which you'd like to elaborate?

So most recently, I actually bumped into someone . . . it was a very late day at work. All it really started out with was me looking at my watch in my kind of "Hey, hey, hey, it's kind of late. What are you still doing here?" way. Being a member of a leadership team . . . generally, people expect me to be one of the first people out the door. So this person was a little surprised that it was 7:30 P.M. and I was still at work. So, we got to talking and I could tell from her body language that she had had a really rough day. I just simply asked how she was doing. She replied in that way that we all do . . . being polite, and we just say, "Oh nothing, nothing's going on, really." And I said, "Okay, well, if you need to share, my ears are open," and that's when she expressed some interpersonal challenges that she had in the office. She was at a loss at what to do. I offered up some insights into what was in the realm of possibility, from an HR perspective, and from an organizational perspective, and she wasn't expecting it. She kind of actually left the conversation really happy, really excited. And it's really great to see that change in body language. Ultimately, I would love to be able to convert every unhappy employee into a happy one. In her case, she found other employment, but at least we were able to find what worked for her. It's not always about keeping the organization happy. It's about making sure that the relationship is intact when said person moves on, which is inevitable, and that they look back in a positive light, so that the door is always open for them to come back, or so we can grow that relationship in a different capacity.

Gabriel
I've had one huge, huge disappointment happen where my first movie that was supposed to get made got shut down a month into production. It was after ten years of writing, and I thought, "This is it." It was going to be a huge career-defining . . . life-defining moment. My life would have changed in the most extraordinary way . . . although maybe not in a good way, it would have changed in an extraordinary way.

And that all went away with the COVID-19 pandemic. Not only did the movie get shut down, but the huge actor attached very unceremoniously just dropped out. It was devastating. It shook my whole world. Nothing is real, certainly, in this business, until it's done. Nothing can be counted on. So that was in March or April of 2020, when the movie got shut down, due to the pandemic. Then I think it was in July when the actor went away. I work with an amazing team, and these people worked their butts off to make this movie. So at some point, it was slowly getting back on track, but it was having a hard time. We had another wonderful actor come on board, to replace the one who dropped out, and it probably will be an even better movie, but it was heartbreaking over and over again, especially in that period.

I got together with my director, in the early days of the pandemic, and said "I don't want to sit around. We have to do something else. Let's write another thing." That thing became *Otherwise Engaged*. That movie is now moving ahead and it looks like it's going to get made before the other one. It's shaping up really nicely. We have two wonderful actors on board and there's real momentum. I've learned enough now to know that I can't bank on any of this, but it's just interesting how it's unfolding.

For years, I was stuck in that highly theoretical role of being a screenwriter. I knew that screenwriting was theoretical in the sense that you need a script to make a movie, but it's a transitional document. As I mentioned before, it's a blueprint.

Not if you're Aaron Sorkin.

There are certain writers, like Sorkin, who treat their scripts like works of art, in and of themselves, and I think I actually agree with that. I love curling up with certain screenplays, or plays, and reading them. I'll read plays and think, "What a beautiful document." But that's really not what scripts are about. Even Sorkin would have to admit that it's to mount the play, or to film the episode. If anybody curls up with your screenplay, it's because they're either another writer, or because they're such a huge fan, that they would want to do that. So, being in that role, I thought to myself, "I really can't wait for the day that somebody makes these movies I've written."

The reason I brought this up is that the whole shut-down experience was kind of the beginning of me realizing yes, being a screenwriter is a job, and it's an essential job. You can make a living from it. Somebody's got to do that part, but I always thought, "One day these people will let me make a movie. They'll give us the money and they'll green light the picture, and then I'm going to be on set, and I'll finally get to learn how to make a movie. Then I'll be a filmmaker. I'll be a producer, and I'll know how to do it." And it just would not happen for me. So I realized, "If this is going to happen, I think I need to make it myself. I need to save money, scrape together my savings, and ask for help from as many people as I can. I need to carve out this role for myself because, yeah, it could happen, but it could happen in five years. It could happen in ten years. It could never happen. Why am I waiting?"

So that's really why I did the short film I just did. And, the moment I started stepping into not just the writer role, but the director and producer roles, I realized . . . and it was a little bit unsettling . . . that being solely the writer is a great way to not have to put yourself on the line.

Those other jobs, especially a director, are very public. If the thing succeeds or fails, it is largely because of, or at least it feels like it's because of him. He's the captain, and when you're a writer, you don't have to be that. It's very safe. I didn't even realize that was part of my psychology until, "Oh, now that I'm doing it . . . .." This was precisely the feeling I was avoiding by staying in my room all day, writing, thinking that was my job, and that's where I was supposed to be. "Well, yeah, it is, *and* you're afraid of actually making the thing."

This ended up being three stories in one, but I think what I was trying to say was that one of the more joyful moments was stepping out of that writer role, that was kind of keeping me safe, and stepping into the producer/director role that felt *very* exposing, and finding out that that's where life happens. Somebody's got to be in the closet for a year writing the script, but it's all in service of getting to the point where you're actually doing the project. I suspect that same principle applies to somebody who says . . .

"I really want to build an app, but I don't know how to code."

"Well, maybe you have to learn how to code."

"Yeah, but I don't know."

"Dude. I don't have the brain for it. I don't have that. But what if you did? What if you stopped waiting for some brilliant engineer to come along and you actually learned how to code a terrible version of this app? At least that?"

By the same token . . .

"I want to be a party planner. I can't wait until somebody trusts me enough to plan their wedding."

"Why don't you plan your friends' wedding? Tell them you'll do it for free, or for very little, and that will be your wedding present to them. They save money, and you get to have a cool experience. And, you find out if you have the party planner in you."

I'm very passionate now about this topic, as you can tell. Forgive me for losing the thread a little bit, because I feel like we're talking about a few different questions. But there's something about stepping out of the shadows of your own life a little bit.

Steve
Well, absolutely the story about walking into the Minnesota Opera . . . I can't express what a tangible, real moment that was for me. It was kind of a relief to suddenly realize "Oh, yeah . . . yeah, this is it." And I feel really fortunate for having had that moment because I honestly don't know where I would be had that not happened. So that was a huge moment.

I had another moment . . . a very memorable and joyful moment, when I designed a set for a world premiere show that went on a cruise ship. I designed the show and kind of acted as production manager to help get it built. We put it on the ship out of . . . I think we sailed from Barcelona, so I did two ten-day Mediterranean cruises back-to-back to put the show in and get it all up. We rehearsed in Vegas and then took the cast to Barcelona. I remember sitting in what would have been literally the world premiere . . . the opening night, and sitting in the back of the house of this cruise ship theatre, in the Mediterranean somewhere, and sitting back with a cocktail in my hand, watching it, and thinking, "Holy sh*t. Who am I that I'm having this moment where I'm seeing something that literally came from my mind, and we put it on stage, and people are going to see it, and it's halfway around the world?" That was a moment of joy.

One of the things I love about what I do is that I get to have those moments . . . or, rather, I try to notice those moments, and embrace those moments. I think people in our business tend to . . . and maybe it's any business, but after years and years of doing the same thing, even though I don't do the same thing every day . . . in entertainment, and in theatre, people get cynical and get kind of crunchy and start to say, "Oh, yeah, whatever. This is what my job is." And I tend to try and find those moments where, if only to myself, I can kind of sit back and, again, have those moments of, "Holy sh*t, who am I?" So I truly like to find those moments. And, I think that's part of what makes it worthwhile, and why I continue to do what I do, and not become some jaded old crank.

Victoria
Being able to create my own position with the last company that I worked for, I think that brought me the most joy. Being able to recognize that a multi-billion dollar organization needed an event professional. The tasks were always passed off to an administrative assistant or somebody in a support role. Having the courage to be able to write that plan, present it to an executive member, find an advocate . . . not a mentor, an advocate . . . they're two different things

95

. . . finding that advocate that would go to bat for me with the other executives, and getting the position. I think that was pretty crucial in changing the trajectory of my existence . . . my career.

Would you care to elaborate on your feelings about the difference between a mentor and an advocate?

Absolutely. A mentor is somebody that works with you to develop you in the role or the position. That's my view. So in other words, if I wanted to be a baker, I'm going to find someone to show me how to bake bread. That's simple. An advocate is somebody that understands you, that understands what you're trying to do, and can go to bat for you and advocates for you . . . your cause, your mission. I think that's the difference. And I think that's huge. I think that all people should try . . . all people coming into a career should try to find both an advocate and a mentor. It can be the same person. But I really think that if you can find that advocacy . . . it's just huge to me, that's a person that's going to chat you up.

Jesus

It's the little things that really touch me. I'm trying to think of the first time I felt really proud of myself at work. I had become a Christian after my mom passed away. They had brainwashed me and I was part of this church. I had actually gone to a program called . . . I only went for one day . . . so I wasn't part of the program, but it was something called Worthy Creations, and it was part of the Exodus program, the ex-gay thing, because our youth pastor was an ex-gay and he knew that I was gay because, obviously singing Barbra Streisand, Bette Midler and Janet Jackson, so duh . . . Olivia Newton-John. And I'm obsessed with Lynda Carter. So he took me to this meeting and they wanted to do a play, and they thought I was really funny. So I remember getting up and doing a play with them and everybody was laughing. I don't remember how I felt at that moment, but I'm sure I felt good.

The reason I mention that is because there was someone who saw me, who was part of the church . . . he played guitar, and he said, "Hey, I have a friend, Andy Quiroga," . . . this is thirty years ago . . . "he's an actor and he does shows with this group called CTHML, the Community Theatre of Hialeah and Miami Lakes. You should go audition for them." I said, "Oh, but I've never done theatre. The only training I've ever had is drama classes in junior high and high school." He said, "Oh, you should try. You should do it." And I'm not really a singer, but he said, "You should go. You should." So, I remember I learned the music to "Not While I'm Around" . . . the Streisand version, of course . . . and I went and auditioned and they were considering me for the lead in *Guys and Dolls* and I was flabbergasted. I was just thinking they'd put me back in the chorus, if that. Andy and I were up for the same role and neither one of us got it. Somebody else got it.

So, my first show was *Guys and Dolls*, and they wanted me to play several characters. They wanted me to play a gangster and then, when the lead characters go to Havana, play a Cuban guy at the bar. Well, since I'm actually of Cuban descent, and spoke like my parents and my siblings, I thought, "I'm going to create this character." And I remember I knew what I wanted to do. I just wasn't doing it in rehearsals because I wanted to surprise them. I realize now that was a mistake because it was giving the director a heart attack. He thought, "This guy's not doing anything." I just didn't know how to start it. I remember the lady who worked in the lighting booth said, "Just say 'Azucar,'" which is what Celia Cruz always said. "Okay, that's good. I'm going to do that. I'm going to extend it." I remember on opening night, the director telling me that he was pacing back and forth when the Havana scene came because he thought, "That scene is going to die." The curtain opened and there I was in a straw hat. I don't know why I was wearing a straw hat, but I was . . . no shoes, with my legs spread wide open, on the stage. The waitress came out and I started improvising, and the audience lost it . . . just lost their minds. I could not believe it. I couldn't understand. I thought, "I hope it's funny, but I don't give a sh*t if they laugh or not, I'm going to go for it." When I came out to take my bow, even though that's the only scene I was showcased in, you could hear people screaming like they just really enjoyed it, and that was the first time that I realized the power of performance. I felt loved. I felt appreciated. I felt important. And it went to my head. After that, I wanted to always do a good job, and I had to be the best, and I had to be the scene stealer. And I went to an extreme that I'm not proud of. Then that changed, thankfully. But that was the first time that I felt, "Oh, this is what I need to do. This is where I belong."

I have to say, throughout my entire acting career, if you can call it that, the one thing that has always been consistent with me is how much audience members seem to like me. Again, I don't like to meet the audience. I go backstage while the other actors go out to do that, and I don't judge anybody who does that. I think that's great. That doesn't serve me. So, with the last show I did, I'd change out of my costume and walk to the car, but there'd still be a couple of people left over and they would come up to me and say, "You were wonderful," or, "You were my favorite," or, "I was so moved, my God, that wasn't even acting, when you . . . the grieving part." I just thought, "Great, thank you," and I just wanted to cry with them.

Even now, when I work at the museum, I do a presentation and I make jokes and guests, after I do the docent presentation, come back and say, "Jesus, you were wonderful. Jesus, this is for you. Here's a twenty dollar tip." And I'll say, "Oh, no, no, no. You don't have to. Give it to the museum." "No, you keep that. You're great." And I remember my therapist saying, "How does that make you feel?" I said, "Oh, it makes me feel good, but it feels . . ." She said, "Does it feel overwhelming?" "Yeah, it feels like it's a bombardment that I'm a good person, and I don't believe deep down inside that I am. So I don't like hearing that." It's really, really interesting.

When I was in *Diego and Drew Say I Do*, which involved a lot of improvisation, with each performance, I got more and more comfortable with the improvisation, and I remember there was a point where it was me, the party planner, and the boy toy, after he had done his striptease, and I was kind of making a face of disgust and then he said, "Oh, what are you looking at?" And I said, "Well, you are standing here half naked in the middle of a wedding ceremony." And then he said, "Well, I'm not into *older* guys." I replied, "Oh, and your cougar wedding date isn't *older?*" He then said something else and walked away. At that point, the actress playing the party planner, who is a pro at improvisation, asked me, "Have you ever done improv?" I replied, "Rarely. I never really took any classes or anything," and she said, "You're really good at it. You should really consider doing so." That made me feel good.

I remember in the last show I did, *The Short and Short of It,* the first scene that I was in was about a man who's grieving and is asking his dead wife for permission to date a new woman. Backstage, I go to a dark place, by myself, and I kind of just prepare for the scene, and then I go out. And of course, in the back of my mind, I'm thinking of my deceased father. So when the character says lines like, "I miss you so much," I just lose it on stage. I could hear people in the audience sniffling and getting really emotional. It was so cathartic. It was great to be with other people and know that they understand grief, and I understand grief, and we can grieve together. On stage is when I feel like everything is coming together. It's the best feeling in the world.

Michael

Ooh, unexpected career moments. I have to say that first . . . I guess unexpected is kind of a weird one because, as a professional golfer, you kind of have to expect that you're going to do all the things that you want to do. So, I don't know if I'd use the word "unexpected," but instead, I would say that "unlikely" is a better word. When I Monday qualified for that Korn Ferry event, literally, all of the stars had to align for me to do that that day. And they did. And that was really cool. When I got to call my dad, and call all my family, once I made it through that playoff and told them I was in, that was probably the happiest moment I've had in professional golf so far.

How about the hole-in-one in that Korn Ferry tournament?

99

Yeah, again . . . the hole-in-one was cool, but . . . I didn't . . . I'm kind of weird, where emotionally, I don't react or get . . . I won't say I don't get bothered by things, but I'm just very flatline most of the time, where, if something bad happens to me, okay. Or, if something good happens to me, I just think it is what it is. So, the hole-in-one was really cool. My friends behind me were freaking out. People watching me were freaking out. I thought, "All right, sweet. I made a hole-in-one, but I have 15 more holes to go." So I was kind of just . . . even in the video . . . my friend Vincent was there. He took a video for me. He got a video of the swing, and then you can hear the guy, Matthew Schmitz, who kind of looked after me that week, say, "So did you just make a hole in one?" "I guess so. Yeah, it appears so." It's just a weird trait I have, and I've always been that way. I don't know why.

CHAPTER 7: UNEXPECTED LIFE MOMENTS

What unexpected life moments have brought you the most joy?

Brian

Oh my God . . . becoming an uncle. I don't know if that was unexpected, although I had no clue. I do not have kids of my own. I do not need kids of my own. Would I like them at some point? Maybe, but I don't need them. But being an uncle and getting to play with these little human beings from when they're little, teeny, tiny babies . . .. My oldest niece just turned thirteen. "How are you a human being? Good God." Also, that makes me old. But that was fun.

This one is life/career . . . I worked at Walt Disney World and I've always liked Disney, and I loved working there. I was a singer-dancer in a parade. I got to dance around and make people's dreams come true. I don't know if it's a thing, but I also got paid to ride roller coasters every day. And I got paid to make friends from all over the globe . . . some people I still am in touch with. I'm a firm believer in people being in your life when you need them in your life. I think in the theatre industry . . . actually, it's more like life skills . . . just be a good person. Don't be willing to write somebody off because of somebody else's opinion. This is so not answering your question, but I think being able to have a thought, an opinion, and be able to . . . I don't know. I totally flaked on your question. It's been a long life. I can't really remember it all.

Lisa

Well, this is an interesting one. In high school, I was a cheerleader. My junior year was the only year I did cheer. I was J.V. Cheer Captain, but I competed with Varsity all year, so I got to travel around and compete with them, which was amazing. So that was my first experience as a "swing," which became my norm in theatre . . . always the swing . . . either the lead or the swing. But seriously, I got to be the swing in a lot of things. And because in my senior year they got rid of competition cheer, which is what I enjoyed, I didn't go out for cheer again and instead, I got a job after school. So, I had "zero period" where I could get out right after lunch and go work to save money to take a trip to Europe with my best friend, after we graduated. I was able to save up my money and make that trip possible and get some good work experience. That was fun. And so that was a very . . . I wasn't expecting them to take away the part of cheer that I really enjoyed, and that led to something else that allowed me to have this amazing experience.

Sabrina
Mike. I never wanted to date again after my divorce . . . ever, ever, ever. I was done. I was going to be a single old lady with a bunch of dogs and a ranch. I had no intentions of dating, especially that soon after my divorce, and he just came out of nowhere. And I am so thankful that he did. My partnership with Mike is ten thousand times what my partnership was with my ex-husband. I don't mean to insult my ex-husband. I just mean that in hindsight, we were not a good fit. Mike was the most unexpected life curveball.

Chris
I have those apexes, but also those abysses, of emotion when it comes to being a published writer. It's something where I go up high, and then I go down low, and then I go up high, and then I go down low. Knowing that somebody in Germany has my book is kind of cool. It's a feeling of "I did that." So there's that.

Earlier, when I asked you what you did, you answered it career-wise, which is what most people do, and said you're an author. Why is what you just said a life moment that brought you the most joy, and not a career moment?

I think because when it comes to the authorship aspect, that's the one thing I've done in my entire life that is the most personal. Again, it's the valleys and peaks of it. In putting my writing out there . . . it's the entire process . . . even though it went through several eyes and I had an editor, I was the one at the end of the day who checked up on all the changes and said "Yes" and then put it out there. So it's the most "me" in terms of vulnerability and exposure. I can't sit there and go, "Oh, well, the director made me do that," or, "The playwright wrote this," or, "The stage manager had this going on and . . . the costume designer . . . ." There's nobody else. It's all me and it's such a new experience. It's just really there in my head. But it's every day . . . I'm an author. And I've been writing forever. I've been creating characters and stories that I've just done nothing with. So being published, yes, it's a career move, but it's also a huge jump in terms of my own life trajectory and my sense of how I identify myself. Because again, I can't sit there and say, "Well, I'm just a writer," because I do also act, I do train clients. I feel that those are actually more my "career" than the writing is. The writing is kind of something that, other than being really sick, or fully exhausted, I don't think there's a night that I've gone to bed where I haven't been making up stories before I go to sleep, or writing a scene, or imagining a scenario, or creating characters and deciding where things are going to go in some story that I've created in my head. I just now have validation for it. I've connected to other authors and realized that I'm not crazy, or maybe we all are, but that's the thing . . . this whole idea of laying in bed and just imagining things is not something that everybody does? Nobody else has worlds, and people in their heads? No? What?

Daphne
The key word you're saying is "joy." I've got two answers. One would be my wedding . . . my marriage to my husband, soon to be twenty years. I think I relate things to events because that's what I do. I was thirty-eight when I got married. It was my first time getting married. That's not young . . . it's not old, but I was not young. So for many, many years, of course, as a typical girl, I thought about my wedding. I would duplicate my wedding today if I could, because it was the best day for me for all the reasons that it should be . . . because I finally found someone that I knew was the right person for me, and we were coming together. He'd been married before. He would have cared less about the wedding day. He felt, "We can just live together forever,"

103

but for me, I said, "No, I can't do that." So that was my joy . . . that day . . . bringing us together, bringing all my family and friends and his family and friends and all of us together. It was my dream day because it was what I wanted it to be . . . outdoors, released butterflies, gospel music, amazing flowers, all of my favorite foods. So that day, and my future life, which is beautiful, it's great . . . he's just the right guy for me. So that's one.

And then . . . I love my birthday. I've always had a hard time with getting older, not for any reason other than just the anticipation of the next year. But I love celebrating my birthday, so it's never a question of whether or not I'm going to have a birthday celebration, but I've always had a challenge . . . I think I've psychoanalyzed myself because I believe I'm a psychologist with no degree in psychology. I believe I can figure out what's going on in my world. I had a hard time with my forties, and I think it was because my mom passed in her early forties. So I believed psychologically that I didn't know if I should be there or not. I think when I got to my fifties, I felt a new relief. "I can do this. This is okay."

Although I love to celebrate my birthday, I don't love things being about me. I like things being about other people. So for my fiftieth birthday, I created my fifty favorite things and I had a whole event, for a whole weekend, that was all centered around my fifty favorite things, and having the people that joined me for my weekend . . . we had twenty-something people . . . experience my fifty favorite things. It was so fun thinking about my favorite things and putting it all together, but also sharing it with others. That's just my enjoyment, so it's personal, and I love it. I would create it again if I could because it was just one-of-a-kind.

Heather
Getting married to my longtime love has brought me the most joy. Her companionship has brought me the most joy, hands down. The

support that I receive from her, unconditionally. I'm a Sagittarius and I'm very passionate. I'll come home with many ideas and never, never does she poo poo them . . . ever. She's asking, "Okay, how do we do this now?" So, single-handedly, that is the most joyful thing in my life besides my dog.

What else? Choosing me and moving home in 2018 was probably one of the most joyous experiences, though it was a heartbreaking experience . . . I was transitioning in a relationship and leaning into my life, and though it was painful, it did bring me relief and joy knowing that I was no longer stuck. I had been stuck. I had felt stuck with where I was in my life. So that was a huge turning point.

There are so many, but those are two very big ones. I would say another one too, in life, was realizing that within three years of running my business, I turned it into a six-figure agency and I had never accumulated money like that in my life before. I was always a salaried employee and there's now no cap to my income potential. So realizing that brought me a lot of joy.

Donna
Oh, not related to work? I'm actually going to answer this both ways. Obviously, meeting Frank was the best thing that ever happened to me. There's a yin and yang in most relationships. When I'm training people, and I'm talking about personality styles, I say, "God's sense of humor at work is that you marry the person who's the total opposite of you." So you marry the person who drives you crazy. But the flip side of that is that Frank helped re-reshape me and many of my philosophies about doing business. He has always been a great sounding board, a great influence over me. We say all the time that he has made me a much more patient, tolerant person, and I've made him a more assertive person, in a business sense. So, certainly, finding someone who is truly a life partner . . . we met through volunteer work, which is really important to both of us. We have so many things in common, things that we love to do . . . travel, theatre, supporting scholarships of all kinds. We just have so many activities in common,

philosophies in common, but we've both been able to help each other business-wise as well. So, the most life-altering thing for me was finding a great life partner and having that constant in my life.

I think my dad was a great influence. There was a moment when he did not support me when I told him I was going to start this business. That was very devastating for me. But my father, who never apologized in his life to anybody, had the class to apologize to me and admit that he was wrong when my business really hit and I was doing so well . . . better than any of us ever imagined that it would. He did admit that he was wrong. That was a great moment for me. After that, he was, after Frank, my best supporter. That was a pivotal moment of joy for me.

I have a great, great social circle that I work really hard at maintaining and nurturing, and I get moments of joy from those people every day. And it's a two way street. I hope I'm giving those moments of joy without any expectation of anything in return. Having just had surgery, I think the entire first month after my surgery, there were people here almost every single night bringing food, flowers, asking "What can I do? What do you need?" They were grocery shopping for us, bringing food, helping me however they could . . . you find out who your friends are in moments like that. That brought me a lot of joy, knowing that there are so many people who care about me. I'm very grateful for that. Now, the older you get, the more things like that mean so much because those are people who are like an extension of my family. Some of them are people I've known for thirty-five years, more than half my life. So those are joyful, important moments to me.

Wei
Hmmmm. You would think that this wouldn't be that hard of a . . . it shouldn't be a difficult question to answer. Oh. You know what? That is actually not hard . . .

The day I was married . . . originally, I was scheduled to get into San Francisco in the afternoon . . . early afternoon, probably around noon.

DON'T FIGHT THE FLOW: FOLLOWING YOUR ORGANIC PATH

I can't recall. We had scheduled one of the last appointments at City Hall. This was back when California had enabled same-sex marriage. My husband arrived earlier in the week, and I was supposed to meet him, arriving on the day we were getting married. My flight was delayed by a number of weather-related events. As we're in flight, I'm looking at my watch and it's looking pretty tight. I think from the time that we were projected to land, I had about maybe 30 minutes to get from the airport to City Hall in downtown San Francisco, which is not really doable even in the best of circumstances.

So when we finally landed . . . of course, everybody immediately got up from their seats and they started emptying the overhead bins . . . I motioned to the woman sitting next to me. I said, "Ma'am, is it possible for me to slide past you? I need to be in City Hall in half an hour for my wedding and I am not going to make it." She . . . and this is a story of the wonders of humankind . . . she broadcasts to the entire plane, "This man is getting married. Everybody move aside." And so the entire plane, except for a couple of people, actually parted like the Red Sea and allowed me to grab my carry-on from the overhead, run out the plane and down the ramp. It was just fantastic.

And the miracles of human beings continued from there. As I'm approaching a cab, the driver gets out of the cab to help me load my suitcase in the trunk. As I'm approaching him, I say, "No, no, no. There's no time. I need to get to City Hall, and the quicker you can get me there, the bigger your tip will be."

So he closes the trunk and we both jump into the cab. I'm sitting with the suitcase in my lap and we're off, and of course, it's almost 5:00 P.M. on whatever day of the week it was. We're in full San Francisco rush hour traffic, but we're carefully, and methodically, quickly zipping along. He gets me close to City Hall. We just had to go around the corner, around the block, and we're at a dead stop. The cab driver said, "Sir, this is as close as I can get you at a minute before 5:00 P.M." I said, "Here you go." I think . . . let's say the cab fare was forty dollars, I think I tipped him sixty dollars.

107

You tipped him sixty or twenty dollars?

I tipped him sixty dollars, on top of forty, because he got me to City Hall in roughly thirty minutes, which is just impossible. So I'm running up the stairs with my carry-on. Mind you, there are a couple of sharp objects in my toiletry bag, but I'm flying through the metal detectors, at which point I'm told, "Sir . . . sir, you need to stop and have us search your bags." Ugh. "Okay."

So, meanwhile, the clock's still ticking and I'm flying from one room to another in City Hall. Because they had such a mass of people getting married, the normal places for the registrar and whatnot were not being used, and they actually placed those check-in locations in an overflow area. So I'm running from point A to point B to point C. Finally, I get to the right place, and I'm totally out of breath. I fly into the room, and the woman behind me says, "You must be Wei." I turn around, and I look, and there's my at-the-time fiancé, smiling ear to ear, and this woman says, "Well, we weren't going to leave without you." "I didn't know that!"

So, I think that was the most pleasant surprise because it really showcased how amazing people can be if they're given a reason to be, and how we can all just come together to make something really improbable happen. The fact that I got from the San Francisco airport to downtown, to make it to my wedding ceremony, it just . . . unlikely . . . all these unlikely human happenings . . . that was the most pleasant surprise.

Gabriel

When my grandma died a couple of years ago . . . I was very close with her . . . I worked on the eulogy for her funeral. It was, to this day, probably one of my favorite memories. It was such a wonderful way to send her off. I worked on my eulogy very deliberately. I worked it, in part, because of a moment at a wedding, prior to her passing, that I felt I botched, but actually, for even smaller moments when I have to give a little speech.

I mentioned before that I just directed this short film, and on the night of the second day, when we were supposed to have wrapped, but we didn't wrap, I had to kind of hold court for a moment and get everyone together to say "thank you," and I didn't prepare. I didn't write it down, but I had thought about it in advance. "What feeling do I want to leave them with? How do I let them know how much it meant to me that they came together to work on this thing that means so much to me?" That's probably not really the answer you were looking for, but it's really the one that feels the most relevant right now. It's important for me to express certain things to people in certain moments, and to make those messages mean something. I don't know if it's because I'm a writer by nature, or because that's kind of my love language . . . people saying the things they mean. So I like to do that for other people. There is something about saying exactly what you mean, and baring your soul a little bit at the right moment, when you feel very moved, when you know it matters. That, to me, is the point of living. I missed that at that wedding, and I have tried not to get that wrong since.

Steve
Oh, wow. You know, it's interesting to think about because . . . a little bit of a backstory on this. So, Annie and I have been married forever. We don't have kids. Our lives from the very beginning have always kind of been about us. We never really talked about having kids. That really wasn't what we were into, but what we both are really into is our jobs. I don't often think about life in terms of work and not work, or, life. So, a lot of my joyful moments are around work and things to do with what I consider I do for work . . . creating and building and everything.

The moments that are most meaningful to me are the ones that Annie and I do together. Whether it's going to see a show that I designed, or that I worked on, or going to see a Cirque du Soleil® show that has Annie's cast up there, or going to a hockey game where she has performers doing intermission performances, and we get to go and

109

experience that. Now that to me is a life moment, but that is also a work moment. There isn't a clear delineation of those moments.

Victoria
Oh, wow. The birth of my daughter. The births of my grandchildren. Those are givens. I think being able to train and accomplish climbing mountains, if you will. Now, keep in mind, I want to make sure that I'm very clear that it's more of a hike . . . it's a technical hike more than it is a technical climb. There's a difference. I'm not hanging on with carabiners on the side of a mountain. That makes it sound very exaggerated. I want some clarity there. But I think that training for that, that brought me a lot of joy. The moment that the wheels touched down in Africa, I thought, "Oh my God, I'm in Africa." It was just amazing. I loved it.

What mountains did you climb?

Kilimanjaro Trek in Tanzania, Machu Picchu in Peru, and then trained for the Himalayas in Nepal, but had an unexpected diversion there.

Are you going to try to do that again?

You know, that's so funny you asked that because I contemplated that this morning. I don't know. That would've been a pretty tough trek . . . fourteen days. I would love to go back there some time. Katmandu was not my thing, but I think for a night or two I could get through it to be able to get to base camp and start that.

Jesus
Meeting my husband, Eric. Several weeks before meeting Eric, I had lost my beloved father. I was extremely depressed, and contemplating suicide. As a distraction from the grief, I'd go on dating sites with the intention of hooking up with as many men as possible, without using protection, as a way to punish myself. Then one day I saw Eric's beautiful face and I swiped right. Soon after swiping, I got a notification that we were a match, so we planned to meet that week. I

was in and out of bed and though I promised him we'd talk throughout the week, I never reached out. The day of our date, he reached out to ask if we were still meeting and I said "Yes." When I met him, I was instantly attracted to him, but there was more and I was curious to explore it. I can pinpoint the exact moment, on our second date, that I fell in love with him. I had a reason to want to live, to want to get up in the morning, to keep going and fighting and I never expected to feel that way. That is the most unexpected moment in my life that has brought me, and continues to bring me, the greatest joy.

Michael

Well, yesterday I moved into this house. This is the first time I've ever stayed at a house that isn't my parents', or a friend's, but where I'm actually paying rent. It's mine. That was pretty cool, yesterday. I'm not going to lie to you.

Congratulations!

Thank you. Hmmmm, life moments . . . the only things I can really think of, as far as my life, that were really cool, have all been related to sports. I'm trying to think of something that was just not related to a sport in any way, that was just a very cool thing that happened in life. Being interviewed on Golf Channel that week, last spring, was kind of cool. But again, that's related to sports and my career. That's a tough one for me. I don't really know. Like I said, I'm very much flatline. So if something cool happens, my thought is "Oh, yeah, nice." I don't sit there thinking, "This is so awesome. This is great." But, moving in here was pretty cool. I enjoyed that.

CHAPTER 8: BUT I WANT IT . . . I THINK

Have there been any times when you didn't get what you wanted, or thought you wanted, and it ultimately turned out to be better for you, but you didn't see/recognize it at the time? What were those?

Brian

Sure. I got to college as an overweight character actor and then I quickly realized that is not what I wanted to be. So I went on a crazy crash diet, lost a bunch of weight, and then I said, "I'm a chorus boy." Well, I wasn't even there yet. We were doing *Brigadoon* and I wanted to be Charlie Dalrymple so badly. I auditioned, thought I did decently, and didn't get the part. I went to the director and I said I was curious if there was anything I could have done better. He said, "No, there was nothing really you could have done different. I needed you to be a dancer in the ensemble because the other guy can't dance." Wait, so I'm getting punished for that? I was devastated. But then I realized that I love being in the chorus. I love creating characters and having fun with that. It was such a weird light bulb moment for me. And it took days of being annoyed and days of being pissed off to get to that point. So there's that answer.

And then the other answer would be in 2013, my apartment building burned down because the lady that lived on the top floor overloaded her electrical outlet. It was a very trying time. Rarely in one's life do you have to buy an entire wardrobe of clothes, or buy all new stuff, because you normally just keep acquiring things, and getting rid of things, and acquiring things. I remember at the time, good God, I was devastated, and the day that it happened, I was on the phone with my parents and my dad said, "Well, Bri, it's just stuff." And I said "Dad, I get that it's just stuff. But it's my stuff. And I don't need you to be a . . . this is not a teaching moment. This is a moment where I need you to just hear me out." What I learned coming out of that is it was just stuff. And it took me a long time to realize it, and I don't need stuff. My apartment is not packed to the gills like it used to be with everything that I had ever touched and owned. I'm a bit of a packrat, but I've gotten so much better over time. And like Marie Condo said, "If it doesn't bring you joy, get rid of that thing." It's the same way with people, the same way with things, like a job. If it's not adding anything to your life, why are you letting it take away from your life? Yeah. Marie Condo that sh*t. That's the quote for the book cover.

Lisa

I'm sure there are plenty. Since my brain's in high school right now . . . I really wanted to be part of Irvine Singers. It was boys and girls and they performed together. Because I didn't get that, I took classes at South Coast Rep and started doing stuff over there with them. It's a good theatre here, locally. That led to the development of me as a performer and a really good foundation that served me well. I don't know that I would have gotten . . . I don't know. I can't answer what I would have gotten from the other, but that was something I really, really wanted to get that I didn't get. And because I didn't, then I did something else that turned out to be really good for me.

Sabrina

I can be very general on that and say as an actor, every role I thought I wanted and didn't get probably worked to my advantage because it opened up doors for me elsewhere. I would say there were one or two roles that I really, really wanted that I did not get. But, the opportunities that came from being available, by not doing those shows, probably worked to my advantage.

I'm trying to think of something specific. I would say in some of my cases, the opposite has been true, where I didn't go with my gut for the thing that I really wanted because I did what I thought I was "supposed to do." And nine times out of ten, it was because of my marriage that I didn't go pursue this thing, or didn't go chase this thing, or I didn't get this thing that I thought I wanted, because I was too busy focusing on my marriage. That one's a hard one to quantify. I'm not sure I can give you a specific one. I'm going to have to ponder that one.

Author followed-up eleven months later with the same question . . .

So at the time, I remember I was quantifying personal things and professional things. You asked me if I wanted to add to my previous answer, and yes, I do. So the current situation with my former employer . . . my former employer as of a month ago, because when we did our first interview, I was fully employed with this person, loving it, and learning a lot. Since that time, I thought I was thriving in that job. My intention was to stay. I was supposed to be running the company and then, like, a one hundred eighty degree change happened that I won't get into. It just de-escalated quickly and my expectation of being fully employed with that company went bye, bye, bye.

So I thought I was going to have a career with this company, and now I don't, and I'm sitting here wondering if the universe is just trying to say, "Hey, girl, it's okay. Do something else. You've been working your whole life. You've been burning the candle at both ends. You've been saying "No" to things that you wanted to say "Yes" to because you had this job." And that's always been the case. Trying to accept that maybe it's okay to take a break and maybe it's okay to rest right now, and maybe it's okay to let Mike take care of me for a little while. The bills will get paid somehow. I can always make money somehow . . . unemployment, savings, part-time work here and there, gig work. The stability may not be there for a while, but maybe this is the universe's way of allowing me to say "Yes" to things I wasn't able to say "Yes" to before. So I would say the expectation that I had, and what actually happened, were the exact opposites. But I think it's a good thing because honestly, when I lost that job, I felt like a weight was lifted off of me and I didn't expect that reaction. Usually, when you lose a job, it's panic, it's crying, it's pressure, whatever. And honestly, my feeling was "Cool, bye." I logged off the computer and went and sat by the pool, which I don't do. I just don't do that. So I feel like it's just the universe's way of saying, "Take a minute, recharge, maybe say "Yes" to some things, and figure out what you want to do now. Maybe chase the thing you were trying to do before."

And when I asked you about this follow-up interview, you told me that you had lost your job, didn't elaborate, but were not in the mindset to talk about success. So it's interesting to hear you now just two weeks later, after you've come out of the initial "ugh."

Oh yeah, yeah, you're right. I forgot about that. I think it was because when you had originally contacted me for this follow-up, it had only been a week or two out of losing the job, and I was still kind of grappling with why it happened. I know I didn't do anything wrong. I know that it was not me and I was not the cause of my job loss, but it was also still the right thing. I was trying to equate what we define as success with somebody who just lost their job. How do I talk to you about success when I am recently unemployed? For me, it was hard to . . . I don't know, I'm not sure I'm coming up with the right terminology for this, but, when you're just in that weird place of "Who the heck do I think I am to talk about success when I was just fired?" It was mutual, but at the end of the day, I was terminated. I didn't turn in my notice. She let me go.

Although this book is not necessarily about "success." It's about fighting the flow and following your organic path, which, as you just said . . . maybe this is your organic path, now . . . to be doing something different.

Right. Which is a little terrifying to me because I am not conditioned to follow the flow. I am conditioned to survive. I am conditioned to work. I am conditioned to have a plan. And now the plan has been thrown out the window through no fault of my own. And it's just this weird place to be in, as that type-A personality, thinking, "Now what do I do?" I'm keeping myself busy, in a good way. I'm still working on my recipes, I'm still working on my website, I'm putting myself out for auditions, I'm making connections. I have so much time now just to sit that I didn't have before. It's weird. It's a weird place to be in.

Chris

Disappointment is a common trend. I don't often get what I want. Oh, let's see. Oh, that's a hard one. I have to probably fall back on that Disney trip. I really wanted to go to Halloween Horror Nights that night that I was shooting . . . my birthday. I wanted to get drunk. I was stone-cold sober and starving because craft services did not have anything gluten-free and neither did the online dinner catering. I literally found two bags of Pirate's Booty, the little corn and cheese puffs, and that was my birthday dinner.

Daphne

One hundred percent. The easy answer to that is when I thought I was top runner-up for a corporate job, after I left my last corporate job, and I had interviewed, interviewed, interviewed, was talking heavily with executives of this company, and the former planner, and I just knew I was going to get that opportunity. I didn't get it and I was bummed. I didn't know what to do next. That led to my frustration with corporate America and stopping myself from doing any further interviewing at that point. I said, "I'm done. This is ridiculous." And I pushed myself to at least put in a little time, and give myself a year, in this independent world. And it was the best thing I could have ever done . . . to stop focusing on that and focus more on this, and then having a great end-result, years later. The first few years were hard. At that time, I didn't know the joy or the pleasure I could get from being independent. At that time, the only thing that made me work more towards building my own business was the frustration from not getting that last job.

Heather

Oh, holy smokes. There are probably many, many, many times that has happened. Let me think. Yeah, our wedding, for example. We planned for nine months . . . we found the caterer, the venue just happened to fall in our laps, we found the rings, we found all of it, right? All the vendors, all the suppliers . . . and then all of a sudden, the venue doesn't work out and we have to pivot. UPS loses my wife's engagement ring. We don't have one for the wedding. A hurricane decides to roll up the East Coast after having just weeks and weeks of beautiful, beautiful weather. But I have to tell you that it was designed the way it was supposed to be, because we have received, and continue to receive, compliments upon compliments on what a vibe we gave . . . how authentic it was that they didn't even realize it was raining and cold . . . that it was the most loving wedding. It had to be that way. It had to be that way in order, I believe, for people to recognize just how amazing this love is. And so you have one idea of the wedding and that just gets totally scrapped and what it will be, it was, and it was beautiful. And it worked out better than planned.

Donna
Oh, you're talking again professionally, correct?

It's up to you. If you want to answer both ways, by all means, please do.

Well, you know, I am a firm believer in the statement "everything happens for a reason." You just don't always know at the time what it is. So I'm trying to think business-wise . . . over the course of my career, there have been times when I've been asked to submit a proposal for something for work that I didn't get and I guess earlier on, it bothered me more when I didn't get it. Now I just chalk it up and keep going. I think earlier on it was more of a blow, emotionally, if I didn't get work. But as a percentage, I'm a very good closer, so I get most of the work that I go after. I can't think of a specific example of work I didn't get where later I said, "Oh, good thing I didn't get that," except that I remember there were times where I didn't get work and then something else came along where I said, "Oh, it's a good thing I didn't get that because then I wouldn't have been able to take this." I don't remember the specific jobs, but over the years there have been a handful of times when you're only one person, when you can't clone yourself, when you don't have a team of other employees . . . it's you, yourself, and you, and you can only do so much. There are only so many hours in the day to create deliverables.

And so if I were to get assignment X and then be offered assignment Y, that was time sensitive, and I couldn't do it because I had already committed to X, that would be a bummer. I know that has happened over the years, though I don't remember specific examples.

It's funny because clearly everybody has lots of things in life that they wanted that they didn't get. And I know that's happened to me, but I always tend to focus on the positive and what I do have and did get. I'm sure if I sat and thought about it, I would come up with a whole list of examples, but off the top of my head, I literally can't think of any.

Wei

I think applying for, and being rejected by, the Navy Reserves three times definitely fits that bill. I wanted to join the military for several reasons. At the time, I did not think that serving my country as a civilian was the same as serving in uniform. Basically, I had that mindset that if you're not dodging bullets, you're not really serving your country. But, now, I will definitely enforce that it is not true. The U.S. Government has many thousands of work roles, and every single one of them is as critical as the next. That said, there are things that the military can do because of the U.S. Code that non-armed forces cannot do. So that was one of the reasons why I wanted to join. Title 10 offers certain things that you can't get with Title 1 or Title 18. So, I thought that being a federal civilian, with a reserve background, would be the best blend of the right roles and responsibilities I wanted to match up.

That said, I tried to join the military three times, and each time it highlighted that it wasn't meant to be . . . a different roadblock each time. And if I had actually joined, there are several things that I could not really do as readily. First and foremost, moving around is not as easy an option. You have to get approval from your superiors. You have to then find another unit to drill with, and that would have made my move to Florida, in 2019, a bit more difficult, if not impossible. It would have meant more time away from the family, at the very least, because I would be drilling once a month somewhere else, probably not in my home state at the time.

Another thing that would have been more difficult was taking care of my sick parent in his last days. I would probably have had to drill, rather than take my dad to chemotherapy. That would have been very emotionally devastating. Nowadays, I am very happy that things turned out the way they did, but at the time, I certainly was surprised and dismayed that the universe put so many roadblocks in my path.

Gabriel

Every . . . single . . . time I've not gotten something, it's been the best thing that could've happened to me. Now, I don't know if that's because that's a universal law of life, or if it really helps to be the kind of person who responds to those failures, or those disappointments, by doing other things . . . getting creative, getting frustrated, getting angry, trying it this way, or just giving up and saying, "Oh, that's not my path, *this* is my path." But every single time I haven't gotten something, in time, I've realized that it was amazing.

When I was in my early to mid-twenties, I spent three-ish years at the consulting firm. It was funny because I could have kept going for another year before they kicked me out to go to business school. Once you hit three years, they start talking to you about going to business school. I really did want to go to business school, but I sort of felt, in my heart, that it was too soon. Actually, now that we're talking about it, I think I also felt in my heart that it wasn't maybe my path. Either way, I wasn't ready.

So I left that firm, which was a little bit of a scary thing to do, because the money was pretty good for a young person, and going back to the question you asked me at the top of this, that job really gave me a firm identity in the world. "What do you do?" "I'm a management consultant." Done. Leaving that job was not just leaving the money and the structure, it also brought up the question, "Who am I now? I don't even know."

When I left that job, on my very last day, literally my final day in the office, I got a call from a recruiter at Google. A friend of mine had sent them my resume and I thought, "Well, this is very exciting. This would make a lot of sense. I leave the consulting firm and then I go do this job," which really matched the experience that I had up until that point. Actually, there were two jobs. They were interested in me for two different roles, so I would interview for both and I was really excited. I could see myself working at Google. I was very worked up and it gave me a lot of comfort to know that this would be the next step. Thus began what I think was probably a four or five-month-long interview process.

They flew me up there at least once, maybe twice, and it was just round after round with all these different divisions, and layers, and blah, blah, blah. Long story short, I really was not a fit for one of the roles, and I really kind of panicked because I thought, "Oh, I'm really not very smart and I'm really not as sophisticated as I think I am." And that's sort of true. In that world, I really was not a good fit. But the other role was much more creative. It was at YouTube and it drew on all my weird interests.

At that point, I had co-written my first screenplay for a feature film, which is a weird story. I don't fully understand why I did that, or how I stumbled into it. It kind of came to me because a friend was working on a script and wanted some help. I had zero designs on Hollywood, or trying to be a screenwriter. It started off with me just giving some notes: "Here's a thought here, here's a thought there. What if he said this? What if she said that?" I had no understanding of what a story is or how to make something entertaining. I just was instinctively interested in trying to help. That evolved into me being a co-writer on the script. I loved that. I also had written, with my sister, some lyrics for a pop album that we recorded. So I really had some weird experiences and they all were valuable for YouTube. So, "Cool, this makes sense."

Four or five months of this, and it finally got to a point where . . . I don't know if it's still the case now, but at the time, Larry Page had to approve every single hire. He was CEO, and he would look at every person they hired and say, "Yes." But to get to that, you had to go through this hiring committee. To get to the hiring committee, you had to put together a thirty page dossier on yourself. They told me to put *everything* in there. "Do not hold back . . . every award, every experience, every talent, every certificate. We want people who are good at a lot of different things and interested in a lot of things. And we want to see how you've excelled in all these different worlds. Do not be humble. Do not be shy." So I put together this whole thing and said, "I wrote this pop album, and I wrote a screenplay, and I did this, and I placed in this poetry competition when I was in high school," which was just so dumb. And I just really went ham. The recruiter said, "This is great. Just stand by. We just have to get through this." A week goes by, and two weeks go by, and three weeks go by, and it's probably a month or more, and I just never heard from this recruiter again.

I have to explain now that while I was still working at the consulting firm, I took this class at an acting school, which was not because I wanted to be an actor, and it wasn't even an acting class. It was called "Singing for Actors," and it was about using your voice . . . I can't sing to save my life . . . but you had to sing as an exercise in tapping into different parts of yourself. It was a really transformative experience for me, this class, because I was a very rigid, controlled, shut-down, masculine young man. I'm really not that way deep down, but externally, I was very . . . you wouldn't recognize me. I was a different person. And I went through this class and it was *amazing*. This dude who taught the class kind of cracked me open in a really cool way. It was terrifying and it was awesome.

I went back to my consulting firm, and there were these two partners at the firm who both headed up the media and entertainment practice. I told them that I was doing this class and it was really helping me with my public speaking, and it was really helping me with clients. They were intrigued, so they signed up for the class and it changed their lives. One of them, this guy who I'm guessing was in his mid to late forties, took the class and had some combination of waking up from a dream and having a midlife crisis, which I guess is the same thing. He realized, "I don't want to be a partner at a consulting firm. I want to be an actor." I think he had studied theatre when he was a kid, so there was always that dream in him. He left the partnership, which was a big deal . . . kind of amazing, but it was a little like, "Oh, boy, that's an intense decision to make." He gave it all up because he wanted to be a creative, which I understand. I didn't think that my little recommendation would change this man's life, or perhaps ruin it. Because he had been doing consulting for so long, even after he left, companies would still reach out to him to ask him to consult for them. So Cirque du Soleil® asked him if he would come on and do a year-long strategy project for them to define the future of the company, and help them figure out "Who are we going to be for the next twenty, thirty years?" He asked me if I wanted to basically run the project. I said "Yes" because it felt like "Great, a job just kind of fell into my lap. It's a good interim job." Meanwhile, I'm interviewing at Google, which was fine. It wasn't a secret. So it was a short-term job to keep me going before I could get the Google job.

I was in Montreal, in my hotel room, and I had reached out to the recruiter a few times, asking, "What's going on? I'm not hearing anything." And then finally she called me while I was in the car, driving home, and she said, "I'm afraid that the hiring committee read your dossier and decided that we can't move forward." I thought, "Yeah, I sort of gathered that." My heart was kind of sinking at this moment because I was really excited about it. They were giving me strong indications that it was going to happen. They were asking, "Okay, when could you move up here? What kind of stock options do you want?" So it really wasn't just "We're interested." It was more "This is happening. This is just a formality."

So I was pretty down, and I asked her, "Can you just tell me what happened?" I think she said it's their policy to not comment or whatever, which is, I think, pretty common with some of these tech companies. I said, "Just between you and me . . . we've known each other for five months. Just give me something. I need to understand." And she said, "Okay . . ." She pulled over too. That was funny. She said, "I'm just pulling over . . . so basically, those other interviews, with that other division, the one that we ended up not pursuing . . . the feedback in those interviews wasn't great. It colored your performance in the other interviews." I thought, "Oh, that sucks. But yeah, okay, fine," because it was not great. I knew that. Then she said "And the hiring committee looked at your dossier and they just felt like you had so many interests in all these different places that they weren't sure if you were really a Googler." I thought "You told me to put all these things in there! You wanted all that stuff in there!" I didn't say this out loud, but in my head I'm thinking, "What?!?!" I think what she was saying, and she's probably correct, was that they have so much data on what makes employees succeed, how long they'll stay at Google, and there's probably some algorithm plus human judgment that looked at that and said, "This guy's not going to stay here for more than a few years," or, "If he stays here, he's not going to be great because we need people who are like *this*," and I'm not like that.

It was devastating. I had left this consulting job. I took this weird interim job. I pinned my hopes on Google. You start to construct a whole story out of these moments, and think, "Oh, of course, I'm going to work at Google, and then I'll have a name . . . everybody knows what Google is. I won't have to explain what that job is. When I go out and meet new people and they ask me what I do, I'll say, "I work at Google" and that will be it. As comforting as it was to say "I work as a consultant," this was going to be even better . . . anything to avoid having to be a guy who's just bumbling along, trying to figure it out after he quit a job.

So losing the Google offer was more than just losing the job. It was losing a whole story in an arc to my life. I was pretty down about it for a week or two.

I'm just now remembering also that the guy who sent my resume to Google . . . when he heard that it had gotten to that final stage, invited me to Las Vegas to celebrate. My mom was telling my family that I got this job . . . it was really funny. Talk about putting the cart before the horse and celebrating too soon.

The reason I'm telling this story is shortly after that, I started writing more seriously, and I wrote another script, and I happened to meet a really wonderful, special film producer who has since become my collaborator, one of my best friends, and the director of two of my movies. We met and we hit it off and we started working together. That was really the beginning of my real journey in storytelling and in Hollywood. So many things have happened since the Google thing. This path that I'm on, which I know is the path that I should be on, would not have happened, potentially, if Google had said "Yes." They did me the biggest favor by saying "No" to me. I feel that way about almost everything, if not everything, that doesn't go my way.

When I think back, that is one of those moments where I know my life would have been very different, or I would have just kicked this down the road by five or ten years and I would have had this weird dream to do this work, and I wouldn't have been able to do it because I was too busy trying to figure out how to monetize ads on YouTube.

Steve
Yeah. Oh, absolutely. There have been shows that . . . and this is especially true back when I was more of a company manager . . . but there were shows, and I don't even remember exactly what shows . . . I was on the first national tour of *Rent*. And *Rent* was supposed to do an extended sit-down engagement in San Francisco, and I was the assistant company manager at the time. They decided, kind of at the last minute, once the show got to San Francisco, that they were going to let me go and hire a local assistant company manager so they didn't have to pay per diem, and it wasn't going to be on an ATPAM (union) contract. I remember thinking, "Well, you know, I need to find another show." I was still an apprentice, within the union, at the time,

and I think had I gotten on as assistant company manager for another Broadway tour, or first national tour, my life would have been wildly different. I probably would have gone more towards the kind of button-down, tie, company manager route. So by not getting another tour right away, that brought me to New York and allowed me to work on *De La Guarda*, a very nontraditional show . . . and I always kind of considered myself nontraditional, which was a great fit. And again, everything has led me to where I am right now. So I definitely don't have any regrets about that.

Victoria
Absolutely. There is one particular situation where I interviewed for a position. I tried for years to move ahead in my organization, meaning taking a leadership role. I was able to create a position, but I could not get the support staff I needed. I wanted to get into a leadership role. I was told to apply for a position by the person that wanted to hire me, who said, "You are my top pick." And then the interview did not happen. Actually, I was set up, and in hindsight, it was a gift. It was a gift because the job, the role, and this individual . . . well, that person was let go. But, the role did not turn out to be what I wanted it to be. It wasn't for me. It really wasn't. It was a communications job and it really wasn't the role that was best for me. But, it hurt. It stung.

Jesus
Oh, many times. I think when I was young I wanted a career in Hollywood and I'm glad that it didn't happen when I was younger because I think I'd be dead now.

Also, I'm glad that I didn't come out sooner, because I think I'd also probably . . . maybe not . . . be dead. It was the AIDS crisis in the early eighties. I wasn't ready for it. So let's say I had been out . . . I probably would have . . . I don't know . . . contracted HIV or AIDS and probably wouldn't have lived through the AIDS crisis. The reason I mention this is because I'm friends with Pedro Zamora's sister, and there is a documentary where he talked about the fact that when he was in high school, he had unprotected sex with older men. That's how he contracted it. I think that if I had done the same thing, and I probably would have, because I was so insecure, I probably would have had a lot of sex, with a lot of men, and made some bad choices that ultimately would have resulted in me contracting the virus. So staying in the closet may have saved my life.

Michael

Oh, man, you've got some good ones. You're making me think here. I'm sure there were, but again, I don't . . . I don't attach to memories and emotions quite like that. I literally just kind of live on a day to day basis. I feel like I live very presently. If I was going to say . . . I remember that there was one college for golf, and I think my dad had a friend who knew the coach, or something like that, and I don't know if I ever actually talked to him or not, but that was a thing where my dad was trying to get me hooked up with that coach to go play college golf. Sometimes I wish I played college golf, but obviously I don't think you and I'd be talking right now if I did. So I've got to think it's probably a positive for me that I didn't end up playing college golf, and I didn't end up getting connected with that guy. That's the only thing that really sticks out in my mind right now.

CHAPTER 9: RE-DO

If you could go back and do anything, up to this point in your life, over again, would you, and what would it be? Multiple answers are okay.

Brian

The first answer is "No." I would not re-do anything because I would not be here. I would not be getting to wake up and create every day. I would not be able to have all of the relationships that I have, and again, another life thing that took me a long time to realize is it does you no good to think about what might have been, because it's not. And I'm not trying to make it sound weird and dark and depressing, but what good is it going to do for me to go back and change things, because I'm still here? I don't know. Terrible answer.

So how do you feel about *If/Then*?

The musical? I had issues with it. I had issues with it just as a show and the structure and all of that. But it's the same with *Sliding Doors*, the Gwyneth Paltrow movie. Sure, maybe there's a different universe where another me decided to do something different, but I would like to think that person is just as happy as I am now. But I don't know that. I'm not going to lose any sleep over what I could have changed then, to do now. This is getting very theatre heavy, but theatre played a huge part of my life for a long time. When I graduated college, I went on my first audition four days later, and as I was on the train going up to the audition, I was talking myself out of it because I was thinking, "I'm not ready. I can't do this thing. I wish I could go back to college and be safe and comfortable there." And then I talked myself back into it and I ended up getting cast in it. That was my first national tour. I went out on the road for nine months or so with a musical. It's like that *Avenue Q* song, "I Wish I Could Go Back To College," but why? Why would you do that, because everybody in college wants to get out of college? What I have come to realize is staying in your

127

safety net will only get you so far in life. And that's in terms of people, in terms of what you want to do. That's in terms of so many things. Get out of your comfort zone and then you discover what it is you are really good at or what it is you are terrible at.

Also, coming to terms with failure . . . this is one of the things that I try to teach kids left, right, and center. Crash and burn. Make mistakes. Good God, for the love of anything, get out of your comfort zone, and don't worry if you aren't perfect, because your fear of failure will be debilitating in your life if you don't allow yourself the fear and the freedom to fail. Stop calling it fear of failure. We should call it freedom to fail.

Lisa

That is a challenging question for me because I feel like I would have to have the knowledge that I have now to go back and do something differently. And the reason I am who I am now is because I made the choices that I made. So that sort of lines up with regrets for me. And I don't have those. I have learning experiences, but not regrets. Does that make sense?

Yes, it's a very good answer. Now, let me lay more on you. Hindsight is twenty/twenty. If you could go back with the knowledge you have now, to do something over, would you? And what would it be?

Ohhh, this is multilayered because there's lots I know now. The one thing I do think about would be staying in France that one extra year and just deferring my senior year and then coming back and finishing school and having that under my belt. That's with what I know now. There is no way in heck I was going to make that decision knowing what I did then. And there's another layer to that in that the boyfriend that I had in France, we broke up after that next Christmas. So that might have turned out differently. And it's good it turned out the way it did. So I'm not sure where that . . . there's stuff I still don't know about if I had made that decision. I don't know all the variables of what would've happened there.

I had an agent once that I really liked, that I really felt like he just wanted me to come and visit. And this is just my perspective from the time. I wasn't getting sent out on anything, but he wanted me to come and spend time at the office. It was up in Beverly Hills and I was living in Huntington Beach, so it was not close. I got disenchanted with that. And I left that agency. And I think if I had that to do over again, I would have done more hustle on my own and just used the agency to have the credibility and the person to go through to book jobs. So I would do that differently, now.

Sabrina
I know they say that you shouldn't, but yes. To be honest, I probably wouldn't marry my husband . . . my ex-husband. I wouldn't have said "Yes." Again, I don't want to dismiss the time we did have together . . . it sounds very dismissive when you say those things . . . but I probably wouldn't have married him, in hindsight. I wasn't making the choice for the right reasons, when I said "Yes." I probably wouldn't have stayed in my . . . there's a friendship of mine that recently faded, too. I wouldn't have stayed in that friendship as long either. I think I should have ended it a lot sooner. During the pandemic, it went out with a bang and it was probably over a lot sooner than that. I think the pandemic just exacerbated it.

I would definitely have made better choices for myself in my early thirties. I wish I could take back some of my choices to work around the clock and not take better care of myself, because that did cause health problems later down the road. I wish I could take some of that back. I wish I had heeded the advice that I give everybody else and not been a hypocrite when I said, "Go to sleep, go take a day off, it's okay." I didn't and I burned myself out, and it literally caused a breakdown to the point where my hair was falling out, and I was gaining a lot of weight, and I just wasn't in a good place. And, it made me not a good person to be around. I was very grumpy. So I wish I could go back and not have done that, and slowed down a bit, and

129

recognized that it was going to be okay.

I also wish I had stuck up for myself more. I let people talk to me in a terrible way, several years ago, because I was so afraid of being called a bitch, because it had been drilled into me. It's one of those weird things . . . I worked in a very, very corporate job. And then I was also an artist trying to grapple with those two different lives. In the theatre world, and in the art world, you can be a little bit more brisk because you've got to get things done and don't have time for the please and thank you and all of that. But in the corporate world . . . you would think it would be the opposite, but in my particular corporate environment, it was not. Everybody had feelings about everything. It was very HR. I always thought about that episode of *South Park* where they're doing the holiday show, but everyone's offended by everything, so it just becomes these kids wearing black and they're doing these robotic, chopping movements on stage. It was the most accurate thing I've ever seen because everybody was offended by everything, and I was conditioned at this time to be so worried about pleasing people and the HR aspects of it. It took me a long time to get to the place where I had to please everybody because that's what corporate wanted. I let people talk to me in a way that I would have never let people talk to me before. So I carried that into the theatre company I was managing, where members of my board were just calling me a bitch to my face because I was trying to hold them accountable, like you're supposed to do when you're running a business. It really messed with me for a while. I was battling these two worlds for a really long time. So I wish, in hindsight, that I had a little bit more of a spine to stand up for myself sooner, so I could say "You're not going to talk to me that way. This is how we're going to do things." But having said that, I also wish I had learned tact a lot sooner because I was very extreme . . . one or the other. Now I'm the queen of tact. But, both of those things can be true, where people were talking to me very poorly, but I also probably wasn't responding in the best way, so it perpetuated the cycle. I wish I could take some of that back, too.

Author followed-up eleven months later, after briefly

recapping her original answers . . .

Well, here's what's funny about that, though, and what I'll add to that is that I've gotten much better over the years . . . I don't know if it has come with age, and with age comes wisdom and confidence, or if we just run out of . . . pardon my French, we run out of sh*ts to give. I've run out of "I just don't care anymore," in a lot of ways. I still want to be professional, obviously civil, kind, when possible, but I don't worry about being nice. I think kind and nice are two different things that I didn't recognize until recently. I'm kind, but I'm not always nice. I'm direct, but sometimes my directness is, as much as I try to soften the blow, going to upset somebody. So I've just kind of gotten past this, and I will say my time at the little part-time restaurant job I worked at before this most recent job, as well as this most recent job, helped with that because I was brought on board because they "wanted a bulldog." She wanted me to be that person sometimes, so I was able to be of the mindset that I don't really care if I'm hurting your feelings right now. I still have a job to do. We've got to get that invoice paid. You're two months behind. I don't know why you're acting like the victim here. So it's interesting because I think a lot of that is still true in some ways, but I've learned to stand up for myself a lot more.

I'm actually in a current situation that may or may not be applicable in the theatre community, where lawyers are involved because there's somebody out there, behaving badly. And I'm not going to help you cover for this. I'm getting lawyers involved. So I think I've gotten way better at sticking up for myself . . . way better.

I've always been good at sticking up for other people, and then I'll take the crap. I'm not doing that anymore. So that's also probably partially why my boss had to let me go because I started calling her on her crap. "This isn't okay. I'm not doing this. No, you're asking me to do something that doesn't work. It's not going to work. It's inappropriate. I'm not doing that."

Chris

I definitely think that I should have let myself take more risks when I was younger. I have always let fear drive me. It wasn't until I was in my forties that I felt I should fail big or succeed. It doesn't matter. As long as you've made a leap of some kind. I keep joking about the fact that it might take me years before I ever financially break even on my book, and I don't think I would have had the confidence to do that earlier. I wish I had. I wish that I had had that level of confidence to take a lot of money and invest it into something that could fail big, a lot sooner, or at least have the bravery to audition for the things that I skipped because I didn't think that I was good enough, or that anybody would even bother considering me. Now that I'm heavier than I've ever been in my life, I'm more confident in myself. I'm way more confident than I was ten years ago, where I wouldn't go to an audition if I thought I was too fat that day. There are a lot of things that held me back and I wish that I could go back and redo those with the confidence that I have now.

That's not to say that I feel confident every day, but there's definitely been a shift in the way I approach things and the way that . . . granted, I don't think my personal training career is that successful. And as of right now, my book career is not successful. But both of those were investments that took a lot of guts for me to do. I'm still waiting to see if they ever pay off, but, they're chances that I took. I wish I had taken those types of chances earlier . . . like going to New York and auditioning for stuff . . . going to California and auditioning for stuff. Now, I like my house, I like my dog. I want to hang out here. I don't like Florida, but I don't feel like moving. I'm too old for that. But, again, if I'd had that kind of confidence back then, and could have done those crazy things then and just said, "Hey, if I lose money on this, at least I tried. If I completely fall flat on my face, at least I did it," and that's become a big thing for me. Just go out and do it. You might as well. You only live once.

Daphne

Oh, that's a good one. I think I'd say "No." I can't think of one because every path I took led me to where I am, and I love my end result. I've enjoyed every step along the way. I believe in this, and I just told someone who's young, this, the other day . . . I believe we can always change because we can always go back.

I'm fortunate to have lived in six states, and most of those moves have been because of jobs. I left New York City to go to Alabama for school. That was a personal choice. My first job was in Alabama, which is where I was for school, but I've moved and lived in other states since then, and have never regretted it because it's always the next step. I'm always open for whatever's next, but have enjoyed what it has been while it's been, and I am okay with change.

The only thing I can think of, and I just thought of this . . . I don't know that I wish I had done it, because I've never experienced it, but there is some value to longevity in a job. My husband's retired military. He was in the military for twenty years. My brother just retired from his company where he was an engineer for twenty-five years. So I'm sure there's some value to that. I've never had that, and I would be curious to know what it's like to be with one company. My husband and brother are not in hospitality. It's different in the hospitality world. People very rarely stay in something for twenty-seven years. I would be curious to know what it would be like to be at some place that you retire from, and you have such a great long history in it. That would be interesting to me.

And then, I mentioned that I've lived in six states; however, sometimes I do wonder what it would have been like to stay in one because I do have friends from high school, who I'm still friends with now, who see each other because they all still live in New York, and I don't have that. Or even Nashville, which was my longest stint . . . I was in Nashville a total of ten years and I still have great friends there, and they're still doing things together and I'm not. Now, I have great friends where I live now, in Georgia, that I do things with. I don't know if I miss the career, or professional longevity of the company, but I do miss that longevity of living in the same place, and growing older with people that you grew up with, or knew along the way. And it was my choice not to do that, and I don't regret it, but I wonder what it would've been like to stay closer to people. I don't think about that until I see pictures and think, "Oh, they got together for brunch and I missed that." I wish I could have both, but I can't. So here I am.

Heather
I'm going to say I'm satisfied and wouldn't change a thing, but you're asking questions, so I'm going to give you something. The piece of advice that I would like to give myself, earlier in life . . . I don't even know if we're ready for it when we're young . . . is just trust thyself, believe in thyself, know thyself. Ask questions, realize what makes you tick, document that, pay attention. I would tell myself to pay attention because I feel like my experiences essentially would be a little bit different. Maybe I would be "farther along," again, using air quotes. Maybe I would have a different outcome. But I think I am satisfied. I am okay. I could die tomorrow and be okay. But since you asked the question, I think the only thing I would do, or change, or try to change, is my awareness of myself, and the world, and others . . . just my awareness.

Why do you think people don't?

We don't want to get anything wrong. We want to do the right thing. And we are here to experience satisfaction and pleasure. So anything that goes against that, we're going to rub up against, and we don't like it. We're not here to find pain. I think that we are just so controlled by our thoughts and there's no . . . even from a young age, you're taught to chill out when it really isn't that big of a deal. To happen upon that is hard. You really need somebody guiding you there, saying, "No, no, just chill. You're good. It really isn't that big of a deal," . . . no matter what it is. I say that with respect to all situations that happen. I think it's not part of our culture to chill the hell out. We are trying to do more and more and more . . . be more, have more, consume, consume, consume. It's in our face every single day. Our family members talk about it. We were talking about social media earlier, so I just think it's counter culture to be aware and chill out. And I think that's why it's just not the norm. It's not how we operate.

Donna
You know, I stayed at the insurance company for over six years working for a guy I absolutely hated, who hated me, and treated me terribly. I stayed there as long as I did because once I finished my master's degree, and I started teaching at the university, working for him gave me the flexibility to be able to teach and to then start my consulting practice on a part-time basis. When I was doing training for American Express and Renaissance Cruises, it was during the week, on a workday. The nature of my work at the insurance company was that I did a lot of interviewing in the evenings and on weekends, because I was hiring people who were working. So, I allowed them to come and interview after dinner and on Saturday. I put in the time where I needed it, so that I had the flexibility to not come in on a Thursday, and no one was going to say, "Hey, where were you on Thursday?" I had that luxury. So I stayed there a long time.

If I could do something different in that setting, it would be to not let him wear away my self-confidence, which happened so slowly and insidiously that I didn't realize it was happening until I left there, and started rebuilding my self-esteem, and realized he had really hacked away at it without my realizing it. And then again, maybe it's good that I had to rebuild it myself. To this day, it makes me cry when I think about how terribly I was treated, which is probably why I think people respecting me as a professional is so important to me, because he didn't treat me that way, and I suffered for it. And I don't ever want to treat anybody that way. In my coaching practice, it is one of the things that I beat out of the people I work with who treat their people like crap because they can. If I can get through to those people, talk about a moment of joy . . . to help them get rid of that horrible attitude that they are superior and can get away with treating people like sh*t. I've been on the receiving end of that. And I talk to them about that just like this, because I wasn't always this incredibly confident person that I am today. I know a lot of people who aren't very confident, and I always say, "I wish I could drill a hole in you and pour in half of mine," because I have enough confidence for ten people now. I really do. I really feel that way and I really believe it. So yeah, maybe I wouldn't change that because it made me stronger in the end. I didn't know at the time that would be the outcome, but maybe it's good that it happened and I shouldn't want to change that.

Some of the learning experiences I've had . . . things that I sort of got bullied into doing by clients, or potential clients, because I didn't want to tell them to go jump in a lake, and then afterwards I realized, you know what, I should have told them to do exactly that!

There was a law firm a few years back, that hired me to do some training, and I shipped all my workbooks, and this woman went through them, took them apart, changed my workbooks without my permission, and accused me of being a racist, all because the silhouette images in them were simple, black outlines of people. I should have said "No" to that work because it just was not worth the aggravation. But I keep expecting the best of people. I don't ever want to be so cynical that I don't expect people to be on the up and up, and do the right thing. I think being an optimist and expecting the best from people, until they give you a reason not to, is part of what makes me good at what I do. If I started to become so negative, cynical, and non-believing, I think that would affect my ability to do what I do as well as I do it. So even that, I guess I wouldn't change, because having bad experiences like that gives you a basis for comparison to know when your clients are treating you right. Even though they may not be making you happy, that doesn't mean they're being unfair. They have their own issues and perspectives that you have to deal with. So yeah, I guess there aren't too many things that have happened to me that I wish hadn't.

There are hurtful things that happened with people you thought were your friends, and you find out otherwise. Even those make you realize how good your good friends are. And it also, I think, sort of helps you confirm your own self-worth when you say, "That person doesn't deserve me as a friend. That person doesn't deserve to be my client because they don't respect what I do enough." So I think it's sort of self-validating when you know your own worth professionally and personally. And I certainly think I do. There's not much that I would change.

Wei

I would not do anything over. As much as there are things that were not expected, or didn't go according to plan, every single challenge, every single hardship has, frankly, led me to a life lesson, or professional lesson, that I've been able to use later on. So I really think that everything that has happened in my career, and in my personal life, was meant to be. I didn't really believe in fate much as a kid. I definitely believe in Providence now.

Most recently, I've been telling coworkers, had I not gone down to Florida, four years ago, I think I would be a very different person, and I would not have been as well equipped as I am today, to engage in some difficult conversations that I've had. I really think that a lot of that hardness that I endured was really necessary to shape me as a human being.

So nope, I wouldn't change a thing.

Do you want to elaborate on any of the hardness you endured?

Yeah, absolutely. Florida in 2020 was definitely an interesting place. If you look at the population of Florida, it's only about three percent . . . well, actually, it is about three percent Asian, Asian Americans, Pacific Islanders across the entire state, even in the economic engines such as Miami, Jacksonville, Orlando, St. Pete/Tampa. Each of those cities, even, is only three percent in the latest census survey. So when you have COVID-19 shutting down the entire country, and some of the political rhetoric that was going around, there were instances where there were some very hurt people that executed their frustrations on me, be it in the form of punching, kicking, shoving, spitting. It definitely taught me some valuable lessons and empathy for what certain people . . . for what people of certain demographics go through, when they say that they are afraid of leaving the house every day. I actually got to live that in a micro form for basically two years.

I look at it now and I definitely can understand what some families go through when a mom dresses up her little kid or her . . . I'm just going to say it . . . when a black mother dresses up her black son for school, and hopes and prays that he comes home, every day, in one piece. I got to live that for two years. In the first year before Florida reopened, I happened to have some body armor that still fit me from my EMT days, so I would wear that underneath all my clothes, go out, do my chores, and come home because I was not entirely certain that I was not going to get shot. I certainly was spit on. The last guy who did it was chewing tobacco. So I got to clean that off in the bathroom of the warehouse store I was in.

That certainly highlighted a different side of humanity that I really had not seen firsthand. I had seen it academically. I read it in a paper. But, it was never firsthand experience. So seeing that definitely helped me be a lot more empathetic to my coworkers. It also helped me . . . it definitely hardened me a little bit. I am still someone who tries to look at the best in someone, or the best of a situation. At the same time, I don't put up with as much as I used to. As a supervisor, as someone who oversees a base of employees, I tell the employees, "Look, you can express your frustrations as much as you want. But at the end of your venting session, I really want you to contextualize and present a solution for the problem that you're venting about." These days, you don't get an hour to vent. You get about half an hour. And I really do want you to carry out what that solution is.

So I think those are some of the hard lessons that I learned following my move to Florida, that I really did not have knowledge of before. I certainly, in the past, would have let people go on for . . . there was one venting session that lasted nearly two hours. I don't have the patience for that anymore. Part of that might also be that I'm older. That was four years ago. So I'm four years wiser, in theory, and I've definitely seen some more things. Even in the workplace in Florida, I've often been given credit for being able to navigate a workplace that was traditionally seen as not the most welcoming to someone who is of smaller stature, Asian American descent, openly gay, and . . . it's very interesting . . . that workplace that traditionally has been characterized by some as a place where toxic masculinity exists, they embraced me with open arms. And I have very, very fond memories and connections that I use still to this day. And that job, I just happened to land. That was not something I applied for. That was not something that I expected to come across. And yet it did. And here I am. So I wouldn't change a thing. I would not.

Thinking about my first government job . . . it's funny . . . I was a system admin, back in '09. And I received this phone call. Well, actually, let me rewind a little bit. I was following a computer security blog and had submitted my resume based on one of the blog posts that said that someone was having challenges hiring the right people for the right jobs. I thought, "What the hell? Let me throw my hat in the ring and see what happens." So I did, and I didn't hear anything. Nothing came of it for a while, until a couple of months later . . . April 1st of 2009 . . . I get this phone call from someone who identifies himself as a rank, which is very foreign to me because it's not a U.S. Air Force rank. And he tells me, "Hi, I'm so-and-so calling," and he's got this very thick accent that is not U.S. English. And again, it's April 1st and he says, "Hi, I'm calling from such and such government organization." And I say, "Dude, I'm not buying this, nice April Fools joke, though." Click, and I hang up on him.

Probably two minutes later, just long enough to redial, this person calls again, and he says, "Hi, my name is so and so. I received your resume, and we're really interested in talking to you." It was the same guy that called before. I said, "Dude. This is getting kind of old. I'm not interested in this." Click. About fifteen minutes later, he calls back and he says, "Hi, I'm, so and so," and provides his rank . . . "And before you hang up again, I just want to say I talked to my coworkers. This is not an April Fools joke." At that point, all I could say was "Oh. My. God. I am really sorry. This is not how I am. I am . . . my coworkers know how much I have been looking for another job and I just assumed that they put you up to this." "This is legitimate," and he explains everything. He interviews me on the phone for probably a good hour. Finally, he says, "Okay, you'll be hearing from us." And sure enough, I got a job offer. I actually got a follow-up phone call, and an offer in the mail. And that's actually how I started working for the government. I was hanging up on someone. Which means that the government does have a sense of humor.

So, the short answer to your original question is "No, I have no regrets whatsoever."

Gabriel

I have a more traditional, profound answer, and I have a weirdly specific one that may not be interesting for the book, so I'll tell you the traditional one first.

There was one project I worked on at the consulting firm where . . . it was the worst project I've ever been a part of, I think. It was some combination of the work being really dull, and the people on the team were just . . . the day I showed up at the client site and met the senior manager of the project, she literally wouldn't look me in the eye and barely shook my hand. I thought, "Well, screw this lady." It was like she had decided before we even met that she hated me. That's the impression I got, and I don't feel that way often, but I thought, "What's this person's problem?" Then there was the other person I was working under on that project who was also very cold, and maybe that's sort of indicative of the sort of people who work in that field, but it really threw me and it got under my skin. I also was breaking up with my girlfriend at the time and it was very . . . it wasn't the worst thing I've ever been through, but it was not a fun time. It was a lot of staying up until one or two in the morning, talking. She was staying with me. I lived at my mom's house at the time. Because I traveled so much for work, I didn't have an apartment, and this project was in my hometown, so I was living at home and my girlfriend was staying with us at the time.

I was barely sleeping. I really didn't like these people, and I really didn't like the work. There was a part of me, even then, that questioned if I belonged in this place. It really infected my whole attitude and my whole experience. Instead of going to my manager and saying, "Hey, listen, I'm not doing my best work," I just pretended it wasn't happening. This is not the most interesting story, but there are a couple of moments like that where, back then, I didn't have the emotional intelligence, or the vocabulary, to just go to people and say, "Hey, I need a little help. I don't think I'm doing my best work for you. I'm confused about this, this, and this. I would like to be doing better. Can we talk about it? Can you help me get there," and then just let them help me, and do my best. That was something I didn't know how to do when I was young.

So that's the traditional answer. I don't know why that came to mind, because it literally doesn't matter, except for the fact that at my year-end review, I had the best possible reviews on every project, and then on this one, they said, "We almost fired you," which was really kind of scary to hear. I probably would have wanted to fire me too. It was a disaster.

I guess my mind went to that moment not because that moment is so interesting, but because I think it speaks to a quality that I had, or qualities I didn't have, back then. I literally did not know how to ask for help. If I could go back, knowing what I know now, I would have treated people differently. I would have been more vulnerable. I would have been more in touch with feeling bad about not doing the job well. I wouldn't have thought of other people, which is so easy to do, as adversaries, when they're not. Still, you think, "Well, this person isn't nice and this person is not funny," which is a huge problem for me, sometimes. When I encounter people I can't joke around with, I get a little bit frustrated. When this person's just all about the work, and they're impatient with me, I don't care. I'm not going to do a good job. I think I can change a dynamic if I just go to them and kind of laugh and just say, "Listen, I'm kind of blowing this right now." What a relief that would have been, for me and for them, to be able to say, "Oh, this isn't going well, and can we just all acknowledge that? Then let's figure out how . . . please help me understand how I can be better." It's so simple.

The less traditional answer, which is closer to my heart at this moment, is about Jordan Harbinger's wedding. He asked me to give a very brief toast. They had a few people giving speeches and they wanted to keep them brief. So, he said, ". . . two minutes, three minutes . . . this does not need to be a whole thing." I had never given a toast before, and even though I had done that class I told you about, and I kind of like public speaking, this kind of public speaking is a little nerve-racking.

I love Jordan. He's one of my closest friends. Talk about a guy who has changed my life . . . when he and I crossed paths, that was another moment where . . . at first it seemed like meeting him just sort of played into where I already was, but without him entering my life, I would never have encountered podcasting. It's really extraordinary. So he asked me to give a toast, and I don't know why . . . I don't think I'd been to very many weddings, if any. I think he was the first close friend of mine who'd ever gotten married. I didn't talk about this with anybody, so nobody told me that I needed to, and I didn't plan for this speech, which is terrible. Even if it's brief and off the cuff, you want to kind of have some talking points, right?

So I got to the wedding and in the back of my mind, I realized, "Oh, you don't know what you're going to say." I was just going to rely on my improv skills. I was a bit nervous and I got up there and it started off okay . . . I'm holding the microphone, and the first thing that came into my head was remembering the day Jordan said he met Jen and how they met. She listened to his show, and they met on Twitter, and they started talking, which is so, so cute. Then they met up in person. I remember him telling me some very sweet things about how he felt when he met her, and how they got along so well, but I didn't think about that in that moment. All I thought about was, "Oh, it's so funny that you host a show called *The Art of Charm*, which was his previous show, and you're meeting a woman on Twitter," so I cracked a joke like, "Way to live up to the brand of your company." Chuckle, chuckle, chuckle through the room. Okay, not the worst way to open a speech. I've got this. After that, I had nothing good to say. It was really kind of a bumbling speech, and I sort of said some vague, very abstract things about the qualities in Jordan and in Jen that I love, that brought them together, which came from a good place, but it was not a good speech.

I really didn't feel good when I went back to my table. I could tell from the people sitting at the table that they felt, "It was all right," which is terrible for a writer to hear. It's bad enough for a friend, but extra bad for a writer. I realized that it wouldn't have taken a lot of work, and I should have been more thoughtful about that, not just because I needed to look good in front of all these people, but because these moments matter. They don't change the course of your life, but I want to be able to articulate how I really feel and to honor this wonderful moment, especially for one of my closest friends . . . not take up a few minutes of everybody's time saying some stuff that doesn't really matter, that doesn't really mean anything. I was kind of angry at myself for that, and I've taken that little regret into the rest of my life. I don't always do it perfectly. I've probably made that mistake in a couple of ways, but I haven't made it in that big of a way, in a big public place, when it really matters, ever since.

Steve
So I just got done saying that I have no regrets because everything has led me to where I am, and I stand by that. That being said, I sometimes wonder what would have happened had I known sooner in

life that I wanted to be a scenic designer, which is what I'm doing right now. I sometimes wish that I had taken classes or gone to college for scenic design. As an artist in general, I think, and specifically in what I do now, I'm my own worst critic, and have that whole . . . what is it . . . imposter syndrome. So I go through all of that and sometimes I wonder if I would have more confidence, or if I would be a better designer, had I gone to college for what I'm doing. That being said, I also wouldn't trade where I am right now. So, I don't know. I guess in a perfect world I'd go back and do that, and then sit in the chair right now and say, "Okay, which version do I like better," and then choose from there.

Victoria

Definitely with my career, I would have . . . I don't know how, but I would have found that advocate and that mentor earlier, to help me decide who and what I wanted to be. I would do that differently . . . deciding early on what I really wanted to do. The role that I'm in now, it's just by happenstance. It just happened. It wasn't a career that I went out and chose, so I would do things differently in that part of my career path.

There are a few other things . . . I would have bought a larger house earlier. I'm in a small house now, but it's okay. I feel like I've had a good life. There isn't much, just in the career front, probably, that I would do differently.

With my daughter . . . she's an introvert and I realize now I think I should have taken a more active role in her development. I think there are some things there that I'm just now seeing and I could have supported her differently. So I would do that differently. I would.

Jesus

Well, I'm a determinist. I don't think you can go back and change anything. But let's say we could, hypothetically. Oh, God, I would change so much. But see, this is the thing, if I changed anything, would I have met Eric? Would I have met all the wonderful people in my life? Would I have had those moments with my dad, before he died? If the answer to that question is "No," then I wouldn't change anything. But if I didn't know any of that, if I didn't know I was going to meet Eric and all the fabulous people I know, and friends and family, and . . . then I would change everything. Like I said, when I watch *Stranger Things*, I think if I could go back in a time machine to a younger me, I would say, "Have a plan, go to your prom, make friends, stand up for yourself, get a job, get a car, go to college, study acting, study singing, go to L.A., make it happen, get on Broadway. You can do it." I would change everything because then I would have money. I could have bought my parents' home. I would have told my dad to get his radiation treatment. I would have changed so much. If I could change everything, not knowing the outcome, I would. But, if changing any one thing prevents where I'm at today, then no, I wouldn't change a thing. I'm really happy where I am today, and with who I am, personally.

Michael
Yeah, I would say the main one would be get . . . not even great grades in high school, but respectable grades in high school, because then I do think that golf-wise, a lot more opportunities could have opened up for me in college. Obviously, the "publicity" that I got last spring probably wouldn't have happened, but my golf career could potentially be in a better spot.

I think there's so much learning that goes on in college golf. I was on PGA Tour Canada this summer, and the amount of kids that were twenty-two years old, fresh out of college, out there competing and playing good golf was amazing. I was with my friends Carr Vernon and Taylor Kay-Green . . . those are the guys I traveled with . . . we're in our late twenties, and we're looking at these twenty-two year olds, and I thought, "Okay, maybe I missed something." So, getting better grades in high school and then having a college experience is what I would probably do over.

CHAPTER 10: COMPARED TO MY OTHER HALF

Has your significant other (or closest friend) had a career and/ or life path similar to yours, or has his/her path been more "traditional"? Has that affected your relationship? If so, how?

Brian
Full transparency . . . full everything . . . my husband has his degrees in opera performance, both undergrad and master's. So that would be pseudo in line with having a degree in theatre. He quickly realized he needed structure, so he got a "real job," as an executive assistant and he loves that. He loves the structure of knowing what a day looks like, knowing what a day off looks like. In the world of theatre, every day is different. I love that. I get to plan what I do today. There are some times I have deadlines to meet, but also I get to create the deadlines that I have to meet.

Once we moved to Philadelphia, he got a job with the federal government, which has a really good pension plan and benefits package. But we are so different in terms . . . he loves office culture. He loves going in and having office life separate from home life. I can't do that. I could not sit behind a desk for eight hours . . . the two times I worked for a temp agency, they had me sitting behind a desk . . . all I could think was "Get me out of here!"

I think at times there's a little . . . it is not resentment. It is not jealousy. It is nothing other than, "Oh, well, you get to go away this week. Oh, well, you get to do that." Yes, because that is what I chose to do with my life. It's the same with my father who will say, "Where did you go on vacation this week?" If only it was a vacation. Yes, I get to go to California, but I'm sitting in a cold auditorium for nine hours a day working on *Disney's Frozen Jr.* It's not always a vacation. It's work. I think sometimes people that aren't in the industry don't understand. Yes, it is fun. Yes, I enjoy it. If I didn't enjoy it, I wouldn't do it. I think that is the overarching theme. But, also, it is work and it is what I have chosen to do. It is how I have chosen to network and the life I've created. And you know what? I still have money to pay my bills every month. I still have fun. I still am able to save. I still am able to do all the things that I want to do. So it has never caused a rift between us. I've been in relationships with people in the industry where it becomes a competition. "I don't need to compete with you. I am not you. So I am also not a threat to you." Also, we are not in a relationship anymore because of that stuff.

Lisa

My best friend is also a performer, and she went the corporate route, so she always had a job and did the acting on the side, whereas I did acting almost exclusively for a while, and then did some waitressing and picked up odd jobs and stuff to support myself. I didn't have that steady paycheck until, well, until this year, actually. I never had that steady paycheck where I knew what I was going to earn from month to month. She's always had that and she feels more comfortable having that security. So she's gone more the corporate route and then done her performing . . . I don't want to say on the side, because it's very important to her, but she's had to make that fit in with her schedule doing her corporate work. I don't think that's affected our relationship. She's said to me many times, "I couldn't do what you do. I couldn't just not know where the money was coming from." She wouldn't be comfortable with that.

How did it make you feel when she said that to you?

It was a foreign concept to me because it's literally the way I've always lived my life. I've always had what I needed. It's not that there's been a lot of excess, but I've always had what I needed. I've had what I needed to pay my bills, which is what makes me feel successful. So what she's comfortable with, and what I'm comfortable with, are just different things. I had looked at being in a corporate job like that as being sort of restricting and limiting, and that was the part that would make me uncomfortable. It made me see a different perspective on how I was viewing my life and income.

Sabrina

I first asked her this question about her ex-husband.

His was very traditional. Oh, so vanilla . . . his entire family. We come from extremely different backgrounds. We could not be more opposite if we tried. I'm very blue collar . . . grew up in poverty. I know what it's like to be abused and starved. I know what that feels like on the very extreme levels. He grew up upper-middle class, almost wealthy . . . went to public school. His dad was a lawyer. His mother was a teacher and also a counselor. He's also a double inheritor. They never wanted for anything . . . he got to go to four year university, and never wondered where his next meal was coming from. He was an actor, too, so I can't take that from him. There is an artistic side, but for him, it wasn't a passion, it was just something he did, if that makes sense.

We also have very different personalities. He's very stoic about everything, whereas I am not. I'm cool, calm, and collected in crisis situations, but I'm also extremely vocal about how I feel about things, and I'm open, emotionally. He is not. He's also . . . I'm not saying this as an insult . . . he's also a hard . . . he's Republican . . . and everything that entails, and that eventually became a problem for us. He could never understand why, even going into my thirties, when he had kind of stopped acting . . . he was teaching more . . . why I was so still involved in the theatre. I think he always thought I was going to give it up so that I could be a better wife and a mother. There was always that. He would never admit it. We had marriage counseling for a while and some of these things started to come out. His family is still intact. They've got their problems, don't get me wrong. Every family has its problems. But, he doesn't understand what that kind of trauma is. Eventually it started to deteriorate our marriage. That, and because I had evolved into a different person and frankly, he didn't. He stayed exactly the same, which I don't think is healthy.

Most people have not met him. He was dubbed the unicorn because people thought I was making him up. He would leave shows during curtain calls. He would never come to any social events with me. He would never say anything on social media to boost me up or tell me how . . . he never used the words "I'm proud of you." He basically didn't exist outside of my private world.

I then asked about her current significant other.

Weirdly enough, Mike's path was also very traditional, but he also grew up in a military family, like I did. He understands moving around a lot. He's always been very artistic and his family has always been extremely supportive of that. But, he's also a jock . . . I never thought I'd end up with a jock. In high school, I hated jocks, even though I was a cheerleader. It's a weird thing. I'm a very weird person . . . dichotomies all over the place. He definitely had a much more traditional upbringing than I did, but his family is also very supportive and loving and welcoming. In this relationship, I'm with somebody who's just a better match . . . personality wise, temperament, humor, politically, which I've grown to believe is important in a relationship. You have to fall in line on certain political spectrums . . . not to the extreme and not every single thing, but there are certain things that are important politically because they do affect your reality . . . that you have to be on the same page about. I didn't always think that until my previous marriage fell apart. And then I think also the reason this one works is because I'm more mature and I'm much more willing, than I previously was, to take responsibility for my part of the relationship when it's not going well. I also know what I will not put up with in a relationship. I know what I won't tolerate. I know where the line is. He's the same. We respect each other's boundaries. And, his family is amazing. I would pick his family any day of the week.

Chris

I do have a significant other. His change of trajectory came very early. I was a beginning teacher. I had already graduated from college, had begun my teaching career, so I was on that trajectory at the time that he was actually in med school and dropped out. He did two years of med school before he realized, "This is not for me. I'm not feeling this doctor career. It's just never going to work." And he had been, from the time he entered high school, part of a seven year med program where it was structured that you actually take two years off of the full education. He'd been taking these courses in high school, so that he only did two and a half years of college and then went into medical school. Everything was accelerated. He had been on this accelerated trajectory, and then he was just done. And then it was about a year and a half of him just trying to figure out what he wanted to do. "All I've been focusing on was medicine all this time. Now what do I do?" So he became a substitute teacher, since I was already in the school system, and while he was substitute teaching, he was looking here, looking there, researching this, researching that. He eventually started taking classes in computer sciences, got several degree certifications in I.T., and then, of course, ended up getting hired by a hospital.

We started dating in college, in undergrad. He's been on that trajectory ever since. So the whole time that I was a teacher, he had shifted, did all that, got on that path, and has been working for the same hospital system ever since. He started there two years before we were married and we are going to be celebrating our twenty-first wedding anniversary this year (2023). So, he's been employed in this hospital system for almost twenty-three years. I have had a multitude of careers in that span of time.

Has him being in a more "traditional" job, or at least with one employer for that long, affected your relationship in any way?

He pushes me to make those crazy leaps and to do crazy things. When you're in a traditional nine to five job, which usually ends up becoming eight to six, he sometimes gets the feeling that "I work all the time," while I, on the other hand, am all over the place with when I work. But, at the same time, his regular pattern allows for my craziness to just kind of happen. He's never asked me to go back to teaching and have a "regular" job. In fact, he's always saying "Try this, you want to do it." Other times he's saying "Stop doing that. That is not what you want to do." He says that about one of my jobs that I'm ready to give up . . . it's one of the freelance jobs that I do. He's always saying "Just stop. It's taking your time. It's taking your heart. It's sucking your soul. So stop doing it just to earn a paycheck. Focus on the stuff that might not make you money right now, but might make more money in the future."

Daphne

My husband was in the military for twenty-four years. He retired before I met him, but then he worked in the hotel world and I met him at Opryland. He was there for twelve years. He's very much about the corporate model and he didn't understand why I would want to leave there, even when I knew there was something else, better, that moved me to Atlanta. I've always followed what I believe is the right path for me, but he hasn't understood that because he's very consistent and has had two major careers. Fortunately for me, his last stint was in hospitality, so he gets what I do, which helps. He understands when I'm on the road, traveling. So that's not a problem. But he definitely does not understand why I, at the time, would job hop, because since I've been with him, now over twenty years, I've had three different jobs, not counting being an independent planner, and he didn't get that. "I don't understand why you keep moving." "Well, something else out there is better." He didn't get that.

What discussions did you have? How did you convince him, or at least calm him, to know this is right for you?

That's a great question. There were two.

We were married in '04 and to make a long story longer, but that's how it'll make sense, his mom passed away in '05. So, we went from Nashville to South Carolina . . . his Mom was sick . . . so we went up there and then in the two weeks that we were there, she passed away.

On the way home . . . I remember this vividly. . . . it was in December, I said to him, "Now it's just your dad. We are so far away living in Nashville. We're seven hours from your dad." My dad lived in South Carolina and he was on a different side of the state. So, "We're seven hours from your dad, seven hours from my dad, my brother's in Georgia, all your siblings are in South Florida. I know why we were meant to be in Nashville, because we met in Nashville. I get that. But I don't think that we should stay there. I think we should consider coming closer to home." Well, he doesn't do change. My husband's path is very steady. So the conversation went nowhere. However, I knew it was the right answer, so I had already started the motions of getting my resume together, and was filtering it out to people in South Carolina and Georgia, just to see what I could find.

In March, everything aligned. He was laid off from his job at Opryland. Then I knew. The paths were coming together, because now he was open to "What's next?" By April, I had an interview scheduled with Home Depot, in Atlanta. In May, I went to the interview. By the end of May, I had the job, and started in July. So I had set the stage and he wasn't listening to it. But once that happened, he metamorphosed to "Okay, now what?" "Well, now we're going to do what I thought we should do, which is move back closer to everyone." And it was perfect. Once we got here, and we got the house, within a month or two, every one of his siblings and his dad had been to see us. We were two and a half hours from his family, and I think he then got it. He realized he didn't want to be too close to them, and I get that, but close enough that they can come here and we can go there. I was tired of missing every holiday because we were so far away. So that was good.

And then the second was when I left corporate America, when I left my last corporate job. That was when I was going back and forth between Atlanta and Louisville. When the time came, with all my trips back to Atlanta, I said to him, "I think it's time to leave Louisville." He replied, "Why would you do that? You've got a great job." I said, "I'm just tired." He didn't get that, and there was a little bit of an argument for about a week. Although I knew it was time, he didn't see it, or feel it, or get it. But he knew I was sad and I was bothered and I needed to do it. What I didn't know, until the next week, when I told him I had resigned, and was making the move, was that he was ahead of me. He said, "Well, I've already booked the U-Haul truck to bring your stuff back, so tell me what date you're moving." So he got it. He didn't like it, but he did what he does, which is do the logistics to make it happen. So I appreciated that. And two months later, because I gave him two months notice, we had the U-Haul truck in Louisville, and he brought his friend, and my brother, with him, and we packed it all up and brought it home to Atlanta. So he accepted it. He had a few little nervous moments when I was back in Atlanta, and he started asking, "Okay, now what?" "I don't know. I don't know what, but we'll figure it out."

Heather

I would say she has a semi-traditional trajectory in that I think Megan was like me. I didn't know what the heck I was going to do, so I had to go into a job before I found out about Full Sail University. And I did attend, but I still had to work as I was doing that. She went from high school right into a career, then went back to school, then back to work. So it's more traditional in a sense that she's been with companies for long periods of time. She doesn't jump around.

I would say the only time that it caused . . . it's never, never caused a problem . . . it was my personal issue . . . me working on my confidence, working on myself. Megan also is in digital marketing and she works for a very successful agency in Pennsylvania. She does SMS marketing and I do social media marketing, so we have a lot of the same language. We're both in marketing, but she has a solid income and she gets paid really well, and sometimes that hurts me to see, as an entrepreneur. It's not her, and it's not her company that she works for, it's just me and my confidence level, thinking, "Oh, I feel like I don't have it or I'm not worth it or . . ..*" She's killing it, man. She's so good at what she does and she's being recognized for it. And I'm so happy.

A year ago, two years ago, when she would come to me with that solid income, I would still be very, very happy, but there was a small little part of my ego that would think, "Well, what about me? When am I going to get mine?" I had to come to her and say, "I am so sorry that my crap got in the way and I couldn't be one hundred percent excited for you. I was only eighty percent excited." We had these conversations and we have an understanding. We're very open and honest and transparent and prior to getting into this relationship, that was one of our things that we agreed to. I practice that. It's scary, but on the other side of that, there's compassion. Megan understands, there's empathy, and we're able to grow from it because I am so freaking excited for her. She's amazing. It takes work though, man. It isn't easy. To look at her in the face and realize my ego is getting in the way of my joy for her, but my joy for her is the thing that lights me up . . . I've got to get out of my own way. I have to.

Donna
I alluded to that earlier. When I met Frank, who's five years older, he was already in his own accounting firm with a partner. He was already very successful. So that absolutely had an impact on our lives because from a financial standpoint, he had a very stable accounting practice. When I left the insurance company to take my consulting business full-time, I spent the first six months crying because I wasn't making a lot of money. He kept saying, "You're doing great. Don't worry. Don't worry about the money. I make money, don't worry." And so he was, as he likes to say, the wind beneath my wings. And, he helped me get work. He got me into the Seminole Tribe of Florida, which for ten years, was my biggest client. I made a ton of money from them. When you work for, aside from the State of Florida, the largest governmental entity in the state, the Seminole Tribe, you can then go to any other municipality and say, "Well, you know, I was the management consultant to the Seminole Tribe." Impressed, they say, "Oh?" So that was really helpful to me. I had a lot of beliefs about

being self-employed that Frank did not agree with. We used to have heated discussions about some of those differing philosophies, and with some, I realized he was right, and with some, we agreed to disagree. But I learned a lot from him, from watching how he ran his business. I learned a lot in terms of things I wanted to do and things I didn't want to do.

I learned the importance of doing monthly billing. I learned the importance of being firm about my fees. We bill completely differently, and I would never want to do my billing the way he does. I don't charge "per project," because it has been my experience that when you agree to a fixed price, you get screwed. For my kind of work, which is consulting, when a client wants a flat rate, I have none of that. When you charge a flat rate for consulting, they think they can sit and talk your ear off for hours, because they're salaried at their company, so they can talk and talk. And for me, it's "No, no, no, no. Time is money." So when they're paying by the hour, they think time is money, too.

Having his support and encouragement has been invaluable. One of the nice things, because of my personality style, is that I never wanted to be the little wifey who was taken care of. I wanted to pull my own weight. A good marriage is a partnership. I've always felt like we had that because there were years when he made more money, and years when I made more money. I've had my turn at pulling that weight, and I feel good about that.

When you work for a governmental entity, it's just like in the White House . . . when one president leaves and the other president comes in, they clean house. Everyone who worked there is gone and they bring in all their own people. The Seminole Tribe was like that, too. So literally, one day, we both got, no exaggeration, a pink slip in the mail that said "Your services are no longer required as of Friday." And you're thinking, "What?!?!" You're just done. We both got that pink slip the same day when one tribal chief was out and a new chief was coming in. It wasn't a reflection of the quality of work we were doing.

It was just that that's how governments are. One regime is out and the next regime is in. That was a little . . . it was actually a *lot* scary for us to both lose our biggest client on the same day. But, that was a guardian angel moment of joy for me because my phone started ringing off the wall like someone was sitting on my shoulder going, "Oh, you need more work." And every week, my phone was ringing with new work. It was unbelievable. I was so lucky. That's one of the things that I always say to people who tell me they're thinking of starting a consulting business and ask, "What should I do?" I say, "Plant seeds every day because you don't know when they're going to break ground to bear fruit." And in those ensuing months after we lost the Tribe, many of the calls I got were seeds that I had planted at a chamber of commerce breakfast . . . at a women's networking group . . . it was like everyone I had ever handed a business card to started calling. And it was like, "Whew, there is a God." I remember saying to my dad, "I'm so lucky," and he said, "It's not luck. You've been doing all the right things all along for this moment to hit." "Yeah, but it's lucky that it hit now."

So I think that Frank's career trajectory was, for a long time, a few steps ahead of mine and he was helping me along the way, and then at some point, I started to feel like we were equals in the game, and have felt that way for many years since. I've been able to refer work to him. Now, there are many times when I'll ask him to get on a call with one of my clients, or he'll ask me to get on a call with one of his clients. We joke with our clients that when you hire me, you get the benefit of him, too. Or when you hire him, you get the benefit of me, too. We actually say that to clients . . . "My spouse does this. If we ever need someone with that expertise, she or he will get on the phone with us and help us talk through this . . . no extra charge." And we've done that many, many times. So it's nice to have a spouse with an expertise so different from mine who's willing to share that with my clients and vice versa.

I think my path, as I said earlier, has not changed dramatically in years. He has moved the focus of his business around several times. He was an auditor for years and years. He did governmental audits. Now he's gotten away from that and he's really doing more of the small-business consulting, about how you can save money, and your taxes, and advanced business planning, contract CFO work, contract CEO work, stuff like that. So his business in the last ten years has morphed, whereas mine has been steadfast. I don't picture my business changing much until the day I retire because I like what I'm doing. I have a neat blend of what I'm doing. There are tons of things I say flat out, "No" to, and I have other people who are experts, to recommend, but I'm not going to start looking for new things to do now. So he and I are in different places in that sense. I think our trajectories have dovetailed very nicely and we have been able to support each other's businesses over and over again in a plethora of ways.

Wei
The beauty of us both working in I.T. is that although the paths were similar . . . we both came from liberal arts backgrounds . . . the field is broad enough such that there were times when our careers met, and there were times that they went their own ways, indigenously. What has been really good about that is that from both of our careers, we've both been able to learn and see a different side . . . or see a different perspective, and that's just a minor, little factor. Maybe it's that I'm looking at a problem head on, and he's looking at it from a forty-five degree angle. But it's complimentary. It's never conflicting. And I think that gave us a breadth of perspective that has helped both of us in our careers.

He's currently in the private sector. He was a federal civilian before. There are things that a private company can do for itself that the U.S. Government cannot. For instance, if you look at a company like Amazon, when you buy their products, when you sign up for their services, you agree to Amazon's end user license agreements. You're signing away a lot of your privacy, whereas with the U.S. Government, a lot of that is regulated. And so it's always interesting to see what's in the realm of possibility when you have full, unfettered access to data, compared to government departments and agencies, which basically have to work through the legal constructs of the U.S. Government, or the U.S. Constitution, to ensure that what you are doing as a government is lawful, legal, and moral.

It's certainly eye-opening for some, when you explain what the commercial sector can do, and it challenges their notions that the government can do whatever it wants with their information. I think that's something that the government continues to struggle with . . . helping people understand what it cannot do for itself, what "We the People" have not empowered the U.S. Government to do.

Gabriel

I don't have a significant other. I'm just trying to think about my friends. I guess Jordan and I had parallel journeys in the sense that we were both part of traditional corporate structures and we left. He was let go in the recession of 2008, and I quit a few years after that. His career then became sort of nontraditional. Most of my friends have had career paths different from mine and are somewhat unconventional. It's a mixed bag.

If anything, when my friends are on different paths, it's always complemented or been interesting for me. I don't really want to be the sort of guy . . . and I think this probably happens in the entertainment industry more, perhaps, than other fields . . . you start hanging out only with people who are in the industry. I don't think that's inherently bad, but I don't want to only have friends in one world. I love having friends from different walks of life. I also find that it actually helps. Last week I called my friend Erin, who you've probably heard on the podcast . . . Erin Margolis. She's one of my closest friends, too. I called her to talk. We talk about my scripts and she calls me to talk about psychological theories. We just share back and forth and it's a beautiful thing. So, my friends, being on different paths, professionally, has probably only helped our friendships.

The paths that tend to change the relationship are the ones that have to do with values and deeper interests . . . a friend whom you can only be kind of jokey and funny with, but who isn't passionate about figuring out certain aspects of life. I find as I get older that I don't care what people do for a living, I don't care where they live, I don't care what money they make. It doesn't matter. But if they're lit up about the same questions and they . . . basically if they can sit at a table with me and have a good conversation for two hours, then they're probably going to be in my life forever. Everything else is a footnote to that.

Steve
In our adult life, Annie has had a pretty traditional career path. When we moved to Vegas, she didn't have a job. She didn't come here with a job. I had the job when we moved from New York. She just came and she was temping a little bit just because, again, she didn't know what she wanted to do. There was nothing specific that she was here for. One of her temp jobs, her final temp job, was at Cirque du Soleil®. She worked at the front desk as a receptionist. That was twenty-three years ago. They liked her and she liked the company. Again, it was a good fit and everything. So she has progressively, or steadily, moved up within the ranks of Cirque du Soleil®. She now is Director of Communications and she's got a pretty sweet job. So that has allowed me to explore the path that I've taken. I feel really super fortunate that . . . we kind of joke sometimes that she's my sugar mama, because I get to do what I want. I get to be an artist. I get to be flakey, and I get to not really know what I want to do because she has that steady income and job. She has always been my biggest supporter and I literally would not be here, where I am today, without her, because, again, she's supported me and what she loves to do has allowed me to do what I love to do. I'm lucky. I say that to myself every day. I'm not kidding you.

Victoria
I think so. I think that he too is of the generation that I am. We're in our third quarter of life. He went to school. He didn't really have an idea what he wanted to do. His sister basically said, "Hey, you're going

to school and you're going to get into technology . . . I.T.," and that's where he's been. He's been in the same role for . . . the same type of role for at least . . . he graduated in 1978. He has been in his career for decades now and is absolutely . . . he's sitting at home right now, behind a computer, and just absolutely bored out of his freaking mind. He was never challenged, and he never wanted to take that next step. I don't know if it's a fear, and at this point, it's moot, because he's going to retire soon, but he still wants to work, which is interesting.

He retired in late spring of 2023.

He found a lot of fulfillment by finding a role as a football official for high school, and did that for fifteen years. Now he's officiating lacrosse, and absolutely loves it. He found his outlet that way, and it's a little side hustle providing some extra cash. That's the benefit of it, but it's his love, it's not the fifty bucks he makes doing a game. It makes me so happy to see him loving this, but I feel sorry for him. I really do. I feel sorry for people that are in that position and that can't . . . he didn't have a mentor. He didn't have an advocate. Again, I think advocacy and mentorship are so important. I think I need to do more of it myself, to help others along the way . . . have an influence on people, and be able to help them. Not that I'm anybody great, but I still probably could help. I have enough knowledge that I could help someone.

Has that affected me? Yeah, I think that there's a lot of potential. I think as a spouse or significant other, you can see the potential in somebody else and when they fall, and they don't see their potential, I think that's harmful. It hurts to see somebody not use their full talents.

Jesus
He's had a more traditional life, but there is one element of his life that I think helped bond us. Eric grew up in a cult, but at the time he didn't know it was a cult, obviously. He was made to feel that the world was going to end before he turned nineteen. So he got married at eighteen and he had kids before he was twenty. He was living that

160

life. He had convinced himself that this was happiness . . . being with this woman and having these kids, being part of this church, all of that . . . even though he knew deep down inside that he was gay and he was attracted to men. Then everything fell apart and things changed.

He had a plan. Eric is the planner. I'm more of the spontaneous "Let's see what happens" type. So, he had more of a traditional life. I think that's why our relationship works. Nowadays, in fact, I'm too much of a planner, and I think it's because I was never a planner before. He's more about the practicality of stuff, and remains calm, and approaches things in a sensible way. I'm more of that "Let's talk about our feelings. How are you feeling today? How did that make you feel when the person said that? Did that hurt you? Are you carrying any anger with you? How does this make you feel? Let's have a conversation." Even before we're intimate, I have to have a conversation because I need to feel connected in that moment. So, I think our personalities work beautifully, together. We balance each other out really well, but our lives were very different.

The one thing that is similar is we're both humanist, secular atheists, and anything other than that is a deal breaker for me. When I first met him, I asked, "Are you a religious person? Are you a believer?" He replied, "Oh, no, I don't believe in God. I was a Jehovah's Witness for many years," and I said, "So are you an atheist?" He said, "I don't really believe in God, and I don't know if there's an afterlife." So that was the thing that really bonded us and why we're so . . . we carry that anger at indoctrination and what's happening in the world today, the threat of Christian nationalism. That's the one thing we have in common. The other thing we have in common is that I think we're good people, and we care about people, and we care about doing the right thing, and wanting to be the best versions of ourselves. In every other way, we're different.

His family . . . I would love to trade families, extend my family to be with him, and his family to be with me. Every time we go to New

England, his grandkids will say "Oh, get ready, Jesus is coming. Get ready to talk about your feeeeelings. Get ready to cryyyyy." It's not done in a malicious way, because when I get there, it's almost like they're thirsty for it. I remember his granddaughter once saying to me, "No one ever really asks me how I feel. No one ever really listens to me." Recently, she called me because she wanted to vent about something, and I remember asking her, "Well, is Shawn," who's her ex-stepdad, "like a father figure to you?" "No, he's more like an uncle to me. Actually, my father figure is Poppy," which is what they call Eric. I said, "Really?" and she said, "Yeah, because I'm struggling a lot now, but when I think about what Poppy went through and how he survived it, I realize if he can do it, I can do it too. He's a great source of inspiration for me." I tell that to Eric all the time, and he brushes it off with, "No, I don't think so." Then when I shared with him what his granddaughter said, he said, "Oh, wow."

Eric has a young grandson, Cedric, who reminds me of me, because he comes to the house when we're there and he hides behind a chair, because he's so shy. Eric's daughter has a dog. One time, when we were visiting, I started tossing the ball to the dog, and then I purposefully threw it where Cedric was. Cedric went and grabbed it and I said, "Oh, I'm so sorry Cedric. Did it hit you?" He just nodded "No," and rolled it back to me. I said, "Cedric, would you mind," because he's always grabbing the ball from me, "if we could toss it and make him run back and forth? Would you mind catching it?" He nodded "Yes," so we started tossing it and he moved from behind the chair, to next to the chair, and we started playing. Then we started doing a competition where it was me and Cedric. That night, when we were leaving, and would not see him again on our visit, Eric gave him a hug and said, "Well, Cedric, it was good seeing you and I hope to see you again when we come back another time." He said, "Well, I might come back tomorrow," at which point I said to him, "I'm going to play outside tomorrow, and I hope that you come because I would love to play with you. You're so good at this." He did come back the next day and we played and he laughed. All of Eric's grandkids were playing. When we were done, Eric asked me, "Do you know what my son just told me?" "What?" "He was watching you playing with Cedric and Aiden," who is also super shy, and he said, "You know what, Dad? Jesus brings out the best in people." I said to Eric, "I just see so much of myself in Cedric. I think I know how he feels."

So Eric's had a more traditional route. I had a completely nontraditional route, but our personalities work together to balance each other out. The common bond is that we share the same idea about indoctrination, and we're kind human beings.

Michael
I could speak to both if you want. I do have a girlfriend right now. We've only been together for five or six months, and she's not playing professionally, but she is in the golf social media space. She played college golf, so she's kind of been . . . she kind of agrees with me on the fact that if I played college golf, my career might be elevated right now. But it might not be. Obviously, it's all speculation.

But let's talk about my friend Taylor, who I'm actually renting this house with. He played four years of college golf at Trinity College, which is in Hartford, Connecticut, my home state. He's from Needham . . . Boston area of Massachusetts. I would say his path has definitely been kind of . . . I don't want to say the standard, but the more usual one. He played four years of college golf. He turned professional after that, and he's basically been chasing it ever since then. I know he has a decent support system, financially, so I don't think he's ever really had to work or . . . I guess it's just been golf. That's not a shot at him. That's just kind of the typical path for professional golfers coming out of college. A lot of these young golfers have somebody, whether it's a family member, or a sponsor, so they have the money to do what they need to be able to do. That's kind of the normal path.

So has him having that normal, or traditional, path affected your relationship in any way?

No, because most of my professional golfer friends probably have something similar to that. Not all, but most of them have support in some way. And now I have one sponsor that pays all my entry fees. To be honest, I don't know any professional golfer that does this on his own. It's so expensive and golf takes up so much time. You can't have a full-time job and still make this happen. So that's kind of the normal thing. I'm very grateful for the people that have helped me. Obviously, the Venmo donations that came in that week last spring, when I Monday-qualified for the Korn Ferry tournament, and received all of that press, were a huge help. Unfortunately, all that money's gone because I spent it all in Canada this summer, but, I do still have my one sponsor that pays my entry fees for tournaments. As far as the travel expenses and hotels, that's still on me, but I've been making it work up to this point.

CHAPTER 11: COMPARED TO MY PARENTS

Did your parents have career and/or life paths similar to yours, or were theirs more "traditional"? What jobs did they hold? Did that affect the career and/or life choices you made in the past or do now?

Brian
Yes. Yes, they did. My mother was a teacher. She retired ten years ago, after thirty plus years of teaching. My father worked for two companies, I think, during his entire life, as a cost analyst. So when companies were building major structures, they would come to his company and say, "Great, how can we legally save money? What can we do to still pass all the inspections, make sure everything is good to go, but not make this project as expensive as it needs to be?" My mother worked the school day, so she was around after school, and in the summer. My father worked a four-day workweek for most of his career, where he worked ten-hour days, Monday, Tuesday, Wednesday, Thursday. Then he was home with us on Friday, Saturday, Sunday. My father did all the laundry. My mother did all the cooking. I am a middle child of three boys. We're very close in age, so we're very competitive, still to this day. My little brother is a doctor and he's always been the smart one. I feel like my parents felt, "Bri, you can do whatever you want because Kevin's going to take care of us." They've always supported me going into this career. They didn't always get it. I feel that way with my husband, sometimes. I feel that way with my friends, sometimes. People don't always have to get what you do, but they should at least support what you do, otherwise why are we wasting time?

I don't think I personally went out of my way to not have a traditional career, but I feel like where we are now, traditional careers aren't a thing. That's a very generalized statement. But our parents' generation, our grandparents' generation, going back and back and back . . . company loyalty was a huge thing. We were taught and told, "If you stay with them, they'll take care of you." It's not a thing anymore.

Also, all of these smaller mom and pop businesses have gotten decimated and bought up. There's a handful of companies that own every other company now. This is all my personal speculation on the world of business, and there's no real reason for that.

That whole idea of staying with one company for your entire life, that's what you do, you know your part . . . and maybe it was our generation sitting there saying, "Yeah, that might have worked for you, but you were able to buy a house in 1974 for six buttons and three pennies." Now we can't even afford a tank of gas all the time, but the minimum wage is still seven dollars and twenty-five cents an hour. So many "Boomers" sit there saying, "Well, get your act together. You're killing the doorbell industry." I'm thinking "No, I don't want a doorbell because I don't want anybody coming over to my house because it's too small. Let's go out. Let's do something." Cut. Print. Moving on.

Lisa
I have two different examples. I think my dad always had the traditional job that got the insurance and the benefits and all that stuff. He traveled a lot for work. He worked for several different companies within pens and office products, let's say, and he was typically a regional sales manager. So he traveled a lot.

My mom stayed home with us until I was about five and then started her interior design business. She was self-employed, and had her own business, so she could be more flexible with the hours to have time with us, to be able to pick us up, to be able to work around our schedules as kids. I think one of the things that I found challenging was I felt that since my mom was able to do her own business, and do her thing, she would better understand me wanting to do my thing. From her perspective of wanting to make sure I was taken care of, she felt she was able to do that because she had my dad, and he had all the benefits and protections and stability. So she was able to do that. Since I was by myself, I needed to do that for myself, to have that stability. So she is pleased as punch that I have this new job and so am I, by the way. I love it there, but she really wasn't terribly comfortable with me not having a steady, full-time job with benefits, previously.

Sabrina

Like I said earlier, neither of them went to college because Dad enlisted in the Army and Mom did what she was supposed to do. She married my dad at nineteen and had me at twenty. She did work various jobs. I remember her, very specifically, working at a bank when I was in elementary school, because we used to hang out in the downstairs break room, after school, while she finished working. I also remember her working as a manager. I think it was a Home Depot or some sort of store like that. So my mom has had various jobs throughout the years. My dad was always in the military and he was always overseas. When we did see him . . . I won't say there were many good memories because that's a whole different personal thing, but he was overseas a lot. So it was a much, much different upbringing than . . . it was a much different path than I am on.

Has that affected the career and/or life choices you made in the past, or do now?

Yes and no. Yes, because growing up that way taught me time management, responsibility, and commitment to a task. Despite my parents' and my differences, they taught me a great work ethic. But "No" in that I'm the only artistic one in my family. No one else in my family has ever pursued a career in the arts. Nobody else sings. I was an anomaly. Also, I'm the only one that got out of high school kind of whole, if that makes sense. I didn't drop out. I made it to some sort of college education. I got the heck out of my hometown and broke that cycle of just popping out kids right after school, and living in these small towns, following your husband around everywhere.

Earlier, you said you married your ex because that's "what you did." Did that come from your parents specifically, or your grandparents, or your hometown . . .?

I think it's a combination of my upbringing and also society. I think I was very susceptible to the message that women receive. Plus for the stability, frankly. At the time I was in an unstable environment, living in New York as a starving artist, and it seemed like a good deal . . . I'm going to move in with this person who loves me. Let me go back to the family influence, and then I'll get back to this because it all makes sense when you hear it.

My familial upbringing was very traditional. It doesn't matter whether it was functional or not, it was, "That's what a family looks like. And this is what your role is in that family. The women do the cooking, the women do the cleaning." As feminist as I am, I bought into that message because again, I was a people-pleaser as a kid. I didn't know that I was allowed to say "No" until I was an adult. Plus, it was a very dysfunctional family. It was very . . . I'll be very honest, it was very abusive. So when you're at that age, you're susceptible to these messages. Then society teaches that message. We teach women and girls that their job is to be a homemaker. We're getting better, but it's still a very prevalent message, the gender role. So I very much bought into it at the time. I was very much a dual personality in my early twenties, where I was a strong, independent woman, but I was also going to marry this man and be stable. I was very conflicted and I can't pretend to understand it now, but at the time, it made so much sense to say, "Of course you say "Yes," that's what you do." I didn't know I was allowed to say "No" to an engagement because you don't do that . . . it's rude . . . when a man asks you to marry him . . . do you think you could do better?

This also leads into the other reason . . . I was in a previously-abusive relationship with another man for years prior to that. So why would I say "No" to this? This seemed like heaven, right? Even if it wasn't a good match, why would I have said "No"? You don't deviate from that path because that's what you're supposed to do. That's what's "societally acceptable." No matter what we tell women, that's the path we're still being pushed towards.

Chris

My dad worked in the elevator industry almost his entire life. He began working as a mechanic right after high school, and he and his high school girlfriend got married because they had a kid on the way. Before that, though, he had wanted to be a visual artist, and he was a rock and roll drummer in a band. He actually did a lot of art fairs and things. In fact, I've got some of his stuff in my place. So he was a musician/artist who, because of family responsibility, got a job as a mechanic, which then turned into a career in the elevator trade, up until he was forced to retire. That was because of health reasons. Once that happened, he got back into art and creativity. But that was his path. He went the traditional route, but his heart was always . . . he never regretted it, but there was always that part of him that I think from the time I was little, always had that feeling of, "If this is what drives you, and this is where your passion lies, do it." So that had a huge impact on me.

I started out traditional, but the first time my dad got cancer, and I had just lost my grandmother to cancer, caused me to stop teaching and pursue theatre. It was that real sudden, powerful message of "You only live once." My father was always upset that I had not pursued any of those avenues. He always wanted me to be a writer. He always wanted me to be an actor, and unfortunately I am that person who is a ping pong ball in terms of my energies. I've never been diagnosed with ADHD, but I have that inability to constantly just single-mindedly stick to one thing. When I was a public school teacher, I was singing in a band, and doing community theatre, and writing fan fiction. That's how I work. So stopping teaching allowed me to at least pursue one thing, but then the other things always kept popping in, and I think that's been a frustrating element for me. I've never been able to really focus on one thing. But again, my father taking that path and encouraging me to kind of explore mine, caused me to do it later. I didn't go straight into that weird ping pong path.

My mom was traditionally a housewife who got a part-time job at a law firm, and ended up becoming a county clerk at the courthouse in

Osceola County. So she just kept working for lawyer, lawyer, lawyer . . ..

Did their career paths or choices affect the decisions you made? You mentioned your dad's first bout with cancer, but did seeing what they did for work affect you at all?

My dad had the traditional nine to five job, at least when I was growing up. He drove me to school on his way to work, and my mom was the traditional high heels, business suit woman, once my brother was old enough to go to school. That's when she started working part-time, doing the work in law firms. That lasted up until she retired. There's a part of me that, when I first started teaching, thought, "Look at me. I'm doing the business suit and high heels thing." That lasted until I became a drama teacher, and then it was jeans and comfortable shoes.

Daphne

Both of my parents always had steady jobs. My mom was a dietitian, and worked in the school system, so her work was very steady. She passed away when I was young. I think my mom's position affected me because as a dietitian, I watched her, nightly, create meals and plans for the school systems, at home, because that's what she did. While I've never been a cook, and I've never liked to cook, personally, I love to do the planning. I later learned her planning all those meals was just part of her. We had a lot of family parties and functions at our home, and I didn't realize how organized and detailed she was. That spread to me because I watched her growing up, and I became that person. I am that person now.

And then for my dad, he was very traditional. He worked in postal services. He was a postmaster in his final job. He retired after thirty-something years at the U.S. Postal Service. For a minute, I actually thought about getting into it. One of my summers home from college he said, "You need a job. I will get you a job at the post office." My first thought was, "The parcel desk girl is horrible," so I had a moment of thinking that maybe I could get into that for the steadiness of it. He did get me involved in communications with the public relations person at his post office, because I was a communications major. For a moment, I thought if I got in with the Postal Service, that would be one of those jobs you stay in forever. So my thought, at that time, was consistency, a traditional path, get somewhere and stay forever. But then I knew that I wanted to be in the hotel world, and I didn't know until I worked at my first hotel job that hotel people don't stay at the same hotel for long. They move around a lot. So as soon as I got into the path that I wanted, which was the hotel world, I instantly became fixated on the notion that it's okay to move around. In fact, my first hotel job was in Birmingham, Alabama, at a hotel that was only going to be open for nine months, because it was going to be renovated and come back as a different brand. I took a job knowing it was only going to last for nine months, but I was excited about the job. It was a great opportunity, and I got something somewhere else before the nine months ended. But, at the time, I didn't know that would happen, and I never had fear. I've never had a fear of not knowing. I like security, but I always know there's something else for me that's bigger and better out there, somewhere.

Heather

Both of my parents were very traditional. They're a generation above us. I believe that generation had the idea that you go to a job, and you retire from that job. I don't think that . . . well, obviously that's not the case anymore, but I think that's the last generation to feel that way. My mom got into finance and worked for a financial institution and retired from that. My dad made Reese's Peanut Butter Cups his whole career. He worked for Hershey. I think he was with the Hershey Corporation for forty-two years. For me, looking at that, specifically from my dad's point of view . . . mom didn't really complain about work too much, but Dad . . . he was a great employee, but corporate life and the suits . . . he felt, "Oh, the suits make all the money and blah, blah, blah," and "I have to work and work and work and this and that." For me, I can't go to the same place every single day. I'd drive myself nuts. So seeing that, hearing that, sort of did help me be honest and see that I can't do that.

So to clarify, was he on the assembly line?

He was an engineer. He would fix the assembly lines and stuff. I don't know where he started . . . maybe in the same role, but where he ended up was high in the engineering department.

I'm going to tell you, I'm sort of a lone wolf, man. I get my experiences outside of my family. So, observing and watching or reading, that's sort of where I think maybe I have developed my desire for how I want to design my career.

Donna

My mom had a high school diploma. She was a bookkeeper her whole working life.

My dad lied about his age to go fight in World War Two. He came back, got out when he was nineteen or twenty, wasted his GI Bill and didn't go to college with it, which is what he should have done. He totally blew that. He had a whole bunch of jobs until he "found himself" in the computer industry. That was when he finally went back and got a two-year degree. My father would have been a brilliant trial attorney. If you think I can argue, you ain't seen nothing. I am, to use the cliched phrase, a chip off the old block. I am my father's daughter. I got all the best of him and I got the annoying parts of him, as Frank will tell you. I got the ego, the overwhelming self-confidence, the confidence that I'm right ninety-nine point nine percent of the time, and the lack of tolerance. I got those things from him. When he retired, he was a senior director at a very large computer company. He was the only senior director in the company who didn't have a master's degree. He didn't even have a four-year degree. He worked his way up on his own merit, and he was very, very proud of that. They both followed very traditional paths. My mom, not just in terms of what she did, but being of that generation where if the wife has to work, because most World War II vets didn't want their wives to work, it was because they needed the money. So she worked because she had to, not because she wanted to.

My parents' paths were very traditional in that my dad was way brighter than my mother. Any decision of importance in the house was made by him. She got to voice her opinion, but then he decided. He was very authoritative. And yet, while he was that way with my mother, there was always the expectation that my sisters and I would all go to college. It was not open to discussion. It was an expectation. My dad absolutely said to all three of us over and over, "You can do anything you want. You can be anything you want. You don't have to be barefoot and pregnant. You can go to college and choose a career." My older sister wanted to be a doctor from the time she was eight years old, and that's what she became. My middle sister always wanted to be a teacher, and that's what she became. Financially, I was the most successful of the three, but the oldest is an M.D. That's a tough path, especially back when she started. In 1970, there weren't a lot of women in medical school. So I think my dad shaped us.

He probably had the most positive impact on me because I was eight years behind my middle sister. I got the benefit of my dad being more financially successful by the time I was a teenager. Emotionally, psychologically, he was in a better place, and I got the benefit of that in terms of his business philosophy, which we talked about all the time. I was the closest to my parents, geographically. My oldest sister never came back home after college. My middle sister came back for a year and then got married and moved away. I came back from college and lived with my parents for a few years, until I finished my master's degree and bought my house. Even then, I was only four miles away from them. I had a close relationship with them my whole life. So they had a big impact on me.

Even though both of them followed traditional career paths, they were always very encouraging of us to do whatever it was we wanted

173

to do. Once we got past that initial hurdle, when I started my business, my dad was very supportive of me. Frank and I have talked about the fact that it was logical for him to be worried about me starting a business, because he had never run a business. It was scary for him to picture me being one hundred percent reliant on myself, as opposed to a company that was going to give me a paycheck, and give me health insurance, and give me a 401(k). That was what was "normal" for him, and the thought of me not having those things scared him, for me. I was able to grasp that once I got over the emotional impact of his lack of support. I just decided that I would prove him wrong by being successful. And I did. And he got it.

Seeing how hard they worked, above all else, regardless of what the career path was, I learned a work ethic from them. To be in your own business, it goes without saying that you have to be willing to work your ass off whenever you have to, 24/7, in the middle of the night, on the weekend when your friends are out with their kids, or doing something fun, and you're at your desk working because that's what you have to do. You do what you have to do. If you don't have that work ethic, you're never going to make it in your own business. So I certainly would give him credit for that.

Wei
My parents empowered me with all the skills they could have. What's interesting is that my dad held down three jobs when I was growing up, so I didn't really see him much until my high school days. By then, I think a lot of my personality had already gelled. My mom definitely influenced me more than my dad did. She was a stay-at-home mom, although towards the end of my high school days, she did go back to work as a social worker. I think that while both of their paths were very different from mine, universally, one of the things that they both drilled into me was a strong work ethic, and my dad really did teach me that I had to look out for number one. I had to be the advocate for myself because no one else was going to really do it for me, and that no matter how hard things were ever going to be, I had to power through and come up with a solution. So I think that's actually the

biggest influence in my career. More than their actual paths are the soft skills that they may or may not have intended to give me.

Do you think that your dad telling you that you needed to advocate for yourself, and look out for yourself, was him, or was that a cultural thing? I don't mean to sound like an idiot, and I certainly mean no disrespect. I'm genuinely asking . . . is that a Chinese cultural thing, or do you think it was just how your dad was, and it wouldn't have mattered if he were Chinese, or Native American, or Hispanic, or . . .?

Yeah. So my dad was a hard ass. I don't think it had much to do with being of Chinese descent. I think it was just simply that it was probably, honestly, a culmination of his own life experiences, and how he had to work hard for everything that he had. So I certainly think it was some of that. I don't really think it had to do with cultural influence.

You said he worked three jobs. What were those?

You know, it's funny . . . he was everything that me growing up did not understand. All three jobs were basically either data entry, computer programming, or some type of management. As a kid, I wanted no part of computers. My feeling was they were nothing but trouble. They were only good for video games and I didn't want to have anything to do with computers growing up. That might have actually been another influence of mine . . . that I wanted nothing to do with computers. As a result of that, I actually, when I did finally go to college, and being four hours away from home, had no one to fix my computer for me. So I had to learn to fix it myself, and that led to a career. Go figure.

So again, you said he worked three jobs. I interpreted that as simultaneously. Were they, or were they chronological?

He did all three at the same time. It's funny, there are only twenty-four hours in a day, and when you do eight hours times three jobs, that's twenty-four hours. So, my dad would come home . . . and of course, I was young, so I had my own priorities in life, and that was basically twiddling my thumbs on a control pad and school. So I don't know . . . I don't recall the timing of it. I do remember there were times when we had to drop him off at work, and between jobs he would come home, sleep, eat, and rinse and repeat for the next job. Now that I think about it, one of the jobs may have been just simply a weekend job. But all the same, my dad was pretty much always working for a living, so that we could have a decent life as kids, which definitely did shape things for me, after the fact. I didn't have the student loans that a lot of people did because my dad worked so hard to build a nest egg for us.

Gabriel

My parents were both very unconventional people in many ways. My mom was definitely kind of a free spirit. She didn't have a traditional job until my parents divorced when I was twelve, and she had to get one. She had a very strange and interesting life. She basically ran away from home when she was seventeen or eighteen and moved to New York and then moved to Europe . . . moved around in Asia. She was a model in Europe in the mid-seventies to mid-eighties, but she really wanted to be a writer, so she started writing and she quit modeling. She just didn't really love it after a while. She started writing songs in French, and she invented a little writing career for herself, which was very cool. Then when my parents divorced, in what is probably the most amicable divorce in human history, she had to get a job to support us, so she talked her way into being a tabloid journalist. She was a tabloid journalist for twelve years and very good at it. She broke, actually, some big stories. This was before tabloids became ridiculous, where there's nothing real in them at all. But, back then, they were actually breaking real stories.

My dad is an extremely creative man, always liked to be an entrepreneur, and started multiple companies that would do really well for short periods of time, and then they would sort of stumble, or they would change, or evolve into another company. He's done that for a long time. He's an extremely thoughtful, sensitive, not detail-oriented, but . . . he worked in fashion and in apparel, mostly. He loved clothes, and textures, and fabrics, and merchandising, and such. I worked in his factories from when I was about eight or nine. I worked there every summer. I'd spent a lot of time there and I didn't love it, but I did soak up a lot.

I'm sure their paths have affected the choices I've made, but probably in less conscious ways. Clearly, I inherited some interest in writing and words from my mom. She taught me how to write for school, when I was a kid, but she taught me how to write in a very linear "This is how it's done" kind of way. It was an amazing education. It's how I learned how to string a decent sentence together. I've had to learn, since then, how to let go of a lot of what she's taught me, so that I could become a better writer, or I could become more myself. That's a whole other topic that clearly is about more than the writing, but I guess my parents being . . . oh man, this is one that I could go on about forever.

Steve
Okay. So again, with my dad, I think his path was very traditional. He worked at what's called Plastics Incorporated. They made plastic things: injection moldings, ashtrays, and car scrapers. He worked in the office in accounting and inventory. I think that absolutely influenced me, in that I knew completely what I did not want to do. I didn't get along great with my dad back in the day, and I certainly didn't understand what he did. I thought he was a big nerd, and not in the cool, hip sense of the word. I knew, I think, that I didn't want to do that, to be that. I think he had a couple of different jobs through the years. He's retired now and, as a note, he is now truly one of the most amazing people that I know. I have the utmost respect for him, and understand him better than I did back in the day. I look up to him more for what he does personally, than whatever he did professionally.

My mom was a stay-at-home mom for a little while. Then, I remember she was a cashier at Target. I still remember walking into the

Target . . . any time now I walk into a Target, and smell the popcorn, I'm immediately transported back to going to meet my mom at work. She was also a respiratory therapist and worked in hospitals for a lot of years. I think I probably get some of my vagabond nature from her. I think she probably got bored easily too, with her jobs. She also owned a business for a while . . . she started a business in nursing . . . in the medical field. They sent out nurses to cover for shortages and strikes and such around the country. Now she answers phones, at home, on the computer, for one of those companies that provides mobile receptionist services. So, she was fairly nontraditional.

You said that you look up to your dad more for what he does personally, than whatever he did professionally. Do you want to elaborate on that?

He worked in an office and he worked on books. I don't know that I even know, or knew, especially at the time, exactly what he did. I don't think he was ever particularly happy doing what he did. You asked about those moments of joy, and maybe he had them, but I certainly never experienced any moments of joy from my dad, professionally. Now that he's retired, he is now . . . he's seventy-something and he just did a fifty mile bike ride this past weekend. He doesn't run marathons anymore, but he still is a big triathlete and he cross-country skis. He is amazing. He's really inspirational in that way that he's almost eighty years old. And he is always, always the oldest guy, or one of the oldest guys doing these races, and does really pretty well. And he'll say, "Well, I finished. I finished top in my class. There was nobody else there, but I was there . . . the oldest." That, I think, is why I like and respect him more now than I ever did. I look at him kind of as an inspiration. If only I could be in that good of shape when I'm seventy-something years old.

Victoria

Absolutely. I feel like I'm sitting on a couch somewhere or something. Full disclosure, my mother grew up in eastern Kentucky and she was a high school dropout. Later on, she went and got her GED, but she always struggled trying to find and hold a job. My parents were married until I was thirteen. My father grew up in a very professional household. His parents, and my aunt, came over from Germany. He got his undergrad and his master's degrees from Northwestern University. My grandfather, whom I'd never met, was a corporate attorney in the Chicago area for a piano company . . . I want to say it was Baldwin or something. I couldn't tell you which one it was, but he was very predominant in the legal field in Chicago. So Dad always took that very professional approach. However, my dad had trouble finding a job. He worked for the Postal Service. My grandparents and my father owned thoroughbreds. They raced thoroughbreds and that was their passion, or my dad's passion anyway. I think that impacted him quite a bit, not being able to see somebody take . . . they took the nontraditional route, let's just put it that way.

So did that impact you in a positive or negative way, or is it just a matter of fact?

I think in a negative way really, because I never knew what it was like to see somebody get up every morning and go to work. I never experienced that routine. So I never was able to see that come through. It was nontraditional for sure.

Jesus
My parents' career paths were similar to mine. My father was a musician and my mother was a seamstress. He made his living that way until we got to the United States. Then he had to get a job working in a warehouse. But up until then, for the first forty-some-odd years of his life, he was a successful trumpet player and composer in Cuba and in Spain. My mom did costumes and alterations in Cuba and Spain, and then here in the States.

I think their work affected the career and life changes I made. I don't know that you can control what you choose. If you listen to a certain music, you either like it or you don't like it. You don't choose to say, "Oh, I'm going to choose to like opera." Being around music, and

179

seeing my mom be creative with costumes, and making my Halloween costumes and such, it influenced me. I saw television, I saw musicals, I saw costumes, I heard music. It's not something that you control or choose. It is calling you. It is saying, "Hey," and you say, "Oh yeah, I like that. That resonates with me. That speaks to me. That's what I want to do. I want to be in the arts."

Michael

Neither of my parents ever had any career aspirations in golf, or any career aspirations in . . . my dad might have had, at one point, some career aspirations to play professional basketball. He's six foot eight. He played in college. They both went to college. They both have degrees. They both have very good, stable jobs at the moment. So, like I said, how this all amounted to me doing what I am, I'm not really sure, but it is what it is.

My mom is a social worker. My dad is a psychotherapist. So they basically do the same work, just in different ways. Again, like I said, I think that's part of why I'm so emotionally . . . I don't want to say stable, but just . . . I like to use the word content, in that I don't let things bother me. I'm okay with whatever happens, most of the time. I'm sure it's because I was raised by them. My mom obviously deals with emotions in her work. I believe social workers, from what she tells me, explain and help families cope with loved ones passing away, or getting sick, stuff like that. And then my dad does a lot of family therapy, relationship therapy, drug and alcohol counseling. Both my parents are, I believe, thirty-plus years sober at this point. I've never had a sip of alcohol or done any drugs in my entire life. Obviously, it's because my parents are sober. That's how my life was. That's who they are. And it is what it is. But how that all connects to my career in golf, it really doesn't. It just is what it is.

CHAPTER 12: SUCCESS!

How do you define professional, or career, success today? Have you always defined it that way? If not, how did you define it, formerly? When/what made you change your thoughts on that? There may have been more than one time you changed your mind.

Brian

This is something that I am adamant about teaching. I always give three top takeaways from my workshops and one of them is confidence over cockiness. You've got to be confident, you don't have to be cocky. The biggest one I always tell students is networking, and the third is that you have to define success for yourself. Do not take somebody else's definition of success. Do not think success, in the world of theatre, is only Broadway. If your only definition of success is Broadway, great, good luck, likely not going to happen. You've got to find these little micro levels of success along the way because . . . and this isn't just theatre advice, it's life advice . . . find your big goals, and also the smaller goals to help you reach your big goals. If you're standing on the ground and the closest branch is twenty feet above you, you're never getting up there, but if you're standing on the ground, and there are branches every couple of feet, you can climb your way up, eventually.

In high school, my goal was Broadway. My goal was literally "I'm not successful unless I'm in a Broadway show." Well, friends, what I have discovered over this career is with Broadway, your show is going to close, your contract's going to end, and then you're going to be right back to the thing you were at before. So my definition of success, and it ties back to ninety two percent of what I've already said is, "Am I able to pay my bills at the end of the month, doing the thing that I love? Am I able to make money by creating, by figuring it out?"

With the pandemic, pivoting into the world of events . . . I was invited to be a beta tester for a virtual game show for a team building company. I talked about it with the person that invited me, and I then talked to the creator and said, "Here are my thoughts on this. Here's what I think." He was super receptive and we had a really great collaborative chat about it. I was then asked if I wanted to try hosting one of them. It was like figuring out . . . here's what I'll say . . . success . . . there's financial success, and then there's life success. I think with life success, I want to feel successful because I've surrounded myself with people that care as much as I do . . . people that want to be involved and want to help people out. In this industry, and in life in general, there's so much fakeness, so when you actually find those real people and those real moments of connection, as happened being a beta tester of that game show, I feel like that's success too.

Define your own version of success. My definition has changed over time, but the biggest change came in college and probably right after, when I was moving to New York and I was taking over the world, and then I realized that wasn't happening right away. That also meant I was having to work in restaurants. I had to quit a restaurant or two because, while I was making very good money, I got to the point where I was not happy. If I'm not happy, why am I doing this? If I have money in my bank account, but I'm miserable, am I any better off? I don't know. Maybe somebody would say "Yes," but for me it was "No." Is that any better than having no money and being happy? My other big catch phrase lately is "Somebody else's success is not your failure. Somebody else's strength is not your weakness." I think that's good life advice for people to hear sometimes.

Lisa
Well, since I was little, really, I've felt that success is doing something that I love and being able to support myself doing it . . . pretty simple explanation or description or expectation. Some bumps in the road for that I suppose were others' expectations for me, and that it wasn't always the easiest thing to do. Sometimes I was working a lot and sacrificing social, or personal, time to be able to make sure that I felt comfortable that I had the money coming in to support myself.

The success thing, I think, is a fascinating question. I grew up in an upper middle class neighborhood, so I had everything I needed. Success to me, then, was having the money coming in, so I could buy a house and support myself. Buying a house was a big deal. That was a big part of the success I had in my head. That's what you do. You make enough money so you can buy a house. Then as I got into my twenties, it was really pursuing the things that made me happy. It was more the little things. I felt successful when I could pay my bills . . . when I wrote the checks . . . back when we wrote checks for bills, I would write my checks and send them off. I know! Who does that anymore? I just had to buy stamps again. You know, I don't remember the last time I had to buy stamps, but I had to mail something, so I had to get stamps. I thought, "Well, those will last another ten years." So it really became that success for me was more that I was getting jobs, I was constantly working, and that I had money to pay my bills and buy groceries.

I guess now what may have shifted a bit for me is the goal that I have. During the COVID years, all my savings were used up, because what I was doing for work went away, and I didn't have another source of income. All my backups were in-person gigs. I always thought, "Oh, I can always go back and bartend." Well, not during COVID you can't. So I had to really pivot at that time and find other work, and my savings went to support me during that time. So with the goal of building back up the savings, I'm looking more now toward what I want to have coming in, to not just support my daily life, but to also have the savings, to also be able to save for trips, to be able to save for retirement. So it's expanded a little bit.

Sabrina

I used to buy into the traditional idea of success. You're making money, you're moving up the ladder, you are respected in your field, you stay with the company for thirty years, and then you retire. It was that very black and white view of success. Maybe you get awards, maybe you don't. The definition of success that I used to believe was constantly moving, constantly going, making money, being promoted, moving up the ladder in whatever industry you're in.

As the years have gone on, I've started to recognize maybe success cannot always be related to finances. Maybe success is also how well you balance your work and your life, which is kind of where I'm at now. I consider myself a successful person . . . having to battle my own thoughts on the fact that I'm currently unemployed, and actively searching for a new job, I consider myself a successful person, because every single thing I've been through, professionally, up to this point, has gotten me in other doors that maybe I wouldn't have been able to get into, otherwise.

Sabrina landed a new job shortly after she answered the above, and is very happy and thriving in it.

It's also taught me about work/life balance. I'm more insistent now on that balance than I was before, because of the lessons I've learned from previous employers, or from life. So I think the definition of success that I had before, that very traditional, upward trajectory . . . about financial success has changed to the success that I have now, which is that I'm well respected in the fields that I work in, and the fields that I choose to enter. I have a lot of skill sets that other people do not have, in my industry. I have good connections. I have a great relationship. My home life is secure, even though my financial life is not, and because I have that foundation under me, I can thrive in whatever I choose to do next. For me, that's become my new definition of success. It's weird how it's shifted in just the last year, alone.

Chris

I think my definition of career success now is being able, and this I think probably has always been the same, really being able to make a living at your career . . . being hirable . . . being the person that people want to hire to do the work, and being able to actually earn an income, doing that work, successfully . . . meeting the requirements of the job and not hating the job. That, I think, is the key . . . you're doing something you like. It may be your favorite thing in the world, and you're generally happy doing it. You're making an income at it. People are happy with the work that you're doing. I think that those are the criteria for being successful in a career. That's pretty much how I've always viewed it. I've never looked at it in terms of being wealthy, being famous, getting accolades. Half of the time it's luck. Other times it's completely subjective opinions of things. I think success is just "Do you show up, do you do the job, do you not hate the job, and are you making an income at the job?" That's how I view it. If you get up in the morning and think, "God, I don't want to go into work" every day, that's not career success. You might have the money, but I think you have to have all three of those things. And if you're making the money, but people are constantly saying, "Well, that jerk never does his job," then you're not really successful. Who knows how you got there, but that's not success.

Daphne

What I realized and learned, probably more so when I was leading a team, because I had team members and I was responsible for their development, their training, their growth, their salaries . . . all that fell into my umbrella . . . is that there are different thought processes to what defines success. I say that because for me, it was always the opportunity to do what I enjoyed doing, and with that came money and more money. Always. I never went to a job that wasn't more money. Then it got to a point where it was also about the title . . . not necessarily the recognition, but definitely the title.

There was a point in my career, in the same corporate job, where I stopped and really analyzed things . . . again, I'm a psychologist with no degree . . . I psychoanalyzed my path, and what was important along the way, when I made those choices. I realized that when I asked for an advanced title in the role that I was doing, and with that, taking more responsibilities, whatever they were, I kept earning more money. It was interesting because it was a struggle that I couldn't understand. I'm asking for *this*. I'm getting *this*, and *this* is great, but I didn't need or

185

want *that* at that point. I wanted *this* and that's when I realized everybody at different stages of their lives, potentially, has different aspirations or different desires.

I had a member on my team who had been with the company for thirty years, who was never going to leave that city, or state, or company. She was getting more money regularly, and she just wanted consistency. I had another member of my team who was young, and got married while we were all working together. Then she got pregnant, and for her, she wanted money because she needed it for her family. It was growing, and she needed advancement. She wanted to grow within the organization. So it helped me to realize that where you are in certain times of your life helps determine what's important. And while position and title were very important to me then, previous to that, money was most important. So, at different phases, different things were. Fast forward to now, as an independent planner, I can call myself anything. I can be the president, the owner, whatever. I don't use any of those terms, because I think it's kind of crazy to be that when it's just me, a company of one. I chose my title, which is "Meeting Management Consultant," because that's what I want to do. I want to be a consultant, to help manage your meetings.

I'm blessed. In the past nine years, there have been years that I've made little money. There have been at least two years where I made more than I ever made in corporate America. It's not consistent, but it's happened. So now it's all about enjoying it. And I realize that this is hopefully my last career path. What's important to me could change tomorrow, and I've had to have that wakeup call within myself, because being independent, it can be easy to take everything that comes to you, especially if you feel like it's more money and more opportunity to spread your wings and learn more. But a) you get exhausted, and I've been through that time, where I took on too much, and b) I've also taken on things with people that I don't enjoy working with. This year, for the first time, I stopped that madness where I've actually stopped working with a couple of clients that I just didn't enjoy. I've got to enjoy what I'm doing. Money's great. I need the money. I want the money. I want to keep a roof over our heads, but I want to enjoy what I'm doing. I don't want to walk away or go to my hotel room at night and be miserable. I want to enjoy every aspect of what I'm doing.

Heather
Again, up until I owned my own agency, it was you get up, you clock in, you do your job, you clock out, you go home. Rinse and repeat for forty years, so that you have the nest egg and you can live your life at the ripe old age of sixty-five. I saw that, but I wanted to live a rock star life. I didn't want to have to work. I didn't want to do the nine to five, Monday through Friday, and get two weeks off each year. Hell, no. I didn't understand why I had to go to the office. I didn't understand why I didn't get more than two weeks, if I was lucky, for a vacation. I didn't understand why we have to work between Christmas and the New Year. Nobody should have to do that. So that was success prior to me running my own business. What I call success today is autonomy . . . the ability to have a choice . . . a choice in how much money I earn, how much money I spend, where I spend my time, and how I spend my time. That time is success to me. Owning my own time, doing it for me, that's my level of success. The autonomy . . . woo!

So because you commented on this . . . a friend, who happens to be my attorney, once told me on a Sunday, I believe, when I asked, "What are you doing working on a Sunday," that "When your name is on the door, you work when you have to work." How do you feel about that with what you've just said?

I would, first of all, say bull donkey. I would say that is his reality. I would ask that person this question: "Is that true? Is that true?" My name is on the company, but I choose to take Fridays, Saturdays, and

Sundays off. You have to have things and be committed to these things, and organize yourself in a way that you can have the freedom and the autonomy. You don't need to be chained. You don't need to grind. You don't need to hustle. You absolutely don't if you so choose. But, if you subscribe to a theory that you must . . . if this, then that . . . if you subscribe to that, then that's your reality. But I would call total B.S. on that.

Donna

When I started my work career and I was still in corporate America, success was defined simply as achieving the title I thought I wanted, and making a certain dollar amount. That was it. In a traditional work life, what else is there? Do I get promoted and do I make more money? So that was normal, standard, conventional thought. Once I got into my consulting practice, it was like Maslow's Hierarchy of Needs, where you start at the bottom and you're in survival mode. So, for example, my first clients, I told you, were American Express and Renaissance Cruises. Renaissance wanted to pay me with cruises. I said, "As much as I would love that, no, I need the money." Nowadays, I would love to have a cruise line as a client because I would say, "Just pay me with cruises." I would be thrilled. So what you define as success in the early stages of a consulting practice is completely different than now.

When I started my business and I was in survival mode, it was based on how many new clients I was closing. I had lots of business opportunities because I was out there attracting them, but the measure for me was how many I was closing, Like I was saying before, of the ones that I actually do a proposal for, versus the ones that see me speak and just hire me, how many of the opportunities I have, am I closing?

Another measure over the years was the dollar amount that I was charging. To go from being a personnel manager, or HR director, into a consulting practice, is a very difficult transition. I don't know if it's the same for people who leave other types of corporate positions and go into a consulting business, but with HR people, most of us are people people. That's why we go into HR. We're warm and fuzzy and we want to help people and we almost feel bad asking people to pay us a lot of money. The people who feel like that don't make it. I had a friend who had been in a consulting practice for a number of years, that I met through the National Speakers Association. We're still friends today. Whenever I was frustrated, after I talked to Frank, I would call Steve, and he would help me reason through things based on his own experience. One of the things I struggled with early on was "How do I know what my consulting rate should be? How do I know when I should raise it?" He said to me, "When you come home and you think they're not paying you enough to put up with this, it's time to raise your rate." When I think to myself, "I'm not getting enough for what this has turned out to be," and when I come home saying that a lot, I raise my rates.

Interestingly, I raised my rates a year ago, during the pandemic, for the harassment and discrimination work because once people started going back to work, even remotely, harassment and discrimination was happening. It was fascinating to me that even though half the people were still working at home, there still managed to be complaints, harassment, and discrimination, and the demand got bigger and bigger, even then. So, I have raised my rates for that work twice in the last five years. On January 1st, I raised my regular consulting rate for the first time in at least ten years, maybe even fifteen, partially because I had a couple of friends who wanted to start consulting and asked if they could pick my brain . . . I told you I always say "Yes." I had multiple three-way conversations with a woman and a man, not a couple, just friends who decided to start an HR consulting business. One of the calls we had was about setting rates. The rate they wanted to start with was more than I charge. I thought, "Whoa," and I said, "How did you come up with that number?" "Well, we talked to a bunch of people who are in consulting practices and that seems to be the going rate." I said, "Really? For people who are just starting out?" They replied "Oh, well, no, but even though we're just starting our consulting business, we've been in HR for thirty years, so we feel like we're . . .." I had to talk to them about the distinction between having done the work for X number of years, and being in the business of doing that. So that got me thinking. And then I had a bunch of client things happen that annoyed me and I said, "That's it. I'm raising my rates." Frank said, "You can't raise your rates right now. We're just coming out of a pandemic." I said, "Watch me. I'm doing it."

I have a client, a government client, and each piece of work I do for them is on a different purchase order. So I have five purchase orders going on with them, in different departments or whatever. They had a new project they wanted me to do in November. I said to them, "You need to sign this engagement letter before December 1st, because my rates are going up on December 1st. Anything you do with me after that is going to be at the new rate." We closed that purchase order and then two months later they needed me to do something else and it was at the new rate. So they have purchase orders now at two different rates. I didn't blink and neither did any one of my clients . . . not one. So as I'm sending out new engagement letters to existing clients, it's the new rate. And no one is saying, "Oh, wait a minute, wait, no, we want the old rate." The change is a ten percent increase. No one is blinking. I did that with the other piece of my business, and like I said, I raised those rates twice in the last five years. So, yeah, that piece is significant, obviously.

For me, success is both the financial win and the feeling that when I lay my head on the pillow at night, I feel good knowing that I helped somebody. Whether it's that I did coaching that day, or I helped people manage their teams better, or I worked on an investigation that is either helping someone who's truly a victim of something, or teaching someone that they can't falsely accuse somebody . . . I lay my head on the pillow at night feeling like I made a difference in life. So there's the altruistic piece, which is that I made a difference. Then there's the realistic piece, which is that I made money doing it. I don't think those two are mutually exclusive. I don't think that it's wrong to want to make money. I'm a capitalist and I'm in business to make money. I don't do this for charity. I don't feel bad that I want to make money. People who feel bad about that are never going to succeed in a business. You can't feel bad that you're successful. I definitely don't.

One of the things that I've learned is, for the most part, except for the jerks, your clients will treat you the way you train them to treat you. By that I mean . . . I had a client, my law firm client in Buffalo, the one that I really liked, with the lady president. . . . there was a great HR director there. I loved him. When he got my bill, it would hit his inbox and the check would go out in a couple of days. I remember one time, thirty days came and went, and no check from the firm, which was very unusual. So I emailed him and said something along the lines of, "Maybe my invoice got lost in the pile. I don't know if you received it. I'm attaching another copy." The next morning, Frank and I were getting dressed to go to work, and our home phone rang, and I answered it on speakerphone. Frank was standing right near me and it was the HR guy. It was around 7:45 in the morning, and he said, "I'm sorry to bother you at home, but I just wanted you to know I feel so bad. I'm so sorry. Your invoice . . . someone put it in my inbox and it fell to the bottom and I didn't even know it was there. I want you to know I am walking it down to accounting as soon as we hang up and they will send out your check today. My apologies." I said, "No problem. Thank you for letting me know." I hung up the phone and Frank was standing there with his jaw on the floor, and said, "I've never had a client call me to apologize for not paying my bill fast enough." "Well, my clients understand that I need to get paid. I'm me, myself, and I. I don't work on one hundred clients a month. I work on seven or eight clients a month. When I send out my bills, I need to get paid." So I think that's a really important piece . . . setting the right expectations with your clients. When you have clients who rush to pay you, it means they value what you do and that's a great feeling too. I think that's a measure of success . . . not having to chase your clients to get paid. They want to pay you.

Wei

Growing up, we didn't really have that much. We were definitely middle class, maybe lower-middle class, which is probably why Dad worked three jobs. So I defined success as the Norman Rockwell image . . . picket fence, cats in the yard, a dog at play, significant other, and two kids. Certainly all of that went out the window when I became an adult. Success professionally for me, especially as a government worker, is are we correctly, legally, morally, ethically serving the people? Are we doing everything that we can to make sure that the country is on firm setting, and is safe from attack? That's success for me. Heaven forbid there is another 9/11. That is failure.

How do you define your personal success?

My personal success . . . I'm not sure. And I think maybe that's a good thing. It's dynamic. I don't have a grand, overarching goal, and a rigid construct of what success looks like anymore. And maybe that's part of why a government career works for me. It gives me that flexibility to change my expectations to meet what the needs of the day are. For instance, success for me today was going through all my emails after a week of being in meetings. Success tomorrow is probably making sure that my leadership has all the information they need to answer the questions from above. But overall, I get to live in the moment and I think that's success, or at the very least, it's happiness.

Gabriel
When I was younger, and I was working at that consulting job, and the job after that, I think I probably defined it in terms of status, though not entirely. I mean a little bit, in that way of "Do I have a cool job? Is it an important job? Do people see me a certain way because of that job?" Yes, that's part of it, but it was actually more of an internal thing for me. It's that identity piece that I touched on earlier. "Do I have a job that gives me some solid place in this world?" It's a weird way to define success, but back then it did matter to me.

The other metric was money. I don't know that I was obsessed with the dollar amount, I just thought that it was a useful proxy for whether this was a good job. That has changed pretty dramatically. I still think that having money is really nice and very helpful, and when the money you make is a reflection of the value you create, it's wonderful. I don't think it's irrelevant, but it's not the most important thing. I really do view it as it being a reflection of the thing that you do well. That's what makes the money feel good to me.

Now my definition of success is probably, "Am I doing work that I'm proud of and am I working on problems, or topics, that are meaningful to me?" I still can't really believe this because it seems kind of dumb, but I would do a lot of the "work" that I do professionally if nobody were paying me.

A couple of months ago, I went to see *Avatar 2* with my childhood friend. It's not something I would have seen had he not invited me. It's something like three hours long and it's kind of intense. When we walked into the movie, he offered me a weed gummy . . . a very weak weed gummy. I have not smoked or eaten weed for probably seven or eight years, and before that, it was pretty sporadic. I was very apprehensive. The few times I've eaten weed edibles, it was a little dicey. He said, "It's just going to relax you. It's fine." I ended up basically having three panic attacks during *Avatar 2*, and it got so bad I had to leave the theatre. I was sitting on the stairs, outside, with my head between my legs, deep breathing to calm down because . . . I don't know if you saw that movie, but there's some really disturbing stuff in it, which I did not expect. I think I would have been disturbed even if I had not eaten the two gummies . . . I took two. It's a story as old as time . . . you take one and you're thinking, "It didn't do anything. Let me take one more," and then you're dead. Regardless, it was just a very upsetting evening. I was aware of how funny it was while it was happening, but it was really upsetting because there's this whole sequence where they . . . well, I'm not going to ruin anything big, but there's a sequence where the villains do some really disturbing stuff to some animals. I don't know if it's because I love animals, or because I took two gummies before I watched it, but I was truly . . . it was horrifying. I had this physical response to the movie.

The whole evening ended up becoming . . . I was high for hours. I didn't know if I could go home. I had to walk around for a while and the whole evening turned into this really funny experience. My friend's mom and I ended up in this really funny conversation. Eventually, I did drive home, after I calmed down a little bit. The drive home was really funny, and getting home was funny . . . the whole evening was really funny. I was stoned until one in the morning, probably, and I got to the movie around 5 or 6 P.M.

I came home that night and I was in a state of "Oh, I can't watch a movie and I can't read a book . . . I can't do anything . . . but I think I need to write about what happened tonight." I sat down at my laptop and just started . . . I just went ham from the beginning to the end, up until the moment I walked in the door of my apartment to open my laptop. I narrated the whole evening. I continued to work on that essay for a week or two, taking it very seriously. This is not something I intend to submit to any magazine or put in a book. It's just . . . I love doing it and I take great pleasure in narrating, and trying to get down and make funny, and make interesting . . . trying to suss out the meaning of the stuff that happens to me. The less important, or significant it is, sometimes the better.

I bring this up as a prime example of my metric of success being when I'm working on things that I care about and that move me. For some reason that I don't understand, and I don't have to understand it, this moves me. I like embarrassing myself in public and having this incredibly borderline traumatic but also really hilarious evening, and then coming home and writing about it. What happens is that I can then re-read it, and I can share it with my friends and make them laugh. Maybe one day it'll be in some collection of essays, *maybe*, but that's not on my mind. I'm doing it because I want to do it. I hope that feeling never goes away. If I can make money from that, if I can make good money from that, I would be thrilled. I'm not saying that the money is irrelevant, but I just don't know if I'll ever be the kind of person who can make a lot of money, or enjoy the status of a certain job, if the work that I'm doing isn't meaningful, and isn't creating some kind of value, even if it's just to make somebody laugh, because everything else for me flows from that.

Steve

I don't do anything to be successful. Take scenic design, for instance . . . I've got a show running right now. It's a small summer stock production of *Cinderella* that I designed for the Vegas City Opera . . . how is it successful? Honestly, it truly is about, when it comes down to it, if I can sit back and look at it and say, "You know what, I'm proud of what I did." I don't always have to like it and I don't always like it. I have those moments of, "I'm such a sh*tty designer," and someone will say, "Well, why didn't you do that?" "Oh, yeah, you know what? I should have done that. It's because I'm horrible at what I do." And then again, I can have those moments where I'm sitting out in the house, watching something and I think, "This is the show that I literally conceived in my mind, and put down on paper, had someone build, oversaw the whole process, loaded in the show, went through technical rehearsals, trained all the technicians how to move everything, and it's all done safely, and it's visually interesting, and the lighting designer said, "Hey, nice job. I don't mind lighting this.'"" So to me, that's what makes it successful. It's maybe a combination of personal satisfaction with what I do, and also that it ticks off the boxes that it should tick off in a more "traditional sense," which are, again, is it safe? Is no one going to get hurt? Does the audience like it? Do the other design disciplines like it? Does it work for them? Does it compliment costumes? Can the lighting designer light it? Is the producer happy because I didn't go over budget? I think it's kind of a culmination of those things. I feel like . . . and again this is awesome because I've never thought about it in terms of . . . I've never been asked that, but if it does what it's supposed to do, which is entertain, ultimately that's what it is. Do people come and are they entertained?

I used to say this, and it was kind of cliche, but if I could just change one person's life, with seeing a show . . . if they come in and look at the set and say, "Wow, that's an amazing set. Yeah, the cast was good and the lighting was fine and the costumes were good, but you know, the set is really what did it." I think I've gotten beyond that because it's really not about that. It's about the whole and how I am part of it. So that's maybe kind of how I define success . . . when I sit back and look at it. And if I'm okay with it, then it's successful.

I absolutely did not always define it that way. When I was younger, money was certainly one way of defining success. I have never made a lot of money. And entertainment, theatre, is not a way to get rich for most people. You do it because you love it. I have friends, and even some colleagues, who made a lot more money than I ever made. And I thought, "Man, if I could just . . . ." Maybe this goes back to what I was saying about landing another company manager job on a tour . . . I made bank even as the assistant company manager, and I had a cool job, and I got to travel, and I thought I was successful, at that point. I don't know if I was necessarily satisfied or happy, but it was still kind of a cool gig. And money certainly was the definition of success.

Getting back to my dad . . . I remember more the stories from my mom and brother and sister . . . my mom and dad are divorced, so my mom kind of gives my dad sh*t because he was never into the money. I remember one time, hearing my mom and dad fight about the fact that my dad had turned down a promotion that would have meant substantially more money. My mom was so pissed. "Why did you not take that job? That would have been more money." My dad's reply was "Well, I didn't want to do the job, so I didn't take it." "Yeah, but you'd make more money." "But I didn't want to do it."

I don't remember a moment where the definition went from money to whatever it is now, for me. I think that kind of morphed, and maybe it was when I realized that I was never actually going to get rich doing what I wanted to do, and coming to terms with that, and being okay with it. Now, that being said, we're not poor. We're fine. I make a living. I feel really lucky that I get to draw pictures for a living, and I can actually pay my bills. I wish there was a moment that I could pinpoint, and say "That was it," but I think I kind of mellowed with, not age, but with the experiences, and it just became less about the money and more about wanting to not be miserable. Again, I look at friends who work in more traditional jobs, and . . . I have one friend, in particular, who makes a ton of money in I.T. and bitches about his job all the time. He complains about corporate politics and blah, blah, blah. But, he comes home with that check and that's great because that's him. That's what he wants. He's okay with it. He couldn't do what I do. And I certainly couldn't do what he does.

Victoria
I think that career success, starting off, was basically bringing a paycheck home. You had a paycheck, you had insurance, you were doing good. When did it change? I just always had a desire to be a different person than I was. I always wanted more. I knew there was an opportunity for more and I knew I had an opportunity to make more money. At one point this was true . . . you look at somebody and you say, "Okay, forty hours a week. I could work those forty hours making X amount of money, or I can make more money working those same forty hours." I knew that there was an opportunity for evolution.

I stayed in administrative type roles, if you will, support roles, for years, and went back to school, which was always, always the desire for me . . . to finish my degree. It was through an evolution of changing jobs that I was able to always advance myself a little bit more, a little bit more, a little bit more, until I got to this last job. At this last job, there was an opportunity to evolve and grow into different roles within that situation. So that helped the evolution part, and I could see an opportunity to grow so far, but then at one point, it just tapped out. I couldn't go any further. So it's just through evolution that my definition of success has changed. I can't say there was one defining role or anything like that.

I did take a sales job once, though, where I had to get out and just hustle with the old sample bag. I sold industrial chemicals for two years. That meant, back in the day, you could walk into a factory, or a hospital, or whatever, and that really helped me to get out of my comfort zone, to be able to talk to people . . . to try to influence people and solve a problem. I think that helped quite a bit.

I think defining professional, or career, success today is very individualized. Before it was title, title, title, getting better, getting better, getting better. I think today it's very individualized, because what you consider to be success in your professional career, and what I consider to be success are two different things. That's it. You have to define what you consider to be success. Maybe it's a series of small wins along the way that makes you successful. That's how I define that.

Jesus

Today I define success as anything that makes you happy. If it brings you joy, then it's a success, whether it's financially successful or not. Before, I didn't define it like that. I defined success as having to be financially successful. If you're not making a living as an actor, or a singer, or a dancer, or whatever, then you're not successful. Today, if you work at a museum and do community theatre, or community dance, or whatever, and you're happy doing it, that's successful to me.

My mind changed probably twenty-five years ago, when I was watching an episode of *The Oprah Winfrey Show*. This guy got up and he was talking about Michael and Janet Jackson and he said, "Oh, look at Michael, look at Janet, look at how successful they are." They were talking about abuse, and he was saying, "Yeah, the father may have been abusive, but look at the results." Oprah said, "That's how you define success?" I thought, "Wow. Huh." That stayed with me. That is how I was defining success, and then I realized, "No, it's whatever brings you absolute joy. I want to do art just because it makes me happy and doesn't matter if I'm making a living out of it or not." That's really when that seed was planted.

Michael

For me, it's always been like a ladder, or stepping stones, as the goal is to accomplish this. And then it's, "Okay, I've accomplished this." Now you reset your goal. What do you want to do next? I want to accomplish this. The first goal for me in professional golf, once I turned pro, was to win a minor league, which is like the little mini tour events that happen down here in Florida. They're usually one or two days, they cost two or three hundred bucks to enter. You can win a thousand or two thousand dollars. That was the first stepping stone.

Like I mentioned before, I always compare it to baseball. Single-A baseball is comparable to the minor league golf tour. It's the bottom of the bottom as far as professional golf goes. And then I won one of those, and I won a second one. And then it was a matter of, "OK, now I've got to try to go up to the next level." As I mentioned, I was on PGA Tour Canada this summer and my feeling was, "Okay, I got on PGA Tour Canada. So that means I've achieved another step on that ladder. I achieved another level." So I'm always kind of reevaluating once I accomplish things. That goal, the goal for me once I got my Canada status is that I wanted to Monday qualify into a Korn Ferry event before I went to Canada for the summer, which I did.

So now I've been proving to myself what I can do in professional golf. At this point, the main goal now is to . . . I made it through First Stage of Q-School a few weeks ago. I have Second Stage coming up. Obviously, the main goal is to make it all the way to Final Stage and get on to either the PGA Tour or the Korn Ferry Tour, which is one step below. It's the developmental tour for the PGA Tour. That's my goal right now. If I look back to two or three years ago, when I hadn't won on the minor league golf tour yet, that goal seemed crazy and so far out of reach. So the fact that I'm at this point now is really, really cool.

Will you explain what Monday qualify is?

Every PGA Tour-sanctioned event, except for few, has a qualifier on Monday the week of the tournament. On the Korn Ferry tour, the top eight guys in that qualifier make it into the actual tournament. On the PGA Tour, the top four guys make it into the actual tournament. It's extremely unlikely that you'll make it. The odds are very slim. It's usually somewhere between one hundred to one hundred fifty guys playing the qualifier for the top four or eight spots in the tournaments. So that's why I said earlier that all the stars aligned that day for me to make it through that qualifier. I think there were a hundred and . . . I actually don't know how many, exactly. There were over a hundred people playing in one of two qualifiers that day. In the qualifier I was playing, I happened to be in the top four to make it through. So it's a very unlikely thing, but it's also one of the best opportunities in the world for professional golfers, because you have the opportunity to play one round of golf and just go straight to the highest level, which is really, really cool. That doesn't happen in any other professional sport, anywhere.

Will you explain what Q-School is?

Q is for qualifying. It's kind of a weird name. It's not actually a school. In professional golf, Q-School is . . . I don't want to say the most important, but it's what everybody . . . if you have the money, you play it. It's how you get your status on a bigger tour. For example, last year I played Q-School for PGA Tour Canada. I finished solo tenth. I made it through. I got my PGA Tour Canada card to go play the tour. This time of year, the fall, is when Q-School for the PGA Tour and Korn Ferry Tour happens, which are bigger than PGA Tour Canada. They are the upper levels of PGA tours. The one in Alabama, last spring, was a Korn Ferry Tour event that I Monday qualified into. So pretty much every professional golfer this time of year plays Q-School and tries to get status on a tour, because once you get status on the tour, there are bigger purses, you make more money, your career is in a better spot, all the opportunities open up.

They have a weird way of naming it. There are technically four stages of Q-School: Pre-Qualifying, First Stage, Second Stage, and Final Stage. Being on PGA Tour Canada, I was exempt from Pre-Qualifying. I went straight to First Stage, which I actually ended up winning a couple of weeks ago. I shot eighteen under par and I won it. So that gets me status on what is now called PGA Tour Americas. It's the Canadian tour and the Latin America tour combined. They're combining them this year. I played badly in Canada this summer, lost my card, won First Stage, got my card back, and now I advanced to Second Stage, to try to get to Final Stage, to get my status on a higher tour. It's not easy to understand for people who aren't involved in golf, and I wish they would make it easier and more understandable. I really don't even tell my mom's side of the family what I'm doing because they don't understand what it is. If I do something and I play well, I'll let them know, but as far as, "I'm going to do this next week and it's for this and that," they don't know what it means. It's just honestly easier for me if I don't tell them. So, Q-School is basically mini tournaments to get your ranking. You're trying to work your way up the ranks and Q-School is the main way to do it.

So back to defining professional success, do you feel like you are at a new level of success now because you're in your own home?

Not really, because I'm still not in a financial spot where I know exactly how I'm going to pay the rent every single month. If I had fifty grand in my bank account right now, I'd probably be thinking, "Oh yeah, I feel like I'm doing really, really well right now." But I don't. I know I have enough to pay this month's rent and then I'll figure it out after that. That's kind of how my life's always been. I just kind of move one week, one month at a time, and just figure out how I'm going to make everything work. My girlfriend thinks that's very, very stressful and I can see why. But for me, that's how my life's always been, so it's not anything new to me.

CHAPTER 13: SEPARATION OF POWERS

Have you ever felt that you needed to keep different parts of yourself separate from certain parts of your life?

Brian

I'm very much an open book. My husband and I joke about this all the time, where I am hyper-aware of situations and settings, and I will go out of my way to not waste somebody's time. I'm very much a cut to the point person. So if I can assess in a situation that somebody actually doesn't care, I'm just going to wrap it up. Or if I can assess in a situation that a topic is not going to bring anything to the conversation, I'm not going to bring that up. Could some people take that as me hiding or compartmentalizing, I think was the word you used? Possibly. But I overthink a lot. So I will go out of my way to think, "Well, what's the answer you want to hear?" And that's something I've gotten much better at not doing over the years. Previously, I would try to play into the "What's the answer you want? How can I give you the thing that you need in order to hire me, in order to do this, in order to do that?" Now, if I'm the person you want, great. If not, great. Here's my thought on the matter: I might not be the person that you want, but I'm still going to be honest with you, because it's not going to do me any good to hide that for the rest of time, if this becomes a thing for us, together.

Lisa

Oh, man! Well, going back to high school for one, nobody even knew, except for my very close friends, that I was performing and I was doing shows, in places other than my high school. I kept that separate and I kept school academic. I think part of that was because I didn't get into the performing aspect I wanted to at school, so I just did it somewhere else. Those were very separate, and I didn't share with people that that's what I was doing. One thing I know for sure has helped me in corporate training, especially walking into a room of gentlemen who are older, and I'm there to teach them something, or train them on something, was bartending in a sports bar. I have to tell you, that has come in handy for corporate training and team building like you would not believe. And yet, I don't always know if that's an appropriate thing to share because it might make people look at me differently, or less, because it was a Hooters knockoff sports bar that I worked at. I do know, though, the skills I learned there have come in handy throughout all of my team building and corporate training work.

So basically you know how to talk to guys.

Well, yes, and deal with people who are drinking, because you get that a lot in corporate team building. Companies feel there has to be alcohol in order to reward people. So you're doing team building programs where people are drinking. The murder mystery dinner theatre is what helped me learn how to relate to women, because the characters I was playing, especially when I was younger . . . well, the characters I'd been playing most of my life were the little sexy ingenue ones, and for dinner theatre, what I learned was I didn't have to work on men at all. I just walked in, dressed up, and I got them. I had to work with the women. I had to make them all my best friends and relate to them. I could ignore the men and they were fine. That helped me feel more comfortable, and more genuine, in relating to women and what they respond best to, especially if they're feeling at all threatened.

Sabrina

I'm very good at compartmentalizing. Because of the varying fields I've worked in, I did it. There was work, and then there was personal, and then there was family, and then . . . I would put things in boxes because I think, again, it's conditioning, and it's also the way I've viewed things. I used to, when I was married, keep things very separated. My home life was different from my work life. I didn't tell my ex-husband personal things, because emotionally, we just weren't on the same page. I wouldn't talk to my boss about certain issues I was having because that's inappropriate. You don't do that. You don't bring that to the office. The same thing happens in the theatre. You keep it at the door. And now I will say I have lessened that a little bit because I recognize, as someone who's a leader in my community, and a leader in the jobs that I've done, you can't ask human beings to check it at the door all the time. There's always going to be some sort of overlap. There has to be a little bit more compassion for ourselves, and compassion for your employees, and compassion for your partners. Things are going to bleed into each other, especially in the last few years, working from home, where it's impossible sometimes to not have that overlap . . . your office is in your house, so it's bleeding into the kitchen sometimes.

I used to be very much someone who believed, "This goes in this box, and this goes in this box, and this goes in this box." And now I think, "Maybe this box and this box can be friends. Maybe my work life and my personal life sometimes have to meld together a bit, because I'm a human being. Maybe I'm having a bad day at work. I need to go talk to my boss and say, "Look, this is where I'm at today. I'm going to do my best. I'm here. But you need to know that this is what's going on with me, so that you understand why I'm responding the way I am.""" The same is true with my partner. I need to be able to talk to my partner and say, "Look, this is what's going on with work right now. This is why I'm reacting this way." Again, with my marriage, there were things that we just didn't talk about because I didn't know I was allowed to talk about them. They were *my* issues, not *his* issues. And now I've become very much aware that they were *our* issues. In my professional life, there's more empathy. I can bleed some of my personal into my professional, while maintaining a professional discretion, obviously. So I think there's much more balance to that now than there used to be.

I'm very good with discretion, too. Mama . . . she's a steel trap. You tell me something and it's confidential, I take it to the grave. I think that's still the one thing I hold very strongly. I assume if somebody tells me something, it's told in confidence. I think that's different from the compartmentalizing of personal and professional and all of that. I don't know if that made any sense, but there it is.

Chris

I'm incredibly shy. I know this is crazy, but I am super shy, so I've always had a kind of protective barrier around myself, that I learned to maneuver around in a way that hides just how painfully shy I am. I think that for a long time . . . I didn't know I had Celiac's Disease until I was thirty-three . . . so from the time I was fifteen, until the time that I was thirty-three, I was in constant pain. I never let anybody know. I just kind of cultivated a . . . it wasn't a mask . . . it was just easier to get through the day by drawing on, and channeling, and trying to project positivity. I didn't want to be the person that when you walk in a room, everybody says, "Oh, here comes Miserable Milly." I wanted to be the person that when I come in, I smile, and you smile, because then there's a reciprocation of energy. So I did that.

Once I tackled my Celiac's Disease and I felt better, it became easier. I had a little extra energy. Sometimes I get a little nuts, but it's still that outward display of confidence, because growing up, I didn't have that. I didn't know how to do that. People thought I was a stuck up bitch because I didn't talk and I was academically up there. I graduated number three in my class, so I was that kid. I had issues with making eye contact, I didn't talk, I didn't know how to break out of my shell, and because I was this person who was known for academic excellence, people thought that of me. I found this out later. I was in high school when I found out what people thought. "I had no idea that you were nice." I'd say, "Why? What? What did I do? Did I hurt you?" "No, you just kept to yourself, and you were super smart. I just thought you looked down on everybody." "No!" I was miserable. I thought everybody hated me and I didn't know what to do. So that's definitely a part of me that I try to keep out of certain other parts of my life.

Then, of course, when there's personal drama, or family drama . . . that stays over there and work stays over here. That kind of drama should not, unless it absolutely has to, if it literally breaks down the wall and gets in the way, be mixed into anything else. You keep those things separate.

Daphne
My professional and my personal lives stay separate, and it's intentional. I have great colleagues and/or team members that I've worked with, and some of whom I think of as personal friends, but most of whom I think of as professional friends, allies, coworkers, colleagues. I have many, many personal friends, none of whom, now, are in the industry.

It was very, very different in my former life. When I was in Nashville and I worked at Opryland, I was in my thirties. I grew up there, and all of my closest friends . . . we all grew up there. We all got married. Many of us working at the hotel met our significant others there. We all knew each other in our personal lives. We all went from the hotel, to the bars, to dinners, together. We spent our holidays together. That was my existence. Many of them still spend time together, but I've moved from that world. Not many of them are in the industry anymore, so there's not necessarily a connection in that way.

In my current life, none of my friends work in the industry. It's very separate, to the point where I have two phones. I'm one of the few people in the world that still keeps two phones. Even though I work for myself, I have a professional phone, and I have a personal phone, each with different numbers. Obviously, my brother, my husband, and maybe one friend have both numbers. When I'm working and I'm crazy, and I'm all over the floor, and I'm on site at hotels, my personal phone usually is still in the hotel room because I don't need to see the seven hundred-text chain about something with all the in-laws. If my folks are calling me, they're not calling me with an emergency. They're calling because they want to talk for an hour, but I don't have an hour. If they needed to, they would reach out to other people who could find me. So I keep it separate.

Now, the same holds true on weekends. If I don't have a work function, I may touch my work phone every day just to make sure nothing's blown up, or to check if somebody's texting me that needs something, but otherwise, I don't look at my work phone. I keep it very separate. I try my best. It's especially important when you work from home and you're working for yourself. I could work all the time, and I do often work past . . . I don't have set hours. I work late at night and I don't mind that. If I need to put a spreadsheet out to work on it or play with a meeting space, I can do that on a conference table and that's fine. But I do really try to keep it separate and that's just for my own sanity.

Heather

Absolutely. One hundred percent. I mean, I'm a gay woman who grew up in the 90s. Gay was not okay. You didn't tell anybody about that. So that's the vibration I operated on for a very long time. It turns out that if you can be you, things get a whole lot easier. If you're willing to step up and be your true, authentic self, if you know what that even freaking means . . . go back to that awareness thing . . . if you're willing to show up, do your work in the way that only you can do it, and show up in life in the way that only you do it, things get a lot easier. I had to teach myself that. I had to break through that mold. I think I was still in my late twenties, trying to hide the fact that I was gay. I had short hair. I am the token gay girl, you know what I'm saying? You looked at me and thought, "She's gay," but still, even in my late twenties, I had to keep that separate. I have since dropped all of that stuff. But, it was strong. That grip was strong.

Donna

So one answer to that is that over the years, a lot of my clients became friends. Over the years, a lot of my friends engaged me to do work for them. Because of all the volunteer work that I've done in the HR world, like being president of my local SHRM chapter, being president of the state SHRM organization, and serving on the national board, I built a reputation for myself in the HR community, both at the micro and macro levels. I'm well known in the HR world. So there were clients who became friends and friends who became clients, and sometimes I have felt like I had to separate those two.

Sometimes the client felt that way and we would have an open, honest conversation about how to keep separation of church and state . . . friends versus professional. Most of the time it wasn't an issue because either we became friends or we were friends. Here was a trust relationship that fostered a great working relationship. Now, there was one person in particular, where it would not have been good if her boss thought, or knew, that we were friends before she hired me. She got proposals from other people and she really wanted to work with me. She did her due diligence and one time she hired a different consultant. Most of the time she hired me. She kept saying, "My boss can't know that we're friends outside of this." "Fine, no problem." So, aside from those occasional examples, I want to do business with people I like. I want to do business with people I trust. I like doing business with my friends. Because I know that I am honest and ethical, and I would never intentionally do something that crossed a line or wasn't appropriate, I don't worry so much about having to separate one situation from another, because if an ethical issue came up, I would address it head on. I can't think of any times that's happened except in that situation where she said, "My boss can't know that we're friends."

Wei

I think "Don't Ask, Don't Tell" was the biggest for me. Again, I was not active duty military, so I could be "out" at any given time in my professional career; because at the time that I entered government service, discrimination based on sexual orientation was not allowed for a federal, non-Armed Forces employee. But, as a courtesy to active duty folks who could not be out, I chose to not disclose my sexual orientation. I played the pronoun games and there were a bunch of people who caught on and told me, "No, it's okay, Wei. You can be honest with us." And I always replied, "I don't know what you're talking about." So when "Don't Ask, Don't Tell" was finally repealed by then-Secretary Gates, I happened to go into Costco, which had only a freaking rainbow cake, and I brought it into work to share with everyone. What was interesting is that, again, at that point, I had three years of government service, and many of my coworkers . . . civilians, contractors, military . . . all came in and thanked me for bringing in a cake. They asked me if there was something that I wanted to share. "No, I just brought in a cake because there's a cause for celebrating life." It's interesting . . . even though I had chosen to hide that aspect of my life, enough people had figured it out. It's pretty telling when someone's using gender neutral pronouns to speak about their significant other. Granted, that was back then. These days, a lot more people have non-gender assigned pronouns, so it's a different conversation. But back then, even though I chose to hide that part of my life, many of my coworkers wanted to share. They wanted to know more about me. They wanted to see me in my full, authentic self at work. They honestly wanted me to just be happy. So that's one time when I had to hide and compartmentalize a piece of myself from work.

Have you ever felt like you've had to hide your work from your personal life?

I think there's value in the way that people in Florida approach you, versus people in, say, the Washington, D.C. area. Having lived in the D.C. area for well over twenty years, on and off, it always amazes me, or it shouldn't amaze me, that when you strike up a conversation with a stranger at an event, usually it's an introduction of their name. Then, the very first question is always, inevitably, "What do you do?" And the implication is "What can you do for me?" Now, when I go back to Florida, anytime I strike up a conversation with someone, that first question is actually any number of things. It could be, "Where did you move here from?" or, "What do you like to do?" or, "Hey, what did you do this weekend?" So it's always nice when the conversation does not revolve around what I do for work, because that is only, in theory, an eight-hour portion of my day.

That said, there have been a number of times when I hid what I do for work, not because anything is so secretive, but more because I didn't want to delve into politics, or I didn't want to go and get into an argument over whether or not something being done by the U.S. Government was controversial, for whatever reason it may have been. As a government civilian, you are always representing the U.S. Government, whether you're on the clock or you're not. And so there's value whenever I can steer the conversation elsewhere, toward the person that they really want to know about.

Gabriel

Oh, wow, what a great question. Well, certainly I have. I think it's probably just a general human impulse to hide and to cut off parts of yourself, to function in different environments. We do that in our families before we do it in work environments. We do it with our friends.

When I was in that corporate environment, I was masquerading as a corporate guy for sure. I wasn't like a robot, but there were moments when I would let out the real Gabe, and it didn't always go very well. I'm not the best person to ask about how to behave in corporate environments. I'm clearly not a corporate guy, although I can function. One of the joys of stepping off of that path and getting to do something more creative is that it doesn't just *allow* me to be more myself; I *have* to be myself. Otherwise what am I doing? So when I'm writing scripts and such, it's all about, "Well, what's the embarrassing thing?" It's like the *Avatar 2* story that I told you. That story only works when I can admit how sensitive I am to watching fake people hurt fake animals. Being a creative person is mining all of the stuff that would be completely inappropriate in a corporate company.

As I've gotten older, I've realized that there's such a huge role for vulnerability and authenticity in every aspect of life. The people who really succeed in the corporate world, I suspect, are probably inviting more of themselves to the table than other people. But you can't be a crazy person. HR is a real thing. You can't talk about the terrible day you had with your employees. It's inappropriate. So, there are definitely stronger boundaries, and there probably should be.

I also feel that this new generation and this moment in our culture has really invited . . . people are talking about things in corporate life that you would never talk about, before. They're talking about mental health. That, even ten years ago, was taboo. And you could argue that we've gone too far. I've seen emails, on the internet, of Gen Z people writing to their bosses saying, "I can't come into work today. I need a mental health day." "Yeah, but there's no such thing in our contract as that." And I'm not saying that it's right or wrong. It's just an interesting question . . . how much do we allow for people's foibles and vulnerabilities and idiosyncrasies . . . it's fascinating. I truly don't know the answer to that, even though it sounded like I was kind of putting that down. So to answer your question, yes, I've definitely put away parts of myself.

Steve
I don't think so. I feel like I've always been pretty much like a chameleon. Company management and scenic design: two very different sides of the brain . . . and even though, like I was saying, I always wished I was a better scenic designer, I think one of the the benefits of maybe not being a great scenic designer is I'm also pretty good at company management and spreadsheets and budgeting. I love budgets. I love Excel spreadsheets and doing . . . oh, I know it sounds so odd, but I love that. I can, on one hand, sit and do that. How does that relate to the scenic design? So I feel like being kind of well-rounded in that way has allowed me to, again, get where I'm at now because I've never had to do, or be, just one thing. So, I've never really tried to keep things separate. Say, for instance "I just want to dance, but I can't dance because I'm an accountant." There haven't been those moments in my life and I feel pretty fortunate for that.

You've said a few times now that you don't think you're a great scenic designer. One could argue that being able to use the left and the right brain equally well does make you a great scenic designer.

Yes. And that is a . . . not even a skill, but I really truly like, or

211

appreciate, that about myself . . . the fact that I can do both of those things. I like that I'm not any one specific thing. I have those moments when I'm sitting watching a play, or something I designed, and see it come to life, and again, someone will make a comment like, "Oh, that's great. I love how you made those trees have bumps on them like they do in real life," and I'm looking at that and say, "Well, that was actually a mistake. I never intended for that to happen, but thank you." So, yes, you're right, but there are moments where I wish that I was a better artist or a better scenic designer or . . . ultimately, we put these labels like "artist" or "scenic designer" or whatever on ourselves. I wish I was more creative sometimes. I wish I had that freedom.

I think there's an assumption that people who are really creative are really messy. Their desk is always a mess and they can't find anything. It's because their brains are all over the place and they're just so creative that they can't be bothered with being organized. I tend to be kind of the opposite of that. My desk is very neat and I have a place for everything. I sometimes wish that I was less organized, or more messy, because I feel like then I would be a better artist. I'm totally getting off topic here, but I wish I were more creative, sometimes, than I maybe either allow myself to be, or as I come across.

Victoria
Oh, absolutely. My personal life was totally separate from my career. Absolutely. I rode a motorcycle. People knew I rode a motorcycle, but I kind of kept that . . . I don't really publicize that because sometimes motorcycle people, unfortunately, get a bad rap. They're wonderful human beings. The fact that I was vegetarian for years, and I worked in the agriculture organization, I kept that secret for years and years because that would be . . . I'm eating meat now because my hair fell out. That's been recent, but for years and years, I kept that part of my life to myself. It was nobody's business, and I knew that I would be, I wouldn't say condemned, but judged. I can't imagine somebody having to keep something to themselves and how that makes them feel. I mean, something on a more significant scale. Let's just say that I'm neurodivergent and I have a problem with ADHD. I'm not going to

go out and tell people at my work that I have ADHD, but that shouldn't be the case. You should be able to be who you are, and be accepted. But it isn't always so. We judge people. We judge people all the time. You're judging me now. Well, that's the truth, right? So. yeah, I definitely separate.

Jesus
Oh, yeah. As a queer person, yeah, definitely. If I'm out in public, especially in today's climate, I won't hold Eric's hand because I'm afraid it could result in some kind of confrontation, and then it will escalate. I'm nervous about somebody taking an AR-15 and shooting us.

Are there other parts of me? Yes. I suffer from imposter syndrome. I'm very quiet, I'm off in the corner, I'm reading a book because I don't want to show people the real me, because I'm afraid that if I do, and they don't like me, it means I'm not likable. So if I pretend to be different from who I really am, then that person is okay. I do that a lot.

Do you think you're a different person at work than you are at home, or when you're out socially?

At work, it's still me, but it's the frustrated, annoyed me. It's not really an imposter. It's just another part of me, a different side of me.

I'm really dealing with the imposter syndrome and getting better at it. But the gay thing, I think that's always going to be in the back of my mind. We live in a dangerous world, unfortunately, and we just have to protect ourselves. I would like to throw it in people's faces but no, I don't.

Michael
I have, and I do. You've seen the taglines. I do rap and make hip hop music a little bit. I like to try to keep that separate from golf because I think that's kind of like . . . music is kind of like my outlet from golf.

When I don't want to think about golf, or I'm not happy with golf, I listen to music, or I make music. During a couple of the golf interviews I did back in the spring, people asked me to rap. "Yeah, no, sorry, no shot." I don't mix the two. Those are my two main things in my life . . . golf and music. I try to keep them as separate as I can. They are two very different personalities for me, and two very different audiences.

CHAPTER 14:
IF I ONLY HAD A HEART . . . A BRAIN . . .

There is a quote, in various incarnations, that has been attributed to a number of individuals, including George Bernard Shaw, Otto von Bismarck, Winston Churchill, and even Kevin Spacey, in the film *Swimming With Sharks*, which is where I first heard it. The gist of it is that if you're not a liberal in your twenties, you have no heart, but if you're not a conservative, or haven't turned to the establishment, in your thirties, you have no brain. How do you feel about that?

Brian
I'm very tempted to say, and I will say, that a quote like that I think hits different in today's . . . I'm going to say political climate . . . by saying liberal and conservative. I feel like I understand what the gist of it means in terms of being financially liberal and financially conservative. Not necessarily *value* liberal and *value* conservative, because I feel like there are so many different definitions.

Now I feel like the soundbite is going to come back to bite me in the butt at some point because somebody is going to read your book and say, "Oh, you're a bleeding liberal." I guess I'll go with this . . . it's hard to hear that quote and not automatically take it into today's political climate, to a political side of Democrat or Republican, when you say liberal and conservative.

I understand where it makes sense to some people. In the topic of what you're going for with the book, in terms of career paths, and life paths, and stuff like that, I feel like I've gotten to the point where I've realized how to monetize my strengths, and how to be able to not necessarily have to be "conservative." Especially coming from a performance world, you hit a point where you don't have any money. You need to do anything just to make some money. But, I feel like where I am now, I'm able to still be liberal when it comes to finances, but not necessarily . . . I don't feel like I'm selling out. And again, I don't know that that's exactly where that quote goes, but I feel like my brain just went there in terms of . . . I don't have to just shift, or give up on certain things because of finances, where I thought, maybe earlier in my life I might have had to do that . . . "Oh, if I get to thirty and I haven't done this, then I might as well quit and get a desk job."

Lisa

I have not heard that before. This is new. Boy. I've told you this before, I think . . . my favorite saying is "All generalizations are false, including this one." So I, just on principle, have a hard time with those kinds of blanket statements that say "If you're not this . . . if it's not this, then it's that." I'm a shades of gray person. I think for a lot of people, but not for all, that we tend to be more liberal in our youth because we're more idealistic. I don't see being liberal or conservative as being so cut and dry about heart or brain. That makes it sound like you're stupid to be liberal and I'm not comfortable with that.

Sabrina

I've heard that too, somewhere. That's a hard one because I guess it goes by what your definition of a liberal and a conservative is, in politics, these days. That's changed even since the start of the nation. So I feel like that is very unnuanced, and I don't like things that don't have nuance, because it's putting people in categories based on one aspect of their character, and one aspect of their personality, and maybe there's more to them than that.

I don't like how limiting that is. If we're speaking specifically politically, someone could share an ideology that is similar to someone that they don't necessarily identify with. I consider myself a liberal and a Democrat, but once upon a time, back when things were more bipartisan, there were things on the Republican and conservative side where I could say, "Oh, I can see the point. I can take their side on that. I agree with them." So I think it's very limiting when you say quotes like that, because it puts people in these categories that don't necessarily fit all people. You're identifying people by this particular ideology.

It also seems so incorrect. I feel like I've gotten more liberal as I've gotten older because I've gotten wiser to the establishment and I've gotten a little smarter. I've become more empathetic as a person and I've opened my group of friends and family to more types of people, so my ideology has changed. I think a lot of people have gotten more liberal as they've gotten older. I don't even know if I think that statement is true. That whole quote to me just seems so backwards . . . something about it doesn't seem wise. It seems very judgy and limiting.

Chris

I think it's bogus. I grew up with very, very liberal parents. They were hippies in the sixties. I was in a folk music band with my dad for over a decade, and we sang lots of political protest songs, and environmental conservation songs. I grew up anti-establishment, I guess, and I don't think I've ever settled into the establishment. I like to skirt the edges. It's the same with my parents. My mom's in her seventies now and if a bunch of white-haired ladies got together to protest something, she'd be there. So I don't think that's true. I know a lot of people who, when I was younger . . . late teens, early twenties, were very conservative and still had a lot of passion, a lot of heart. They were conservative in certain views, but when it came to other things, were very, very compassionate and liberal. I don't think that you have to be liberal when you're young to have a heart. And I definitely don't think you have to be conservative to have a brain when you get older. I think that's confusing ideology with soul.

Daphne

I don't know. I think it's unfair to make any full statement about any grouping at all. I need to think about that one. I sometimes wonder, perception-wise, what people think in that realm. What you just said caused me to think about myself. I asked, "Do I have a brain? Do I have a heart?" It got me thinking about myself and thinking about other people. I don't think I know many people that are brainless. I think there are people that are heartless, and that bothers me. I don't know what to make of that one. That's a hard one.

Heather
Is that true? I don't know. That's just an opinion. I don't know . . . I think that . . . man, how do I answer that question? "Don't box me in," is what I'm going to say. You don't know who I was in my twenties, you don't know who I should be in my thirties. Who's dictating this? This question pisses me off, actually.

Don't yell at me.

No, I'm not yelling at you. It's so absurd. Who says I can't both have a heart and be smart about my fiscal responsibilities? I think that question confuses me. I don't know if I can give you an answer.

Donna
That's very funny. I am not a liberal. I've never been a liberal. I'm married to someone who doesn't know he's a liberal. He thinks he's a conservative, but he's not. I have always been a capitalist. I used to call myself a Republican. Now, that to me is a dirty word. So I consider myself a conservative as opposed to a Republican. Frank likes to say that he is socially liberal and fiscally conservative. I am liberal in absolutely no way. When Frank and I were trying to have children, he used to tell people, "If Donna has anything to say about it, our kid will be working a paper route when he's three-and-a-half because she thinks character building is to work their asses off and suffer, because she suffered." There's a lot of truth to that.

It was in the news this weekend that they did away with affirmative action in the colleges. We had a bingo dinner yesterday. All of our liberal friends were here. Someone said, "Oh, did you hear about this ruling," and they all started in with, "Oh my God, it's just terrible. It's just terrible." And I said, "Yeah, I'm really glad they did that. But I'm walking away now."

So, yeah, it is true what Frank says. I had to pay my dues. I had to work hard. I paid off my student loans. They weren't forgiven. The government didn't forgive them. Nobody forgave them. I paid off every goddamn penny myself. And I want everyone else to do that, too. I don't want people to get a free ride because I didn't get a free ride. I want people to work their asses off. I want kids to learn the hard way. I don't want them to get a car when they're sixteen. I don't want them to automatically go to college. I don't think everyone's entitled to a college education. I am a hard ass. I am not a liberal and I never was because I didn't get those things. And I turned out okay. Now, Frank's response to that is, "Well, I got some of those things and I turned out okay." I say to him, "Yeah, but if we had had kids, you would have wanted to give your kids way more than what was given to you, right?" "Well, yeah, they're good kids, right?" We have this conversation with all of our friends. "Well, my kid's an A student, why shouldn't he get a new car?" My reply is, "Did you get a new car when you were sixteen?" "No." "Weren't you an A student?" "Yeah." "Well, how come you didn't get a new car?" "There was no way my parents were going to do that." "Well, why should you?" So, yeah, I'm a hardcore, hard ass, tight ass, mean bitch. Call me whatever you want. I don't want people to get handouts because I didn't get them. I think there's a lot to be said for believing that you have to do things the right way to get the payoff later. I know there are people who go into business who had a silver spoon in their mouths, and they're successful. So obviously it's not true that you only learn if you do things the hard way. But that was my experience, so that was my measure. I was never a liberal in my twenties. I have never been liberal. I will never be liberal. I have always been conservative. Now, I will say that I believe everyone has the right to live their life.

Wei

I think that's a very rigid way of looking at the world. Certainly both sides have their merits and on any given day I can sway from being liberal in one stance to more conservative in another. Life is not very black and white. It's shades of . . . not fifty shades of gray, but probably a million shades of gray. Although every single one of those people mentioned are extremely influential, potentially extremely bright, I think it's a very unnuanced perspective of life and I certainly hope that every single one of those people had the opportunity to literally stop and smell whatever flowers were on their way from point A to point B.

Gabriel

It's a funny question to ask someone like me because I don't identify politically as anything, although I probably have views that would slot me into both camps in different circumstances. I also have a bit of an allergic reaction to categorizing myself as one thing or the other, especially when it comes to politics. So I don't know if there will ever be a point where I think of myself as liberal or conservative, ever. I know what the quote is getting at. It's a very interesting one. But I don't know. I might have to pass on that question.

Steve

Well, I love that. I think what I love about that is one of the things I believe about who I am, and my nature, is my reaction to that is a big "F you." Maybe that's true for you, but that certainly is not true for me. I will do everything I can to disprove that or to buck the system. So that's it. That's a great question. I like that. I wish I had a better answer.

Victoria

I think what that means, to me, is that we lead in the beginning of our lives by emotion and what fulfills us. In our twenties, everything is driven by the heart. Then, as you get older and you see what works, what doesn't work, I think you tend more to be a conservative. In other words, how I value my time and how I value my employment, things that I do, the people I hang out with, those are choices. You realize that in your twenties it's all heart. "Oh, what makes me feel good? This is great!" Then as you get older, and I wouldn't even say thirties, to me, and I know this is a quote, but for me it came about later. It came about much later in life, say forties. Then you say "Okay, okay, this has driven my decisions thus far. Now it's time to stop." Now everything gets judged. Everything becomes more conservative. I'm not saying my heart is not involved, but it definitely is my brain, more so.

I feel like especially now, I look at my life, and the clock is ticking. There's only so much more sunlight left. So the decisions that I make need to count. So it's a balance. It's definitely a balance. It's not that I'm emotionless and that I don't have a heart, because I very much do have a heart, and feel the spirit inside of me. But as I get older, I've only got so much daylight left . . . that's a fact. I've lived my life that way for probably about a decade now. You just wake up one day and you go, "Ohhhhh, how old are you now? We're burning daylight here. We've got to make it count," so my decisions become more conservative. Yes, I still have heart. I want to do things, but I really make sure that they count . . . that they're worth something.

Jesus
Well, I don't know if this relates, but I'll share it anyway. John Cameron Mitchell, who created *Hedwig and the Angry Inch*, said something recently, on a podcast, that I thought was really interesting. He was saying how there are a lot of people that he admired growing up who were very punk, and today they're Trump supporters, or supporters of DeSantis. He wonders why they went so far right. He said that there's this thing where you can become so politically correct that it pushes even the rebels to join the conservative side because they're so fed up. He mentioned that he was doing a movie where he used the word "faggot" and somebody told him, "Oh, you can't use that word," and he said, "But I am a fag." Another example he gave was someone writing a script about racism, being afraid to use the N-word, because of offending people, even though it's true to the character. He said he thinks when we go that far, that's when you start to push these people into that other side.

I get the whole thing about being a rebel in your twenties. You're young, you're impressionable, you're idealistic, and then as you get older, you realize nothing's going to change. But it depresses me. I don't know that I agree with that, because basically what it's saying is, as you get older, you become a cynic and you kind of just become a conservative because you give up. It's always going to be a two-party system. The Constitution is never going to change. We're never going to get rid of the Electoral College. So, when you have kids, you have to become conservative. I've seen this a lot. I've seen friends of mine who were partying and having fun, and then they have kids and all of a sudden they say, "Oh, I don't know if I should take my kid to a drag show." "But you were the one going to drag shows with me when we were younger. Now all of a sudden you have kids and you don't want to expose them to drag?" I don't agree with that. I wish we continued to be rebels like Jane Fonda, even into our eighties.

From what I heard, you're talking primarily about the United States. Three of the four people I mentioned who are attributed to having made that statement are European.

It's interesting you mention Winston Churchill, and I know in England they have really bad free speech laws. It's not like in the United States. That may change, but in England, I think if you criticize their religion, or criticize Mohammed, you can get fined for that, if I'm not mistaken. Whereas here you can call Mohammed an asshole and you don't get fined for that. You can't do that in England, and I think those are really bad free speech laws.

Also, even though in Europe they seem to be more free about sex . . . I know the age of consent in Italy is fourteen . . . I don't personally agree with that, but that is the age of consent over there. People say for some things I'm conservative, and for other things, I'm liberal. I'm such a liberal and say, "You know, if it's a naked body, let kids see it. Every kid has either a penis or vagina. Who cares as long as they're not simulating sex?" There are people who grow up in nudist colonies and those kids don't become perverts or rapists. If they do, it's not because they grew up in a nudist colony. I think you should talk to kids early about sex, when it's appropriate for that particular child. I don't think you wait until fifteen to tell a kid, "Hey, consent looks like this." So, because I'm such a liberal and because I'm so on the far end, there's a lot of things with conservatives that I just don't agree with. I don't agree with sheltering kids and I think drugs should be legalized. All drugs should be legalized. I'm extremely liberal.

I know what that statement says happens. I know that there are people who are very liberal in their twenties, and then they become more conservative, especially after they have children, but I wish it was the opposite. I wish they would become even more liberal and more progressive and more forward thinking. You have all the wisdom when you're older. That's when you can really, really say, "This is why these progressive ideas work," and that is why I like Jane Fonda. That's what I have to say.

Michael

I'm not going to lie, I'm probably the worst guy to ask that question. I probably pay less attention to anything political than anybody else on this planet. What it means to be a liberal versus . . . what did you say . . . conservative? I don't think I know how to interpret the question. I'm literally so basic. I golf, I listen to music, I eat, and that's it.

CHAPTER 15: MONEY

We live in a capitalist society and money plays a big role in that. Whether it be cash, a retirement plan, health insurance, or tangible goods, many people focus on money. Is that a good or a bad thing, and why?

Brian

I don't think it's a bad thing. I feel like we have to, as humans, and especially as humans that are in the creative fields, understand that we have distinct value . . . monetizing value. And if we are undervaluing or devaluing our time and talents over and over and over, we're not serving ourselves.

I know there are times that I do jobs to make money, and there are times that I do jobs to be creatively fulfilled. For the most part, with what I've been able to do, those two things overlap a lot, because I've gotten to a point where I've been able to say, "This is what my rate is. This is what my perceived value is. If that aligns with your perceived value of me, great, let's work together. We can make this happen. If it does not, one way or the other, then I guess it goes back to that idea that I'm not the person for you, because I can't devalue myself just to do this thing, continuously." Trust me, there are some shows I would do for free. There are some gigs or choreography events that I would do for free because I know it would pan out in the long run. As artists, we've got two sides. We've got the financial fulfillment and the creative fulfillment, and sometimes we can find how those things mesh, and sometimes we can't. We have to fill this bucket and then fill that bucket and then fill this one again. I've gotten to a place in my career that I have had to manipulate, figure out, scrap, whatever, how to mesh those two way more than I ever thought I would have been able to do, previously.

Lisa

Boy, that seems like a simple question, and yet it really has so many layers to it. I think it is responsible to focus on money, and be responsible, and make conscious choices with one's money. I think that sometimes that focus can be singular or myopic, and can cause disagreements or problems, from what I've seen in couples, in particular, because there are different values behind the focus on money. I think there has to be a certain amount of focus on money if someone's going to be a responsible individual and take care of themselves, and have the foresight to do their best to make sure they're taken care of. Focusing on money is important. It's the judgment that goes around it that can be a problem.

Sabrina

It's interesting. I've been listening to some podcasts recently, run by female business women, because I've been trying to battle in my own mind . . . again that conditioning that as a woman, it's okay to want money . . . that it's okay to ask for more money . . . against how much I despise capitalism . . . the two things that are constantly in conflict with each other, for me.

My opinion is it is okay to want money. You need money to survive. You have to pay your bills. You have responsibilities. You have a mortgage. Some people have massive amounts of student debt. You need money for that. You can't deny how important money is, whether it's cash, credit, retirement . . . all of the things that require funding, they are important, whether we like it or not. I think the only way to change a capitalistic system, frankly, is to become part of it and work from the inside out. I've had to change my thinking on that specifically, just as a woman in this country who is not encouraged to be the breadwinner. We're not encouraged to do that. We're not taught that it's okay. We're taught to be people pleasers and to make your money, take care of yourself, but don't emasculate your man by making more. There are all these conflicting messages that we get regarding capitalism, and we're told how evil capitalism is. There is some truth to that. Unfettered capitalism is dangerous and we do need to be better about that. But at the same time, I don't think there's anything wrong, whatsoever, with saying, "I want to be financially successful. I want to buy a house. I want to own property. I want to make six figures." I think there can be a happy balance between your personal financial goals and wanting to fix the broken system at the same time. But, you can't fix a system if you're not a part of it. That's just unrealistic. It's an ideology that doesn't work.

A lot of people are talking about cryptocurrency now like it's going to change the world, and I don't think we should put morality to it. It's a system of economics that has no morals. The people operating it do.

Another part of the reconditioning of my brain is to not think that money has "good" or "bad" attached to it, because you need it. It's necessary. You can't deny that you need it. But, also not blaming capitalism as a whole, and understanding that it is a system that's operated by people, and the only way to get any sort of change is to become a part of it. It's an unfortunate reality. I think I've learned that over the years, and this podcast I've been listening to has been reminding me of that, and that I'm on the right track thinking that way now.

Chris
I think it's terrible. I actually have lots of very, very liberal cousins who I admire in many ways because they live communally. They still have their jobs, but in terms of the way that they have built their own extended community of multiple families, lots of children . . . it's just amazing to me. One was full-on, almost like rural communal living, with growing your own vegetables and such, and everybody does your dinners together, and that kind of thing. Then the other cousin lives in Boston, and they have all kinds of different jobs. She's a minister. She's been arrested at protests multiple times. I love it. I look up to this woman so much. She's ten years younger than me and she's my hero.

They say money is the root of all evil, and I actually do believe that. If there were a way to destroy that aspect of our society, I would love it, especially now where you just have so many people hoarding, and you can't take it with you. So why? Why? It's just collecting toys. That's what I feel it's like. It's just that "don't take it away" mentality.

Daphne

I think it's a good and a bad thing. I think people focus on money too much, period, across the board. I think we all do. I've had my moments where I have. My husband and I laughed yesterday, when he was talking about somebody that won the lottery and won billions of dollars somewhere. I think California or something. I said, "I wouldn't want to be a billion dollar winner." I don't know why I said that. I haven't ever had a billion dollars to play with. So maybe I would love to be a billionaire. I don't know. But I do believe what messes up society is when people focus on money too much, but more so, we focus on our judgment of others based upon money. I think that's very unfair. I have a work colleague . . . I wouldn't call her a friend, because I don't agree with this . . . she's very stuck on this . . . she likes to brag about where she went to school. She went to Berkeley, and that to me equates to money. That's what her point is; that she has money and she was able to do these things. There are people that could afford to go to these schools that made the choice not to. There are people that made a choice to go to a historically black college or university because of the culture they wanted, as opposed to the money.

I do think people put too much focus on money. I like to be able to buy myself what I want, when I want it. I like to be able to do what I want to do, when I want to do it. I like to be able to give to others without any hesitation. That's what makes me happy regarding money. I know that money has helped me get to the status I am now, in the sense that I have a home and I can pay my mortgage. We have several cars in our yard. They're not necessarily high-end cars. We just like the cars. So I think it's interesting that people separate themselves from others due to their economic impact, or their perceived status that, more so, if anything, revolves around the money that they're able to bring, or things they are able to do. And I think that's unfortunate.

We have two neighbors, that we're very good friends with, who have money, but don't have passports. It's funny because we travel internationally, quite a bit, and they can't go with us. They're always complaining about the neighbors we have on the other side, who just went on a cruise. It's not about money, but they have passports. I think it's interesting that people have perceptions of others, based on money, when it's not about the money, but rather the access to whatever it is you want to do. Those neighbors have passports. They can go internationally. And our other neighbors have money, but they don't have their passports. Who doesn't have a passport? That's a whole different story.

Heather

I think being focused on money depends upon your lens, because money can be the root of all evil, the source of all good, or whatever. It's open to interpretation. I would say that the thought of money . . . it's not even the physical dollar bill . . . it's not the thing you can spend . . . but the thought of money turns people mad because we don't know how to work with it.

It's energy, but we don't know how to harness that energy. And if we don't have enough of it, we could be angry about it. And if we're not using it for good, we could be destroying things. So I think having a focus on money is important. We just have to be very, very, very careful with what that focus is. We have to understand why we're so focused and motivated by it, because in the end, you're not taking it with you. We have to be very cautious. I have a storied past with money. I'm just now getting to the point where I'm learning how to use this new form of energy for me, which is very exciting. I'm reading an amazing book called *The Energy of Money* and it's changing my life. So focusing on money alone, you have to be careful. Tread with caution.

Donna

I did already somewhat touch on this, and now I have a different answer to that question. As I said, we're all in business to make money, and that is certainly one measure of success, but back in the eighties, there was a bestselling book called *Do What You Love and the Money Will Follow*. I have always been an advocate of that philosophy. So that is why, when I talk to people who are thinking about going into consulting, I tell them to try not to market themselves as the answer to everybody's needs. Figure out what you like to do, that you're good at, and just market that. I know there's ten other things you could do, but pick one or two and market the hell out of those. Get your foot in the door with those, and then you parlay that into other things because yes, ultimately we want to make money, but it's first and foremost about figuring out what you're good at, that you like doing, that gives you satisfaction, because . . . not that it isn't nice to make money, and it pays the bills, and that's always important, but for me, like I said, I need to be able to lay my head on the pillow at night and feel like what I did mattered.

An example of that is when Frank and I were both working for the Tribe, they literally turned those invoices around like that. You sent them a bill and within a week you got paid. That was really nice. But, they paid me tons of money and half the time they didn't follow my advice. I would come home from meetings there, so livid, so frustrated, and I'd be telling Frank, "Oh my God, I spent all this time creating this program, got everything aligned, all the ducks in a row for them to roll it out, and now they're not going to do it. I can't believe it." Frank would say, "But did they pay your bill?" "Yeah, they paid the bill, but they're not doing what I advised them to do" and he'd jump in saying, "Forget that. Did they pay your bill? That's all that matters." For me, no, that's not enough. I don't want to get paid to talk. I want to get paid to be a change agent. I want to get paid so that when I walk away, I've left them better than they were when I walked in. If they don't do what I recommended, I didn't do anything. Frank had to tell me, "Yeah, but that's not on you. That's on them." So this is a conversation we've had for the thirty-five years I've been in business. Yeah, I'm a capitalist. Yeah, I want to make money, but I need that intrinsic satisfaction. I need the good feeling, knowing that what I did mattered, because I care about the clients. I cultivate relationships with the individuals that I work with, and the organizations, and those people matter to me, personally. I want to feel like I helped them. So it's both sides of that coin.

Wei

I think it's an inevitable thing because we all need to eat. We all need to have shelter. You know, if you look at Maslow's Hierarchy of Needs, every single one of those things at the foundation requires money, and it's an unfortunate requirement, and it's not entirely doled out in a fair and equitable way, but it is a part of life. Again, it's inevitable. It is certainly unfortunate. So I wouldn't say it's bad but, I think the unique challenge that many people face is caused by the lack of education about how to handle money and how to handle credit. Yes, we live in a capitalistic society which actually feeds on folks' ignorance about wealth. Money is the tangible thing. Wealth is the wisdom of how to handle that money, how to not fall into the pitfalls, and we don't have that. I think, sadly, it feeds into that cycle of, "Well, the less people know about how to handle money, the more they will spend, and the more that will end up going into corporations or universities, which then feeds corporations, and so forth."

One of the things I learned when I was mentoring in a youth development program is that we don't teach finances in school anymore. When I was going through elementary school, even though I didn't understand the Junior Achievement USA program, we had business people, who were part of the program, come into school and teach us all about how to invest, and what not to do with credit cards when you first get into college. And of course, I was probably eight or ten years old, so I didn't understand what they were saying, but it stuck with me. Here was this business person, who came in to talk to us. . . . to spend part of their day making sure that we had skills that we knew nothing about. Fast forward twenty-some-odd years later . . . actually thirty years later, and I'm in front of this class of youths, and I'm teaching them, "Hey, you know, there's more to life than having the latest and greatest phone, or the next Nike Air Jordans." These kids have it ingrained into their being that this materialistic good imparts value to them, and breaking them of that sense definitely took some work. It wasn't until months later, after one weekend a month, teaching them the dangers of money, and what happens when it's not handled with respect and care, that they started to understand. "Oh, wow. I guess I should hold off on next year's upgrade," or, "My gosh. If I can buy this product used, I can save hundreds of dollars and I don't have to be a slave to a cellular phone company." Yes, you can have the label, but last season's product is just as good as this season's.

Gabriel

Let's start by acknowledging that money is incredibly charged, and it means such different things to different people based on how you grew up. Some people take it very seriously. Other people don't take it seriously. Some people are suspicious of it and some people live for it. All of these things can become pathological in different ways. I don't know if I have anything too intelligent to say about that. It's a little abstract and it's so personal. I think it's really important for different people to understand what their relationship to money is, and what it signifies for them. That's up to each person to figure out and to decide.

Steve

You absolutely need some of that. I don't subscribe to being a hippie and living in a commune where everything is shared. The value placed on earning and making a living has its place. I think much like a lot of things, everything within reason. It's like I said before, about my dad turning down a job where he could have made so much more money, but he wouldn't have been happy doing it. In hindsight, I respect that more now than I did at the time. As I've said, I can make a living doing what I'm doing, and my wife and I have a combined income, and we share expenses and so on, and we're not hurting. I don't have a very good retirement account or a very good retirement plan. In fact, it's kind of embarrassing, but in a way, I sort of don't care, which is ridiculous to say, because I've got to care. I'm not going to be able to do this forever, and if I live long enough . . . I don't have kids to take care of me. There's always something. One of the downfalls to not having a big family, or kids, is I don't have that to potentially fall back on when I get to that age. So to be honest, I just kind of don't think about it. I've been pretty fortunate so far. Maybe there's a part of me that feels like, "Well, I'm a good person. I try real hard and I'm nice. So, hopefully I won't get screwed later on."

Do you negotiate your own contracts, and if you do, does this come into your head at all?

I absolutely negotiate my own contracts. There are parameters and acceptable terms, as a scenic designer, depending on the gig. This little summer stock show that I did certainly doesn't pay as much as I got paid when I designed something for Usher for his Las Vegas residency. Does that play into what I'll make in the future? Not really. Again, I don't think along the lines of "My fee for designing this is going to be X number of dollars because I need this much to pay my rent for the next three months, because that's how long the gig is going to take. And then I want to put twenty percent of that into a retirement account." I really probably should think more about that, but I haven't. Part of it is I haven't needed to. Again, I'll bring this back to Annie and how fortunate I am to have someone who is more stable in her career. We have really good insurance. Annie's got a really good retirement plan. She's got life insurance and all of that through work. I get to capitalize on that as well, so I haven't had to think about that.

Victoria
I think it's a good thing. I'm at a point right now where we are both retired. I'm not dipping into Social Security. I don't have to dip into it until I'm in my seventies. I think that for me, now, it is just about enjoying it . . . enjoying what I have and being conservative with what I have . . . not overspending or being extravagant. I've got to pay for my insurance, I've got to make sure all that stuff is taken care of, and then what's left over I get to play with, so I think it matters. Yeah, definitely.

I think that we do need to focus on money. I don't want to be a burden on anybody. I want to be able to take care of myself in the end and I want to give back. I want to leave something. We're in the process of opening up a trust, a foundation trust, so that we'll be able to help and donate when needed. I think that focusing on money has allowed me to be able to do that. I need to give it away. I need to be able to take care of myself, but I still want to leave something for somebody else.

Jesus

Oh, well it's like that quote in the Bible that people misquote all the time. They say, "Money is the root of all evil." Well, that's not what the Bible says. Even though I don't care what the Bible says, in this case, I agree with the actual statement, "For the love of money is the root of all evil."

It has a function. It's paper that's printed and we're the ones that gave it value and power. But I think you really just need to put money in its place. It is a way to get the things that you need. I need money to buy milk and food. I need money to pay my rent. I need money to pay my car bill. I think that's where you need to keep it. When it goes further than that, where money makes someone say, "I'm willing to compromise my art," or, "I'm willing to compromise my morals," then it becomes problematic. I don't think that money is the problem. I think humans are the problem. For me, it all comes down to humanity. People either behave in a humane way, that I admire and love, or people behave in the most horrible, inhumane ways.

My dad always taught me, "Your religion is to do no harm." That's really complicated. "What does that mean, Dad? Harm to whom or harm to what? Are there times when it's moral to harm somebody in self-defense?" I'll just put it this way . . . morality is subjective, and morality only becomes objective when we all agree on something. So if we all agree that rape is wrong, because of how it affects the other person, then objectively, now a rape is immoral. I also think that morality is situational. In one instance, it might be immoral for me to lie. For example, if I lied to my husband about having a terminal illness, and that kept him from spending as much time as possible with me, before I die, that would be immoral because I'm robbing that person of time with me. But if I lied to a bunch of Nazis about hiding Jewish people in my attic, it's not immoral. That's how I see life. So when I look at money, I think if you are a moral person who is always trying to do the right thing, then you're going to handle money as paper. That is just an exchange for goods. But if you are an immoral person, who is not trying to do the right thing, then you're going to use that money to cause great harm to yourself and to others.

A perfect example, and I'll end with this . . . you're an illegal Cuban immigrant, you are working a job, but you're working under the table and they're paying you nine dollars an hour. Nobody can survive on that. But you don't have any papers. And one day you go to the supermarket, and before you go back to live in that little shack that these people rented to you, that has termites, you buy a lottery ticket and you win a million dollars. Now, because you're an illegal immigrant, you can't cash it in. So your friend, who's also from Cuba, but is legal, who got you the job, says, "Hey, I'll cash it." And the illegal immigrant says, "Yeah, if you cash it, I'll give you fifty thousand dollars and I'll take the rest." And the legal immigrant says, "Yeah, you got it. It's a deal." He cashes it and then takes all of the money. Was money the problem or was it the human being? It was the human being. He allowed what this money could give him to cause him to behave in the most atrocious and despicable way.

To me, money is just a thing, just like a possession. People have to be better. *We* are the ones . . . human beings are the ones who have to improve. It's like when people say, "Oh, God's going to make the world a better place," or, "Christianity will make the world a better place," . . . no, no, no. It's not religion. It's not Christianity or God. *We* have to make the world a better place. *We* have to be better people. *We* have to do the right thing. It's up to us. It's up to humans. That's how I feel about that. Wow, I got a little passionate there.

Michael

I think that's very different from person to person. I think somebody in my position, if you're focused strictly on money, I don't think that is ... I don't want to say the right or the wrong reason, but I don't do all this to chase a bunch of money, or in the hope of making a bunch of money. I do this because I love it, because I like seeing how good I can get. And beating people is fun. I'm sure there are people that have a lot of money and that makes them feel more valuable. That makes them enjoy life more. That makes them happier. So I don't think there's any one right or wrong answer. I guess it's just a very person-specific question.

CHAPTER 16:
EARNING A LIVING ON YOUR ORGANIC PATH

Further to the last question, what are your thoughts on earning a living, and how does someone who wants to earn a good living merge that with following his or her organic path?

Brian

Wow. That is such a subjective question. If somebody has created an organic path . . . well, not created . . . if somebody has followed their organic path and not been able to make it financially sustainable, I feel like a come to Jesus moment has to happen to say, "Do I want to . . .?" I've gone through that. As a performer, I've gone down that path of, "Do I need to go . . . do I want to go to another twenty, thirty, forty auditions and not get cast, not get a callback, not get my foot in the door in any way, shape or form? Or, do I still want to . . .?" This is why it's an organic path, and not a created, forced path . . . you have to step back and reassess. I probably have said it previously, but it's great to have short-term goals. It's great to have short-term plans, and it's great to have long-term plans, too, but if you're not achieving any of your short-term plans, you can never expect to hit your long-term plan. You have to constantly be micro-analyzing and reassessing what's good and what's bad. I don't mean by writing everything down and documenting all that stuff, but just constantly assessing, "Hey, did that thing work? Is it pushing me towards something, whether it's more creatively fulfilling, or financially fulfilling, or hopefully, both of those things? Is it pushing me towards that?"

Now I just skirted your question, I think, completely, but I . . . give me your question one more time.

Author repeated the question.

Well, first of all, we've got to define what a "good living" is. I'm not saying *we* have to define it, but the individual has to. That goes back to their definition of success. What is their definition of "a good living"?

And if your definition of a good living is that you want to have beaucoup bucks raining in, maybe the organic path that you are on is not leading you towards that. You've got to find a way to finagle, to move, to switch to what you want, while still being on your organic path. Coming from an entertainment background, we are constantly assessing what we are doing. We're re-organizing our goals. We are constantly . . . manipulating is not the right word, but what's the word I'm looking for . . . constantly in a place of shifting and figuring out where that fulfillment is coming from. Is it enough? Is it sustainable? So much of my world is "All right, so this thing is going to last this long and then it's done. And then what's the next thing? What's the next moment?"

So, I think for somebody that wants to earn a good living, you're just going to have to constantly be scrutinizing and understanding what you need at that time. What's the fulfillment? That's a hard question. Different industries have different responses to that.

Lisa
Oh, wow. Okay, that's a great question because that's a simpler thing when someone's living at home, with their parents . . . I'm not going to say younger, because it could be at any age, depending on what situation you have with your folks. But, typically there's a little bit more freedom when we're younger because we don't have as many financial responsibilities, and we may have a little more wiggle room to find ourselves and to find that path.

I think for me, I've always been willing to work hard, long hours, to make sure I could support my dreams, and my goals, and still try to create things . . . what some people would say "on the side," I just think is a part of my big picture of life.

So if you're talking about merging the two, I, in different periods of my life, have been a little heavier on one side or the other. It's kind of gone back and forth for me. There were times where the path that I felt was my organic path ended up making me more money. So I got to focus on that. Then there were times where I made less, and I would have to focus on other things, so that I had the income to support my life, and lifestyle, and what I wanted to do. So I think for me, the merger has been the willingness to put in the hours and follow whichever way that pendulum was swinging at the time.

Sabrina

I don't know because I haven't figured that out yet, to be honest. I really don't know how to merge the two. My thoughts on earning a living are yes, of course you should earn a living, however you choose to, legally. If nobody's getting hurt, get your money. But I don't really know how to answer that second part because I don't think I figured it out myself. It's a transition that I'm in right now.

Chris

I think that obviously you have to be able to earn a living. Idealistically, creating a society in which people are actually compassionate, and caring, and sharing, and where there's a little bit more of a level playing field would be great. But, where we are, in reality, is that in our society we do exist with money, and we have to use it to get the things we need. We have to pay our bills. We have to pay whatever fees and things exist in our world, buy our goods, buy clothing, buy health insurance. So, yeah, you have to make the money. I think that the difference is making a living, which again was a part of the criteria for a successful career . . . that you're able to make a living, versus being rich. I don't think being rich is important. I think amassing wealth is not as important as meeting the needs that you have as a person. I think if you're doing that, then you're being truthful to yourself. I think that's the difference . . . not hoarding. Hoarding is bad.

Daphne

You know, that's a good question because I think it's very bothersome sometimes when people choose a path based upon the money they perceive they can make in that path, versus choosing something that they just would enjoy doing. My first job in hospitality was as a secretary, and I never thought that I would, as a college graduate, be one. I mentor a lot of youth, and oftentimes, their perception coming out of college is that they should make six figures. I say, "You know, maybe you can, but that shouldn't be what it's all about for you." I took the position as a secretary, and other roles, because I wanted to learn about what I knew I wanted to do, which was work at hotels. And I'm blessed. Ironically, my mom made me take a typing class when I was in high school, so I could make sure I had a skill set that could translate to anything. As a result, I was a very fast typist. I still type very fast. It's a skill set that I have that I can do anything with.

There've been times, probably during the COVID-19 pandemic, where I thought, "Okay, if my independent meeting planner world doesn't come back, I could go be somebody's executive assistant somewhere . . . a big company making lots of money, probably, because I can type. So skill sets, I think, are so important. And, I think people miss the idea of figuring out what they like to do, or are good at doing, and maybe want to do, and doing it . . . and then think about how much money it could bring to them . . . not naively, because I do know money is necessary, but people so often focus on what they think they should make because they believe it is what they need in order to be successful.

I do believe COVID-19 should have changed many of our lives. I feel for the people that were full of sadness because they lost loved-ones, but we all had an awakening moment, learning what we can do without. Well, not all of us, because there are many people in many spectrums that I know who never lost the beat. They still worked. They didn't have a loss of income. But many of us in the hospitality world, encompassing restaurants and entertainment and the theatre, things like that, we had moments of realizing we can make it with less because we had to. I wish people would think more about that. I've been faced with that because, again, I started in entrepreneurship when I didn't have a plan in place. I had to deviate my thoughts on where the money was coming from. I had savings. I could use it. It was more important to me to find the right path, career-wise, than getting the money. People have to have those experiences to get there. And there are those that have those experiences and still focus on just the money. All they care about is the money. I feel sorry for those folks because I care more about the enjoyment of life, and being with people I want to be with, than I do the money, for sure.

Heather
First, I think you have to define what it means to "earn a good living." What does that mean? You have to know what that means for you. What I've come to find out, thanks to *The 4-Hour Workweek* by Tim Ferriss, is that you don't need a whole boatload of money to have the autonomy you want, which is important to me. You have to get real about the actual number that you need. Do you even know, or are you just guessing, "Oh, a hundred grand will solve all my problems." Will it? Is that true? Have you run any calculations, any calculations at all? Have you said "This is what I want to do with my life?" Okay, how much does that cost? What does that take? From there, you design the plan. I think we have it so backwards with, "Oh, I'm going to get the title, then I'm going to get the money." But what do you want to do, and then how much does it take to do it? Do you have to be rich? You have to take care of yourself to make sure that if you get into an emergency you have something that you can fall back on, but otherwise, dude, we can't take this stuff with us. Why are we so hyped about it?

Donna
I guess there's a confluence of events that have to occur to hit it, whatever "it" is for somebody, whether it's a dollar figure, or the number of clients, or prestige, or reputation, or whatever someone identifies as their measure of success. I didn't talk about that, but let me mention that because, obviously, I have a huge ego, and I think that has contributed to my success. I like being in the spotlight. I like being the center of attention. I like being recognized as an expert. I

like being known in my professional circle. People have said to me many times, when I go to an HR meeting or conference, "God, it's like you're holding court. You sit and it's like your fans come to pay homage and kiss your ring." I laugh, but truthfully, I love that! I have a professional reputation that has served me so well, and a lot of that has nothing to do with my ego or my confidence. It has everything to do with delivering on what I promised. That's what makes your reputation what it is. So that means a lot to me.

I think it's important to want to make money, and anyone who doesn't talk about that side of it is lying. We all want to make money. We all want to be successful. The dollar amount that we use to define success might be different, but we all want to make money. I don't know why people are afraid to be honest and say that. I want to make money, and I want to make as much money as I can.

But, the flip side of that is you have to be willing to pay your dues. You have to be willing to admit when you're wrong. That's another thing Frank has helped me get better at because, as I said, I am my father's daughter, and those words didn't cross his lips but a few times, as I recall. To be successful in business, I think you need to have the mission for the organization, and what you're trying to accomplish, and then a personal mission of "How do I define success for myself, in terms of what I get back from the business," and those two are not mutually exclusive. Those two can live side by side. They have to live side by side in an honest place. I could tell you what my dollar goal was twenty years ago, ten years ago, now. It changes over time. It goes up, it goes down, depending on our situation and how hard I am willing to, or able to work. This year, I knew with my surgery, that I would have two months of barely working. So that has affected my income. I haven't lost any clients, and I haven't lost any work. It's just that I'm delayed in delivering it. I finished my investigations that I had open. Literally, I finished the last one the day before my surgery. All of my other work is project HR work they'll wait for me to do when I've recuperated, and they are waiting for me. So I didn't lose work, but I lost income because it was delayed. So, I think people have to be really

241

honest about wanting to earn money. If you can't talk about it, you're not going to do it. That's why we're in business.

It comes back to figuring out what you're good at and doing that. One of the things that I say to people, especially HR people, because as generalists, they may know about training, and recruitment, and selection, and retention, and benefits, and compensation . . . they may know a little about a lot of things . . . they may know a lot about a lot of things, if they've been doing it for thirty years, and I say to them, "Don't go around with a business card that unfolds and is thirty inches long, because no one's going to believe you're an expert at everything. Maybe you are, but no one's going to believe it until they get to know you. Have a business card that has two or three things that you love to do, that you're great at, and market those. Get your foot in the door with those. Then one at a time, like I did with the law firm, dole out one more piece of something you're a genius at, but you've got to feed it to them piecemeal or they won't believe it. And, if you want to command top dollar, or get to that top dollar, you have to showcase fewer things that you do, not more things." So I think that's a really important piece of advice. If you want to command bigger bucks, you have to narrow the scope of what you do, not the opposite. It seems counterintuitive to some people, I think, but a lot of it's about the timing.

Wei
I think following your organic path definitely helps to make a good living. It's not about chasing the dollar signs. Again, finances are a necessary evil, but I think if you are happy, and you're content, and you're doing what you love to do, I think that having that positive energy in your life will end up enriching the output that you give, which then feeds into the compensation that you earn. I know a lot of people who have chased after the dollar sign, via whatever career choice they made, and they've been miserable. And there's a lot more resistance that they encounter when trying to climb that . . . to progress in their career, when they're just simply chasing after a dollar sign. I think the people who have been happiest have been the ones

that were being true to themselves, being true to what they actually like to do. When you're doing something that you like to do, you surround yourself with people that think similarly, which then empowers you to do more of what you like to do, which hopefully should come with its own form of compensation, whether that's happiness, or money, or satisfaction, and it's almost self-fulfilling in that way.

Gabriel

I have not tried to earn a certain kind of living, or make a certain amount of money, in order to do a good job. I've always done it the other way. That's kind of how I'm wired. It's not super deliberate. It's the only way that I feel good making money. And maybe that will change as I get older and I become a real Hollywood asshole and I say, "This is what I charge, that's why I'm going to do a good job."

Maybe that's part of growing up. Maybe that's what the Kevin Spacey character meant when he said that quote about being liberal and then conservative. I think it's generally smarter and more meaningful, and I think in some way it's the right thing to do . . . to do such good work that you can command money that reflects it. If you approach most things that way . . . I've seen it in my own life, and I've seen it with many other people, including people, by the way, who listen to the podcast and ask questions about this . . . it's hard to go wrong when you're just trying to do a good job and create value for people. People who are willing to do that when they're not making the money they want to make, or are not commanding the salary that they should command for that kind of work . . . they just do it because they care, are irresistible. Those are amazing employees. Those are wonderful partners. I would be nervous, myself, going into, say, a manager's office and saying, "I want to be paid this in order to do this job." It's fine if that's how people do it. And if it succeeds, great. I have no ethical problem with it. But I think it's just so much more fun and fulfilling to say, "I really want to find out what I can achieve, what I can accomplish for you . . . for us. So give me three months or six months or a year," . . . the time frame doesn't matter . . . "Give me some time to show you and let me prove to myself what I can do, and let me see how it fits with what you need, and then let me talk about what I want to be paid to continue to do this." That is such a more interesting strategy to me and it makes me feel like I've earned it and that makes the money better.

I was talking to one of my other producers on that short film, and she said something in passing that really stuck with me and it was exactly to this point. She said, "You don't move up to get to do more. You do more so that you can move up." She was speaking in the context of producing, but I think that's probably a good principle for any world.

Steve
Wow. Again, I feel really fortunate to be in the position that I haven't had to necessarily worry about that. As I said before, we joke a lot that Annie is kind of my sugar mama, and she makes a living so I don't have to, and that's fun to tease about, but I do have an income. It's not steady, by any means. It's not regular. Sometimes I get paid really well and sometimes I do a lot for not a lot of money. I don't know how you . . . what's the word . . . not justify, but . . . how you think about those two things working together to . . . ugh, I'm really stumbling over this one. Will you say it one more time?

Author repeated the question.

Okay. My first thought, honestly, is I'm such the wrong person to ask that. Again, I've been really fortunate that . . . I say fortunate, but it's also been a lot of work. As a designer, an independent contractor, I own my own small business, which is just me, so I can do what I do and get paid to do it, but I don't know how you do that. I'm sorry. I really don't have a great answer.

I'm going to jump in and say that I think you are the right person to ask, because you're doing it.

Okay. Okay.

So how have you followed your organic path and made a "good living?" How have you merged those two? Sure, part of it is luck, but really, it's more on you.

Maybe when I think about it in those terms, it's deciding, in my case, which gigs to take. I certainly have not taken every gig that has ever been offered to me, and more so now, I find myself turning things down that maybe aren't going to provide what I hope to get out of them. As a designer, you can expect to get X number of dollars. So I know, going into a gig, I can expect whatever that paycheck is going to be. But what is the emotional involvement going to be? What is that going to require? What are the expectations? What are the producer's expectations, or the client's expectations, and is it worth it? I think after doing that for so many years . . . and there was a time where I would just take anything and often beat myself up asking myself, "Why the hell did I take this job? I knew it was going to be like this. I knew it wasn't going to be worth the money," but, I needed the money, and I needed to get my name out there. In my line of work . . . this gets back to what you were asking about success . . . it's something I didn't think about in those terms, but as an independent designer, literally all I have is my reputation. How do I define success? If my reputation gets me my next job, then I'm successful. And that truly, now that I'm thinking about it, is it. I find myself saying that more and more. I'm not making widgets. I can't say, "Oh, this is my widget. Here you go. I make one hundred of these and I make a living." No, it's my reputation. People want to work with me and hire me to do their next production. It's all about the reputation. That was a little circuitous, but there you go.

Victoria

Wow, that's a loaded question. Earning a living is one thing. Making sure your bills are paid . . . a good living is making sure the bills are paid and you're comfortable . . . you don't have to worry about it. I think that once you're established, and you're able to take care of your bills, and keep a roof over your head, then I think you start focusing on ways to become more fulfilled in what you do, in your career, which will result in more money, hopefully, and set you on a different path. So I know that's really not answering your question, but that's the best I've got.

Jesus
Oh, that's a tough one because I don't think you can always do that. If somebody said to me, "I want to be an actor and I want to make a living as an actor," I think that's great and you can pursue that with all the fervor you have. But the reality of that happening . . . the odds are against you.

Now if you said to me, "I want to be an actor and it doesn't matter if I make a living as one, because I'll find a way to always act, because acting is what brings me joy, not being Hollywood's next big thing," then that's different. You might have a path and you might say, "I want to use this path to make money." That can work out for some people, and for some other people, it just may not. I don't know if that's always going to be the case. For example, my best friend has been in L.A., Atlanta, everywhere, trying to make it happen. I've always told her, "You know, I don't have to tell you this Deana, as a black trans person, it's going to be tough for you." Recently we talked and she said, "You know, I think I'm at a point now that I'm getting older, and I need health insurance, that I kind of want to be where you're at, where I can just work, and do my acting on the side, and have fun and get that artistic side of me out. And if it's not financially successful for me, I'm okay with that." So, I think you can follow your organic path, but you may have to do something else to supplement that . . . you might have to work in a museum, or if your thing is crocheting and you make crochet pop figures, you do that. You might make twenty thousand dollars a year doing that, but it may not be your whole career. You might have to supplement that with being a nurse, or with being a television repair person, or whatever it is. So I think you pursue your organic path, the thing that you're passionate about, but I think at some point you have to realize that you live in the real world, and you've got to pay bills, and you've got to eat. What do you have to do to make that happen? At what point do you say, "Okay, I'm going to go work at another place"? Is it twenty years? Is it thirty? Is it forty? How long are you willing to struggle before you say, "Okay, that's enough"?

There's also pressure from society. I remember when I was struggling, trying to be a filmmaker, and working part-time, not making a lot of money. There were guys that I liked that I thought were cute and I wanted to date, and they were lawyers and they were doctors, and they looked at me thinking, "Loser." "No, I'm trying to make it," and they'd reply, "No, man, you've got to get a real job." Those societal pressures come into play.

Michael
That's a great question. I guess I haven't really experienced earning a living yet. I'm a big believer that the world always has something set up for you, and everybody has their purpose in life. Eventually, if you don't fight that, it'll all work itself out.

> **You touched on this before, and I don't want to lead you, but I'm going to lead you a little. You lived in your car so that you could follow what you felt your organic path was . . . to play golf . . .**

Yeah.

> **. . . and you made Subway sandwiches. I read something where somebody asked you if over the year and a half period at Subway you became management, and you said, "Nope, I stayed a sandwich artist, only." Do you want to talk about that, about why you did that, and how that allowed you to keep pursuing golf?**

The whole Subway story is that I had just moved to Florida. I needed to find a job somewhere. I didn't know anybody. I didn't know any golf courses. I didn't know how I was going to support myself. I went to Subway to eat a couple of nights and I started to get to know the manager. His name was Yogi. At one point I said, "Hey, Yogi, you want to give me a job here?" "You want to work?" "Yeah." I was thinking I'd get free food out of it, I'd make a little bit of money. Why not give it a run? And then I stayed with him for a year and a half because they were very good at working with my golf schedule. If I needed days off, I could just write them on the calendar and they wouldn't schedule me to work those days. That was the main reason I stayed there for so long. Again, it wasn't a whole deep thing where I thought, "Oh, if I work at Subway . . ." It was just a matter of me thinking, "I know this guy. I'm sure he would hire me. I'll get free food out of it." I did it so that I could keep pursuing what I really wanted to be doing.

CHAPTER 17: DON'T FIGHT THE FLOW

What do you think, and/or how do you feel, when you hear "Don't Fight The Flow: Follow Your Organic Path"?

My thought on this question was that the flow was moving people forward, in their most natural, organic manner. Some interviewees interpreted the question in the opposite way, where the flow was "against them," or "the norm," and they were like salmon swimming upstream.

Brian
That is what I wake up, get out of bed in the morning, and live my daily life by. I'm trying to think of the number of times that I've interviewed for a job, versus had something fall into my lap. I think that pertains to this question. I worked as a project manager for an interior design firm because a friend's friend owned a firm that needed somebody and he said, "Hey, you seem like a good person." I also worked as a project manager for a strategic branding consulting firm. Neither one of those are related to theatre, yet I did them because they seemed fulfilling, and part of my path, at the time. I say, "Get up in the morning and do what it is that you want to do." I don't know that I can say it in any more succinct terms, but that is literally my life's mantra. I'm going to follow what I want to do that day, at that time, and hope that it turns into something bigger and better, and can continue to allow me the creative freedom, and the financial freedom, to keep doing that thing. Because if you're fighting it, and you're trying to create . . . not even create . . . you're trying to stay in this position, maybe it's for a financial reason, maybe it's for the housing, whatever it is, at a certain point, are you going to wake up resentful over that thing? If it's a relationship and you want to stay in it, are you going to become resentful towards that person? If it's a job, are you going to become resentful towards that job? I don't want to live that way. So I think I'm following the flow and following my organic path.

Lisa

Oh, my goodness. I have two very different reactions to that. I'll share both with you. When you say, "Don't fight the flow," my first reaction is, "Don't tell me what to do. If I want to get there, I'm going to get there!" So that triggers something for me. And, "Don't tell me I can't do it." Follow your organic path . . . I feel comfortable with that, and yet I feel like there's more to it because . . . or maybe it's the way I'm interpreting it, but following an organic path doesn't just mean letting things happen around you. It still involves being an active participant in creating and walking that path. The path of least resistance I get, and yet that hasn't always been the most rewarding path for me.

Do you care to elaborate on any of that?

Oh, let's see. I'm trying to think of specific examples. This might take me a moment. I'm glad this isn't radio. This would be awful radio. Oh my goodness.

Okay, I'll start here because it's the first thing that's popping into my head, probably because it's the least profound or threatening. When I was in elementary school, I really, really wanted to be part of the talent show. I don't remember what I sang . . . "Put On A Happy Face" or something like that, and I didn't get chosen for it. I really, really wanted to be in it. Somehow, I convinced the head of the talent show to let me perform, because I really wanted it. If I had not fought the flow on that, I wouldn't have had that opportunity to really speak up for what I wanted and gotten what I wanted.

I also remember doing that in high school for my grade four typing class. We learned to type on computers, and I had taken piano growing up, so I picked it up pretty quickly, and then kind of plateaued. The teacher tried to give me a lesser grade than I thought I deserved. I went in and chatted with her about it and said, "Look at the level that I'm at, based on some of these other people you're giving A's to . . . just because I picked it up quickly, doesn't mean I didn't learn it . . . it doesn't mean I don't deserve the A in this class." She changed my grade.

Let's see, what else? So this might be an organic path one. Well, this is actually kind of a combination of the two. When I was in my freshman year of college, I was taking an intro to drama class, because it was one of those things that was a general education requirement, and would also count toward my major. I majored in French Literature and Dramatic Arts with an emphasis on literature. So I was in DA64 with Bert States. He was fantastic. After the course, which was in Campbell Hall, and held five hundred fifty people . . . it was a huge, huge lecture hall . . . he approached me and asked if I would be part of his focus group for something he was working on for his book on the theatre of silence, which is my favorite thing. I love it. It's the things that aren't said that are more important than the things that are said. It's having the moments where there are two different monologues that seem like they're different, but every once in a while, they intersect and talk to one another. I find it fascinating.

So it was these senior B.F.A. students and me. There were six or eight of us in this group, I think. I had this opportunity to be in this class that was high-level, and this was my freshman year. That's still one of the highlights of my college career, for sure. That's the reason I say that it's a combination of the two. There were a lot of things that could have made me say, "Oh my gosh, no, that's so intimidating. I don't want to be in a class with all these older kids. Why me? Blah, blah. blah." We had to write a fifteen-page . . . I don't know if you'd call it a thesis, but a paper to graduate from that class. We also received Masters of Theater of Silence certificates. I just said "Yes" and went with it, but there are reasons I could have kept myself from having that opportunity. So I think that might be a little combination of the two, because that wasn't a normal flow. I guess it was mine.

Sabrina
I don't know. It feels like a conflicting message because what if you don't know what your organic path is? Does anybody really know what their organic path is? Don't fight the flow to me sounds like do

what you're supposed to do. Don't make any waves, blah, blah, blah. But go with your organic flow.

I get what you're saying. It could just be the way I'm perceiving that statement. I like to say, "Trust the universe, because whether you like it or not, the universe knows better than you." You could take that to mean believing in God, if you do, or believing in a higher deity. I keep it very vague. Trust the universe. If something has been given to you, reflect on why it is happening, whether it's a bad or a good thing, and go with your gut. With my years of experience now, I have a well-honed gut. So I guess I would say trust the universe more than go with your organic flow. But that's for me.

Do you feel like you did that when you were younger?

Noooooo. I did not trust my gut. I did not trust that universe. I had been conditioned to a point where I was not sure who I was, who I wanted to be. I didn't have the answers I thought I had to any questions. I was not the same person. I absolutely did not trust my gut, or trust my instincts because I wasn't allowed to, growing up. I wasn't allowed to say "No." I wasn't allowed to be defiant. Plus, in all the jobs I've ever worked . . . every single job I worked . . . in retail, as a receptionist . . . all of those jobs were about pleasing the other person. You weren't allowed to say "No." You learn to start doubting your instincts, because if you feel something is off, you're not allowed to voice it. You have to sit there and take it. So, no, I didn't learn to start trusting my gut until I was well into my thirties. I always had a good gut. My Spidey-Sense was always dead-on accurate, but I wasn't . . . I was conditioned, both through every single job I ever had, and by my family environment, and by society, to tap that down, choke it down, and not listen to that because, "Oh, you're being paranoid," or, "You're overreacting," or, "You're being dramatic. Do what they tell you to do. Whether it's right or wrong, do what they tell you to do. Don't trust your gut." Yeah, none of that. I was terrible at that earlier in my life.

Chris

Ah, it's interesting. I think the only way to really look at it is if you're looking at it organically . . . looking at nature . . . water. Water works both ways. It follows a path, but it will carve its own path and push through boundaries. So the idea is to be like water . . . coast and flow when the path is easy. And, sometimes, you've just got to rage and carve your own way. Canyons are built by water.

Daphne

I agree with that because I have followed what I believe is my organic path. At the same time, I do believe that people, and I can say this in a professional sense as well as personal sense, don't always take the necessary steps. They'll say, "I'm trying to find a significant other, and I don't know how to do it." "What are you doing about that?" They're staying at home and not doing anything. It's the same with a professional path. I, fortunately, have never had a problem with not knowing how to do what I needed to do, whether it was putting together a resume, getting someone to review my resume, applying for jobs, or getting on LinkedIn and reaching out. You have to make your own steps. While I believe in an organic path, I do believe that only you can help take the steps to get somewhere. The flow is the steps you feel like you need to take in order to get to where you need to go next.

I'm a big believer in asking people, "What's your gut say?" Because, as you know, while you may be trying to follow the path you think is the flow, organically, something's going to give you that gut-wrenching that may turn your head another way and you think, "No, I'm supposed to go this way." Listen to your heart and your head, together. Let them mix together. I'm a believer in testing the waters, or maybe a whole different path. Test it and see. I've never had a problem with that. Those who do, frustrate me, and I've always tried to help people see that there's something out there for all of us, we just have to figure it out. Again, in each person's life, at each moment, is a different thing that could make them happy, or what they perceive would make them happy. My question is always "Why?" Why are you focused on that position versus this? Is it because the perceived perception is it's a higher ranking position? Is it the money? If you had to compare apples to oranges, does it equate? What's important in it?

I have a fifty-plus-year-old friend who is right now trying to find another job. Why would you be trying to find something new at this phase of our lives? Now is when we're supposed to be trying to come together and go down that steady path. I'm trying to help him see that. I know he might be miserable. He says he's miserable. Okay. Well, that's a hard place to be at in this late stage of life . . . to change, and start all over again. But I don't think he's following his organic path at all. He's following his own *perceived* flow.

Heather
Hmmmm. That's true, but you have to understand how to pick up on your intuition and tap into your flow. I love that and I think that is great advice. A step further is to be aware of those times that you're in the flow, so that you can repeat them. Again, we are not paying attention to what we're doing. We have to begin to pay attention. We have to start making notes on our phone . . . a voice memo, a journal for goodness sake . . . have we forgotten how to write? Document the times that you're in the flow, because it feels so good. You've got to document it so that you know how to get back into it, later on, when you're out of it. I do love that . . . working from the flow state.

Donna
Well, from a business perspective, I think there are pivotal moments like the old V-8 commercial, where you get smacked in the face with it, and if you miss it, if you don't recognize it for what it is, then you get off track and you're not following that organic path. I'll give you an example. Before, I said, don't try to be everything to everybody. Figure out the few things you're good at and just do those. But, in 1989, there

was a landmark case in Florida that set the stage for the ruminations of sexual harassment to become a thing that people could sue for. After that happened, my clients started calling me, telling me that they were learning about the sexual harassment thing, and that they needed me to come do training. I said to them, true to my philosophy, "I don't do that. You need to find somebody else." In 1993, after four years of getting those calls, I got a call from a guy that my dad had worked with, who had gone to work for Johnson Controls, a huge international company, that had multiple arms of its business, including aerospace. I mean, a huge, huge company in every first-world country you could name. This guy that had worked with my dad called me and asked me to do some sexual harassment work. When he called me, I finally asked myself, "How many work calls am I going to get where I say that I don't do that? This is obviously something people need and want, and it's not just one or two. It's been a consistent pattern for several years now. Duh! I need to add this to my repertoire."

By then, I had already written my book on mentoring. I was already a certified executive coach. So really, when I think about it, that was the last time I added a new piece of work to the scope of my business . . . 1993, when I added that harassment and discrimination piece, and it's now the biggest piece of business I market, and has been for ten-plus years. It was clearly meant to be part of my organic path, because my background and credentials, I think, uniquely positioned me to be better at that than my competitors. I believe that's why some of the opportunities that I've had in that arena have been put in front of me, maybe on a silver platter, or maybe it was a logical outgrowth of the steps that I took. If it was luck, I'll take it. If it was because I planted the seeds, I'll take it. But, I have the credentials to do those things that I guarantee you no other consultant in the state of Florida has. I've been a liaison to the EEOC. I was approved by the Department of Justice. I've trained attorneys for the Florida bar. No other non-attorney has ever been invited to train attorneys for the Florida Bar Employment Practice Group. I have these credentials that I can spout when a client states that my fees are one hundred fifty dollars more an hour than another consultant, and they're looking at me, I can say, "Well, here's why: boom, boom, boom, boom."

I look at those things that were put in front of me that I had the opportunity to take, and do, and add to my credentials, that were clearly intended to be part of my organic path. All of the things that I did led up to that. I'm glad a two-by-four finally hit me on the head, and I realized it. So, yeah, I think there are things that come your way, and some of them are distractions, and you have to recognize them as distractions and say, "No, I'm not getting sidetracked. Here's what I do." And every once in a while, it's something like that, where you have to say, "Duh, this is a logical extension, or addition, to my business, based on my background and qualifications. It makes sense for me to expand in this way."

Here's another example: when diversity became a thing and people started calling me saying, "Oh, we need you to come and do diversity training," I said, "Oh, I don't do diversity training." "Yeah, you do. You do discrimination and harassment." "No, no, no. That's not the same as diversity." "Well, isn't it the same thing? It's proactive versus reactive." I'd say "No, not really. And in fact, I am not a proponent of diversity initiatives." And they gasp and say "How can you say that? You're an HR person." "Yeah, because diversity is like affirmative action. And I'm not a proponent of that. I want to hire people based on their merit and qualifications. I don't want to care what religion they are, what age they are, what color they are, what gender they are. All I care about is whether they're qualified. I don't want people to be admitted to college based on anything else. I don't want people to be hired in jobs based on anything else. I am a traditionalist. I am a conservative when it comes to things like that, not a liberal. And I have always been that way." So I say flat out to people, "Please don't ask me to do diversity training. I don't do it. I will never do it, because I don't believe in it." So, when you talk about following an organic path, I think that organic path has to be a logical step in the evolution of your business.

Now, I'll say that's for me, because maybe there are other people like Frank, who have clients who start a business, grow it, sell it, start a completely new business, something different, grow it, sell it. They have a vision of what the next big need is that people don't yet know they need. They start a business for that and they do it. I guess that is their organic path - to find a need and fill it. For me, it's "What are logical extensions of what I'm already great at?" and I've grown my business and followed that organic path for me.

Wei

I think that's absolutely crucial. I think that whenever there is heavy resistance to something you want to do, it typically isn't your organic path. If it's something that you want to do, I would strongly consider whether or not it's right for you to do. It's interesting, the universe does have its plan for us. And that's something I learned long ago. And certainly there are paths to get to where we were meant to be. Sometimes we kind of take the long way around and we eventually get to it. Other times we kind of take what is organic to us and we just go from point A to point B, we do pass go and we do collect the two hundred dollars. But, I have certainly learned that if it feels right, just simply go with it. Just do it.

Gabriel

I feel it might be one of the most true things about life that I know.

There's a tension between doing and allowing in life. I think sometimes when we think about surrendering to stuff, or going with the flow, it means that things should just sort of happen around you and that everything will work out. That's not the case. There's a simple dance between what you do and what you put out into the world, and the way the world meets you and takes care of it for you. I think the more you put out, the more the world wants to help. If you're doing things right, and by that I mean if you're putting out something that is important to you, that is meaningful to you, if you're doing it with the right spirit, which to me also means doing it with love and curiosity and generosity, which is not always easy to do, it's going to come back

257

to help you. In a way, it's the easiest thing to do. It took me a long time to find stuff that I care about. I still find it very difficult to find things that I care about enough to work hard and to do them with love. But when you find them and you put them out into the world, and you work hard, and you put in the work to make something, or to get this job, or to help this person, or to plan this trip, even . . . it doesn't need to be professional . . . when you do it in the right spirit, the world conspires with you to make it happen. I've seen it. I believe that. It might not conspire with you to make it the way you thought it would be, but it will always conspire to make it good. If it's not, I think that's usually a sign that there's something off. Something's not quite right. It's not the right time. You haven't done enough work on your end. You haven't approached things in the right spirit. I don't think that is so "woo woo." I actually think that's kind of a grounded idea. People respond to the spirit in which you show up.

For example, and again, I don't mean to go on and on about the short film I just made, but I've learned the most from that experience and it's the freshest in my mind, because it just happened . . . when I first wrote the short, it was ten pages. It was the first ten-page thing I had ever written, and maybe the first thing I had written, ever, that made me think that I could see myself putting in weeks and weeks and weeks of my life to make it happen. "I think there's something here that's meaningful to me and original, but I don't know how to do that." I do have one person in my life, who's one of my close friends . . . a very, very talented director. I asked her to lunch one day, just to catch up, and I also wanted to ask her if she would help me with this film. I was very nervous to ask her for help, and she was so kind and generous. She said, "Yeah, of course I will help you do this." My reaction was, "Oh my God, thank you. Because I literally don't know how to make a movie. I can write a movie, but I don't know how to make a movie." She said, "Okay, we're going to figure this out." Again, back then, we thought it was going to be this little . . . almost what you would imagine a college thesis film to be . . . just make it for you. Scrape together a few thousand bucks, ask everybody for favors . . . the sound is terrible, the picture looks . . . and I would have been okay with that. From that moment until now, at every step along the way, this project has gotten better and bigger than I ever thought it could be. And I had to fight for that. I've written letters to the actors telling them why I want them to read for it. I've picked up the phone and pitched people on this thing, which, by the way, is not something that comes very naturally to me, despite the fact that I like talking to people. I've never in my life wanted to pick up the phone and say, "I've got this thing. I'm lit up about it. I need you to give me this . . . I want you to do . . . .." Suddenly that became so easy. I still felt a lot of resistance, wishing I didn't have to pick up the phone and do it, but as soon as I was doing it, I didn't have to think about it. I knew what to say because I thought enough about this project, and I knew in my heart that it was important.

So I definitely put in the work, but every person I encountered, even the people who said "No," . . . by the way, there were actors who said, "Not for me . . . nah, not really," including a couple of kind of big ones and actually, comically, a lot of small ones, too. "Oh, this actor said 'No'? Okay, I have to go to that person," and that person winds up being better. A famous actor I asked said, "I love it, but no." A guy you've never heard of . . . I watched the dailies the other day and I realized this guy is perfect . . . what an artist. And I wouldn't have even been willing to see him if I had fixated on this disappointment over here.

So that kind of gets back to your first question on this interview, I guess, or one of your first questions. My point in all of this is to say that putting this project out into the world and fighting for it created a wave that was so big that honestly, I felt like I didn't have to do much. There was a logic at work and the best way to serve it was to not get in the way too much. I've never had that experience before in my life, and it was so profound that on the last day, at about midnight, I was standing around with my producer, and my director of photography, and we were debriefing on the crazy two days we had, and I was sort of sad. I felt a little bit down, and I felt a little bit embarrassed and I said, "I've got to tell you guys that I'm feeling like I can't really take credit for any of this. I'm sorry to be a bummer, but I just have to get this off my chest. I don't really feel like I did anything. You guys did all the work." If this incredible producer were not showing up and . . . she worked so hard to make everything happen . . . if this incredibly talented cinematographer did not light the room the way he did, and work with his team to . . . the talent of these people . . . the hard work . . . if my actors hadn't really read the script and thought and felt and . . . I thought the script was pretty good, but when you hear good actors doing it, you realize, "Oh, you're bringing something that is above and beyond the language." I could go on and on about this. I felt like they did all the work and I was along for the ride. It wasn't that I didn't do anything, but I felt as though a lot of my job was almost being the conductor in a way, and sometimes not even that. Sometimes it was just watching them do their thing and then saying, "Okay, can we do it a little more like this? Okay, help me understand why we're doing it this way. Okay, cool. Oh, right. Can we go a little bit tighter here? Can we do one more take like this?" And yeah, that's work, but in that moment, it felt like the smallest part of this thing that had been going on for about a year, or more maybe, since I asked for that help.

Then my producer said, "Gabe, what are you talking about? We're here because of you. You wrote this thing." I know, I get it, but writing it almost felt like the first stage of it. It was a very bizarre feeling that I haven't fully resolved. I've kind of just made peace with it. It's like playing a team sport. I'm not a sports guy, but I read the Phil Jackson book. I really liked what I was reading in that book. So much of what he talks about is the challenge of subsuming individual talents into the team, in a way where the Kobes don't become the cornerstone of the team. You don't want one player responsible for that. You can't build a team like that, and you can't win multiple championships like that. It has to be the team working in concert. They each need to subsume their own talent, and their own identities, into this bigger thing. That's kind of how it felt. Since that night, I've actually come to see that as really beautiful, and it's almost kind of nice that I don't feel entirely responsible. Without me, there would be no script. Without them, there would be no movie. I bring that up to illustrate "don't fight the flow."

You might have been talking more about a larger, bigger picture, career thing. I'm talking about a specific project, but I think they both are getting at the same thing, which is, again, to go back to the Google situation. At that time in my life, the worst thing that could have happened was Google saying "No." Zoom out six months, or a year, or a little more, and that was my path. That was it. Don't argue with Google, who by the way . . . my understanding is that they're very smart people, so they might have known . . . they might have been making the right call for both of us. It wasn't a mistake. I feel very passionately that what you have said is true. I think a lot about how to apply it in my own life. I'm only now figuring it out. I've gotten to a point where it's getting easier and easier to not get too hung up on the "Nos" because of this principle. I had a couple of moments with this movie, when this actor I was really excited about said, "Yeah, I might do it." I was excited, and he read it and he said, "Oh, this is actually good. I didn't know what to expect." Fair enough. It sort of seemed like I was going to have this really big actor in my movie, which would have been really cool. Then he said "No," and it took me all of thirty seconds to say, "You know what, you've been told "No" enough times, and every single time it's worked in your favor. Let's not get worked up about this. What's the next thing?" The very next thing was the right thing. I'll put it down there, but I just want to say that the premise of your book and of your question is probably one of the most profound things I know to be true of life.

Steve

That's interesting because I think conceptually, I get what it is you're saying in that statement. To me, everything is kind of flowing. Like I've said, I've worked really hard to get where I am, and made decisions based on that. But it's also been . . . there is no roadmap to doing what I do. I didn't know back then that this was even a thing, that this was even a job, or a career possibility. So I certainly didn't know of any specific route to get there. I tend to feel . . . I don't know,

I kind of want to be a little bit chill and hippie about it, and just kind of go in with it.

Will you ask that one more time?

Author repeated the question.

Okay. I subscribe to that one thousand percent. I think people, in general, would be a lot happier if they just followed their organic path. What do I think of it? I think that's great advice. I think more people should allow themselves the opportunity to do so and not see it as a luxury. So many people think along the lines of wishing they had the luxury of following their heart, or organic path. To me, it's kind of bullsh*t that it isn't the norm, and that you have to "allow" yourself to do that. We all should. It would be great if we could all do that. We all can. There are a lot of expectations put upon us. Society tells us that you have to make a certain amount of money, and some of that makes sense. You have to pay your rent, and rent costs X number of dollars, and you have to buy food, and you want a car, but I wish people were a lot more open about what they want to do. I find in our industry, and it probably is in other industries too, but because this is what I do, and I know it better, the people that I meet who I most want to be around, who I most like being around, are the ones who, to me, are relatable when it comes to this. They're doing the work because they want to do it. Yeah, I can make a living doing it, and I really enjoy it. We all go through a certain amount of politics and the B.S. that you go through, whether it's from family, or a job, or anything. But in general, I think that the people who are . . . I hate saying "happy" because it's such a generic term, but the people I most want to be around and that I think of as the most successful are the ones who truly are doing it because they want to do it, despite, or in spite, of the challenges, and maybe not making a lot of money, or not being successful in the way other people define success.

Victoria
Oh, I think that's very profound. I think that's extremely profound. I

say that, but then I think that through resistance we grow and we change a little bit. Maybe work with the flow . . . find a way to make it work for you. With change, there has to be some sort of resistance. I think there's a lot to be said about that. I think you should follow your organic path. I really do. The trickiest, I think, is defining what that organic path is. Can you define it? If you believe it's truly an organic path, can you say, "Okay, I've got a strategy. I'm going to do this, this, this, and this to get here," or do you just wake up every morning and say, "Eh, I feel like eh."

Jesus

Is that contradictory? Isn't following the flow following your organic path? What is the flow? I would think that the flow is the organic path. I wholeheartedly, today, will tell anybody who asks me, to let things happen organically. Let your performance happen organically. Start your performance with an intention, but then once you're on stage, just react. Just respond to what's happening. It's the same thing with life, or when you're working. When I'm doing my museum presentations, yes, there's a speech that I give, but if someone cuts me off or does something to interrupt me, I try to react to that, in the moment. I think the best art, the best work, happens when it happens organically.

Whatever flows from you can't be wrong, even when it is wrong, if that's where you're at. With my dad, yes I convinced my dad to follow a regiment that I believed in, that he didn't necessarily believe in. So I manipulated my father in a way, to violate his bodily autonomy. But, it was my father's responsibility, too, had he been doing the work, to say, "Listen, this is the way I want to go. That's not for you to decide. You need to go to therapy." So even though it was flowing out of me like that, and that was not the right thing to do, it was still true to me at that moment. Today I would not do that, because I've learned . . ..

I always tell my therapist that I wish my parents had put me in therapy when I was young. Things would be so different, and she says, "They could be. They could also have been worse. You don't know." I had become convinced that alternative medicine was going to keep my dad alive and maybe even cure him . . . against all the science. And for someone who's a skeptic, like me, you wonder, "How does a skeptic believe stuff without real science behind it?" I was a frightened son who didn't want to lose his dad, so it didn't take much to convince me, because I'm a very emotional person. So when I was trying to convince my dad, I could see in his face that he felt, "If you want me to do it, I'll do it." But he didn't really want to. He was fighting me the whole time. I would find alcohol hidden in his room, cigars in different places in the house, and we would fight. I actually made my dad's last years on Earth harder than they needed to be. It didn't have to be like that. So today, if my dad were sick, I would say, "How do *you* want to go?"

I guess what I'm saying is your organic flow changes as you change. I do believe people change. Some people think they don't. In fact, people who know me now, when I tell them what I was like in high school, say "I don't believe it. You? The guy who curses this person out, and curses people out in the movie theatre . . . too shy to say a goddamn word? I don't believe you for a second." Then they'll meet someone from my high school days who will say, "Oh yeah, yeah. I don't know who this person is, because that was not Jesus at all, in school."

Michael

For me that triggers this "everything happens for a reason" kind of energy. My friend, David Healy . . . he's big into philosophy and he told me this ancient parable, recently, about a farmer. When things happen to the farmer, he doesn't view them as good or bad, and doesn't put a label on things that happened as positive or negative, because you never know how they're going to affect you.

The farmer's horse ran away and his neighbors all displayed sympathy for his misfortune and said what bad luck he had. The farmer said, "Maybe. Maybe not."

The next day, when the horse returned, along with seven wild horses, the neighbors were all happy at the farmer's good luck and told him so. The farmer said "Maybe. Maybe not."

The next day, the farmer's son was thrown off one of the horses and broke his leg. The neighbors all expressed how unfortunate that was. The farmer said, "Maybe. Maybe not."

The next day, a military officer came to recruit the son for military service. Because of the broken leg, he was not taken. Again, the neighbors told the farmer how great that was. The farmer said, "Maybe. Maybe not."

That's what I think of when you say that. Life is going to throw things at you. You don't know whether they're good or bad. You just keep it moving and keep doing what you think you should be doing.

CHAPTER 18: OUTSIDE OF THE BOX

What piece, or pieces, of advice do you have for others on how to live outside of the box in a structured world?

Brian

As somebody who has founded a business in the world where I live . . . in that entertainment sector, I get to call my shots. I get to decide if I'm going to do it, if it's bringing either joy, or money, or whatever. Advice for other people . . . if you want to live your organic, natural path, but you box yourself into this structured world, those two things probably will not mesh ever enough for you to say, "Oh, I'm living my organic life. I'm taking my star peg and putting it in this triangle hole." But, I understand too, that not everybody has the opportunity, the ability, or the mindset to create their own thing. It took me a long time to realize that I could monetize what I do, to the amount I do it, in the way I do it. A lot of that came from support. Surround yourself with people who support you. Surround yourself with people who may not understand what it is you do, but support it. If people don't understand what you do, and they don't support it, they're constantly going to be trying to talk you out of it. There's definitely a time and place for the devil's advocate questions and all of that, but if that's all you're receiving, it's going to be really hard figuring out . . . and not even just founding a business, but how you are going to be successful in whatever your definition is.

I joke with my husband all the time about the fact that for the longest time, he did not understand what I did when it came to teaching at conferences and choreographing at schools. "All you're doing is dancing with kids." "Yeah, I am, but I'm also networking, which is way more important than just dancing with kids. I'm also trying to figure out what the next step is, not only choreography-wise, but also business-wise." He supports it, absolutely, one thousand percent, but he didn't always get it until I took him with me to an event, and he watched it happen. He realized that I can't even walk from this side of the room to that side of the room without somebody saying, "Oh my

God, I want to ask you this question," or a teacher saying, "Hey, can I bring you into my school to do . . .? How can we do it?"

So you've got to find people that support you in what you do. If people don't . . . I'm not saying get rid of your friends. I'm not saying anything like that, but, when I graduated college, and I moved to New York City, I had a group of friends that said, "Hey, don't go to that audition. Let's go out tonight. Let's spend our money on alcohol and parties." That's not why I was there. I had to step back. I didn't get rid of those friends, but I had to cut back my time with them, because at the end of the day, especially in a . . . I'm assuming a job that takes you on an organic, natural path, you've got to be your biggest advocate. Nobody else is doing it for you. Nobody else can do that journey that you are on except you. Thank you, good night.

Lisa
Oh, wow. I would say having the humility to be able to take in all of the advice that well-intentioned people are giving, sifting through it, and finding what is really in alignment with you, and what you really want. People around us always have opinions on what we should be doing, and want to see us be secure, and want to see us live a more traditional life, because that's what many of them are familiar with. So taking in the love and the wisdom of those statements, but not necessarily taking them on as our own, and owning them, is important.

The best advice about living outside the box in a structured world is that sometimes, I found I had to be part of the structure. Sometimes I had to create the structure, and that has supported me in living outside the box. Whether people understood my path, or what I was doing, or why I was doing it, wasn't important. It was me following what I felt was my calling. I think it's really staying true to yourself, knowing who you are, and taking the advice with love, rather than as a challenge you have to defend yourself against.

Sabrina

I'm going to couple this with the previous comments that I made about following the flow and listening to your gut. My advice: you are your own worst critic, but you are also your own best advocate. No one's going to advocate for you the way you're going to advocate for yourself, so learn how to do it and learn how to take the hits that come from it. You have to have a thick skin about it. I wish I had said that to myself five years ago. Your gut, or the universe, or whatever you want to call it, is almost always going to steer you in the right direction, and I wish I had listened to that more, to be honest. Other than that, I don't think there's any one particular thing you can do. It's a very structured world. There are rules. There are systems in place that you can't do anything about as a human being, by yourself. The best thing you can do for yourself is go with your gut, listen to your instincts, trust yourself more than you've been allowed. Let yourself be your best advocate and let the chips fall where they may. There will sometimes be consequences, but they are temporary consequences that you'll have to deal with in order to get to the bigger picture.

Chris

I have no idea how to answer that question. I'm still figuring that out, so I have no advice.

Daphne

I'm a believer in two things. One is that nothing is ever just black and white, or even gray. There are so many other beautiful colors out there that make up the whole rainbow, or crayon box. People need to be open to them. I always tell people that it's not just right here, in your specific realm of thinking, even with the black and white. Go outside the lines. I don't actually color outside the lines. I like to color inside the lines, but with different colors. So, color inside the lines, but use colors other than the ones you automatically go to all the time.

The second is that there's some kind of mindset . . . I believe this with anything, whether it's religion, politics, profession . . . everybody has a way that they believe, and for whatever reason they got to believing that way. But, I love to hear other people's perceptions, or ways in which they think. I don't necessarily have to agree with them, but I love to know why they feel that way, because people feel strongly about whatever they feel strongly about. If it differs from what I feel, I'm not going to try to convince them of my way, and I don't want them to try to convince me of their way, but I want to understand how they got there, because I do believe so much of it has to do with our experiences and/or the people that have been in our lives. Some people think one way because that's what everybody else around them has thought, whether it's significant people in their lives, or that have been in their lives, or parents, or grandparents, or spouses, or friends. And that's okay, if that's what has structured their way of thinking. But also try to figure out your own way of thinking. Don't make it be "just because." That's why I always love to know where it came from . . . anybody's perspective in any subject . . . because it's interesting to me if it didn't come from themselves, but rather, came from what they know, and what they've been around. That somewhat goes back to living in different places. I have never had a problem trying a different place. I don't know if I'd ever go to the West. I'm not a California girl, but I've certainly done my stint up and down the East Coast. I have many family members, on both my side and my husband's side, that have never left South Carolina. They have never lived anywhere else . . . forget the state, but in the little town within that state. I don't get that.

So, I've gone around the bend, and I think it's so important to know that it's okay to color with colors other than black, white, and even gray, but also to understand other perspectives on any subject matter. Know that there are other perspectives and ideas, and ask about them. That may just put a little nugget in your head that you never thought about before. And I love getting nuggets. I love nuggets from anywhere they come.

Heather
Oooooh. Have the confidence and fortitude to break it. What I mean by that is to look at your weaknesses, and evaluate them to see where you can build up on your confidence, in order to break out of that mold. The choice simply is yours.

We're conditioned to be conditioned. We're conditioned to be put in the box . . . not to ruffle feathers or make waves. "Sit down. Don't speak until you're spoken to." All of those things. I implore you to challenge that. I implore you to challenge that and break free. Do it kindly. You don't need to burn bridges. Work on your confidence. If your gut is saying that this doesn't feel right, that this situation, this conformity, this box that I'm put in doesn't feel right, then you've got to make moves. The only person to make those moves, and choose to make those moves, is you. So be okay with it. Try it out. Test it out. It isn't going to be the end of the world.

Donna
I think there are so many people living outside the box now that it's almost a mainstream thing, especially with having just had the pandemic, and so many people working remotely, who now don't want to not work remotely. They are, therefore, starting their own businesses so they can work remotely. I think we are at the pinnacle of working out of the box. Having a consulting business is not so out of the box. There are hundreds of thousands of people who do it every day. But I think in terms of figuring out what . . . each person has to figure out whatever the structure is that's right for them. That might be a different box, or no box, or not a traditional box. I think tons of people are doing that every day right now. It's one of the reasons that companies are having trouble finding good employees. A lot of the people who three years ago would have been good employees are thinking out of that box, and doing different things.

When you think about the number of people who have more than one job . . . the aide that I have coming to the house right now, three times a week, to help us, has five different jobs that she does. She was a yacht captain for many years. She's in her seventies now, but she still crews for this yacht captain every once in a while. She has an elderly client that she does health care for. She has multiple different sources of income that are completely unrelated. So here she is in her seventies, working totally outside of that traditional box, in a totally different way than someone like me.

When I was traveling three weeks out of every month, Frank said, "You need to hire some employees because you can't keep doing this all by yourself." I said, "Over my dead body will I have employees." He said, "Why?" And I said, "Because employees are a pain in the ass." "How can you say that? You're an HR person. That's blasphemy." "No, I can say it because I make a living fixing the problems that employees create. I don't want to have any employees creating problems for me." That was sort of a rogue response to him, because if I wasn't going to increase my staff, then the only way I could increase my income was either to create a source of residual income, or to keep raising my rates. Short of writing lots of books, which I'm not sure I want to do, the only way I can keep making more money is to keep raising my rates, and I'm okay with that.

So I think "out of the box" means different things for different people and what I see people doing today is recognizing a need, and filling it, and that could be totally out of the box in a lot of different ways . . . in delivery method, in how they cultivate clients, doing things completely remotely. That's not my bag. I want to have that face to face connection with people. I think it's very different for each individual. I wouldn't even attempt to define what that would look like for someone else. I talk to people all the time who have brilliant ideas and I think, "Wow, I would never have thought of that." So, I think that's a case by case basis. There's out of the box boring, almost mainstream, and then there's "wow" out of the box. Those people are way ahead of me.

You answered that very much about business. Do you have any thoughts in general, about living your life out of the box?

I think Frank and I live a very out-of-the-box life. One of the things we were both looking for in a mate was someone who was a workaholic, because we both are. It was really important to have someone who was as committed to their profession as each of us was. In our first ten years of marriage, we just worked like dogs.

When I turned forty, that's when I started having health issues, and my best friend died, and she was fifty-five. I came home one day and I said to Frank, "Okay, I have news. We are going to stop this merry-go-round ride that we're on, and we're going to change our whole lifestyle." His eyes almost jumped out of his head, and he said, "What do you mean?" I said, "I mean, we're going to stop living to work and we're going to start working to live." He replied, "I have no idea what that means." I said, "It means we're going to start adding a week of vacation every year until you tell me your business is out of control, and then we'll back it up a little, because life is too short, and we're working our asses off, waiting for the day we get to enjoy it, and that day starts now. I'm going to start planning vacations a year in advance. When I put down a deposit, it means we are not backing out of that. We're not canceling it. We're not postponing it for any client, for any project, for any volunteer work. We're living our life first, and doing everything else second." And he said, "Okay." We got to the point where we were traveling five months out of the year before he said, "I've lost control of my business." That was my turn to say "Okay," and I backed it up to three months, and that's what we've done ever since.

We travel approximately three months out of every year, sometimes a little more. So we say to people, we feel like we're semi-retired in some respects, because when we're here, we work like dogs, but, when we go on a six-week vacation, we're living it up. When you're gone that long, you can actually tune out work if you want to. You can leave it behind if you want to. Now, with all the technology, we take it with us wherever we go, which enables us to go for longer, because as long as we're connected, people don't care where we are, as long as they can get us and we can deliver what they need.

So I think we live a very out-of-the-box life and have for the last twenty years, since we made the decision that we were going to have the work/life balance everyone else dreams about, and drools over, and says, "Wow, I wish we could live like the Horkeys." I feel like we're living "the life" and it's a very out-of-the-box life. I talk to doctors, I talk to attorneys, and they say, "I could never be gone for a month. I don't know how you could do that." We can do it. We've created the model and the staff. When Frank lost the Tribe, he went from twenty-five employees to eight employees, overnight. When we decided to change that business model further, he cut it back to six employees: his six most seasoned, most highly-compensated employees that he could leave in charge of stuff. Then the technology enabled him to continue to be in charge of it himself, no matter where we were. So, you know, I think we are living the life that people dream of living . . . that out-of-the-box life, and we're very lucky.

Wei

I forget the name of the person that this is attributed to, but I greatly value the advice in the "Wear Sunscreen" song, that's been going around the internet for decades. Actually, can you repeat the question?

Author repeated the question.

Right. So the "Wear Sunscreen" speech, I'll call it that . . . one of the things it suggests to its listeners is to do one thing every day that scares you. And I think where I have taken that, or what I have learned from that, has been immeasurable because we, by way of our own biases, by being aware of our own perspectives, tend to favor one course of action, or one way of thinking, or just simply, we create habits. Since I first heard that speech, I have done one thing every day that scares me. One thing that basically counters my natural inclinations. As a result, I've seen things that I normally would not have seen. I have done things that I'd have normally not done, like ride a roller coaster, put myself outside of my comfort zone, which forces me to live outside my box, my bubble. It's easy for us to do the same thing over and over, to do what's safe for us. But it's another to intentionally force ourselves to look at a problem, to look at that box and ask, "All right, well, what's outside that box today? What's this other person . . . what might this person be seeing when looking at that box?" So I think there's immense value in doing that; so that you can challenge not only your internal beliefs, but challenge the world's beliefs.

The "Wear Sunscreen" speech that he referred to is an essay by Mary Schmich, originally published in June 1997 in the *Chicago Tribune*. It's a written commencement speech, providing various pieces of advice for living a happier life. Baz Luhrmann later created a spoken word song, using the text as lyrics. The original essay, as well as Luhrmann's song, along with a number of parodies, may be found by searching the internet.

Gabriel

Ooooh, that's quite a question. It's hard. It's really hard. It's hard because there are only so many hours in the day. When you're working in a certain role, or you're fulfilling a certain role, whether it's in a company, or in a person's life, or in a family, or whatever, that's already taking up some time. We only have so much energy. I also think that we all sort of want to submit to the box to some degree. Everybody wants to be free, but being free is scary, too. I guess maybe that's an interesting place to begin, with some kind of answer, which is just recognizing the ways in which you collude with the box, or what you're getting out of the box. It doesn't have to be all bad. I don't mean to sh*t on corporate life or traditional paths. I think these things are excellent in their own way and they can be wonderful. There are people who have had the most fulfilling corporate careers. It's amazing. So I say that partly to qualify this whole conversation. I'm a creative person and I haven't been conventional, but that doesn't mean that I think it's the only way to live. Believe me, there have been times when I would have loved to be part of a structure. But to live out of the box in a structured world, maybe is recognizing whether that box is serving you, or not serving you, or what you're getting out of it, and what you wish you could get out of it, that you're not getting.

I'm trying to put myself in the position of . . . I guess I can only go into my own position, like when I was at Deloitte, in that first consulting role, and I knew, "This is not my box," but I didn't have a better box. I just stepped off of that path. It's a really good question, and I appreciate that it's really hard. When I think about some of the darker moments of the last decade, they've been me asking myself "Who are you? You don't have this job, but you didn't want that job. So do you want the job or do you not want the job? No, I don't want the job. Great." Then you have to be willing to be kind of raw in the process. I think the allure, or the comfort, of the box can be the identity piece. I keep coming back to that.

I do think that maybe part of the answer is figuring out what you really have to offer. I know it's so simple and it's kind of trite, but it's true. If you have something to offer, that only you can offer, in the way that you offer it, which is an important distinction . . . I don't think there's any skill or talent out there that millions of people couldn't offer, but it's amazing how few people can offer it in the way that *you* can offer it, and that takes some development. By that I mean, how many comedy writers are there in L.A.? Thousands of them. But the ones that probably . . . and I'm not even saying they're necessarily going to make a ton of money, or that it's going to be an easy road, but the ones you respond to, and who tend to get work, are comedic in this very specific way. Or, they work in a way that's loving and productive and passionate. That's really important to me.

I have a friend who, coincidentally, quit Google to be a writer for companies. She's a ghostwriter for brands and she'll write anything from their pitch decks to articles to . . . she ghost wrote a book about marketing for some business people. In a way, that's a creative role, but it's a little bit of a commodity. There's a job out there called Copywriter, or called Editor, and that's what she does, but she's a very loving, present, curious, hardworking, productive, funny person, and that all seeps into the way she writes, and the way she collaborates with people. She gets a ton of work because of it. She's a good writer, no doubt about it. She has to be. But I don't think she's as successful as she is just because she's a good writer. I think it's because she figured out this thing she could offer, but she offers it in the way that only she can offer it. She is a person who comes to mind when I think about stepping outside of the box in a structured world, who was terrified. She asked, "Am I really about to leave Google to go be a writer who . . .?" and she rented a house in the woods . . . before the pandemic . . . two hours outside of San Francisco . . . a very unconventional life. She's not just surviving, she's doing quite well. She offers a skill that, in a way, is very traditional. She's not doing Reiki healing in the woods, which by the way, would be fine, and she'd be great if she wanted to do that, but she's offering something that real companies need, from real solid people, and she's on her own. She's off the map. She's in the Wild West, a.k.a. freelancing.

I hope that illustrates what I'm really trying to say, which is maybe the way to step outside the box in a highly structured world is to know how to operate in that structured world just fine, because it's necessary and it's appropriate, but maybe to get to a point where you take your assets seriously enough, and you develop them to a point, and offer them in a way that maybe allows you to do it on your own terms. Again, it doesn't have to be that way. I don't think she's any better than somebody who shows up to an office five days a week. It's not like one is the right way and one is the wrong way. But if you want to live life on your own terms, it probably has to be because you have something unique and meaningful to offer. That is a whole journey. That takes work and it's an ongoing process.

Steve

I think there are two things. You have to have a sense of humor about everything. Sometimes it can be self-deprecating a little bit. Sometimes I find that helps, at least for me. Maybe a sense of humor and not taking things so seriously . . . the adage "Don't sweat the small stuff, because it's all small stuff." That is one of the big things. Chill out a little bit. I'll use that to encompass a sense of humor and not taking things too seriously. That's one thing.

I think the other thing is something that I still work on to this day . . . confidence. Be confident in what you're doing and know that what you're doing, what you want to do, where you see yourself, is all about you and isn't about fitting into everyone else's expectations. I love what I do, and that has to be enough, because really, when it comes down to it, in any moment, that's what it is. Are you okay with it? Do you love it? Do you love what you do? Are you happy? Are you moving forward? And if not, are you happy where you are? That's okay too. It's not about anyone else's expectations. I go through enough bullsh*t with myself, that I don't need to add on what anyone else thinks about how I should do something or where I should be at fifty-five years old.

Victoria

Hmmmm. I think one of the things that people need to do, and do more of, is to bring up creativity first thing in the morning. I'm a big fan of doing three pages, and I literally will take a half sheet of scrap paper and I will write every day. I'll write out three pages, and it may be, excuse my candidness, "This is sh*t. What the hell am I doing?" It's just kind of like flow, flow, flow. Then all of a sudden, it's "Yoga. Yoga is a business. Yoga is . . . I love being an event planner," or, "Event planner and you bring in wellness . . . what does wellness mean?" And then writing about the dimensions of wellness. It might be just something like that, just writing it out. Then it may be something like, "Life doesn't happen organically." It can happen organically, and unfortunately, we often rely a lot on it being organic. I was thinking about that this morning. I'm going off on a tangent here . . . I raised my daughter pretty much organically, a go-with-the-flow kind of attitude, and now, seeing her kids, I realize that there needs to be a little strategy. There needs to be more strategy than I used. Growing up, for me, it wasn't that way. It was kind of organic. That's just the way it was. So that's how I did it. I think there's a big transition in generations now.

So I think, number one tip, do the pages . . . write creatively to live outside of the box. Find things that interest you. What is that? Is it yoga? Is it wellness? What are you passionate about, or even just have interest in? You don't have to be totally passionate about it, but find out. Explore that. Today we have so many more tools available. For instance, YouTube . . . I'm a huge YouTuber, as my grandson says. I love YouTube. Recently, I taught myself how to crochet. I had an interest in that, so I researched it on YouTube. I want to eat healthy, so I type in something like that, and it's at my fingertips. Find out what you have interest in, outside of the box, and start exploring. There's no investment. It's just your time, right? It doesn't cost anything to go out and Google something, or to watch a YouTube video, and then say, "Okay, this is something I might have an interest in."

And start thinking about your future. I know this is so cliche . . . setting your goals three years out, five years out, ten years out. But start thinking further out than where you are today. What would you like to do? Would you like to live comfortably? You may not know what that means, but you know you want to do it, and then start thinking, how can you get from point A to point B? Those are some of my tips. That's what I would do. And talk to people. Talk, talk, talk, talk, talk to people.

Jesus

Get rid of labels. Stop labeling yourself. Whatever your name is, whatever name you chose, that's who you are. I'm Jesus. Follow your gut, whatever your gut tells you. If you want to be an actor, figure out how to be an actor. If you want to be trans, be trans. Some people consider me non-binary because sometimes I use purses. I like purses, and I like wigs. That's the only thing I've ever envied about women, that they can change their hair all the time. It can be longer, it can be shorter, it can be blonde, it can be brown . . . and purses. I've never really been into makeup or anything like that. Sometimes I use a purse and people will ask, "Are you non-binary?" I say, "Well, I identify as male, but yeah, sure, non-binary, that's fine. I don't care." So at this point, it doesn't really matter if I identify as he or they or who cares.

"I'm Jesus. It's nice to meet you."

I had one person, who is from my generation, say "My issue is are you gay?" I said, "Yes." He said, "So, for example, if you're not identifying as male, I don't know if you're gay, bisexual, or straight. So how do I know if you like me?" I said, "Well, I'd tell you. I'd say, "Yeah, I like you. I think you're hot. And I'd like to have a relationship, or sleep with you, or whatever." And then you would let me know if you consent to that. That's it. It's that simple." He replied "Yeah, but then what if you end up leaving for a woman?" "Well, what if I end up leaving for a guy? What if I end up leaving for nobody? What if I just left?" There's always going to be a certain level of uncertainty. So let's get rid of the labels.

Follow your gut. Do what brings you joy. If you do that, you will always be outside the box. How could you not be, because structure, to me, is your parents telling you to study to be a lawyer. You know, we always hear that. "I want you to study to be a lawyer or a doctor or . . .." "What if he doesn't want to be a lawyer or a doctor? What if he wants to work at a record shop for the rest of his life, selling records, selling vinyl? What if that makes him happy?" "Yeah, but he doesn't make a lot of money doing that." "Well, what if he does that and he Ubers and then he lives in a little efficiency apartment in Hialeah and he's content? If he's happy, that's all that matters." To me, that's going against structure. Even if you decided to be a lawyer and you studied to be a lawyer, but you were a lawyer who identified as non-binary, or you were a lawyer who fought only for civil rights, or LGBTQ rights, or you were a lawyer for forty years and then decided you don't want to be a lawyer anymore, you want to be a fireman, do it. I just think whatever makes you happy, follow your gut, get rid of the idea of the "should." I should do this. I should be this. I should . . . should nothing! Whatever your heart tells you, that's what you go after.

Michael
Don't take anything personally and don't take anything as representing

the value of who you are. If you're living in a car while everybody around you is graduating college, getting a home, living life the "textbook way," don't let that define you. A lot of people would let that put a negative energy on them. Don't think you're less of a person, or less successful, because you're not doing what everybody else is doing at the moment.

My friend, that same guy, David Healy, told me the other day that he didn't know I was living in my car at that point in time. He didn't know until after. That's not something I really went around and openly told to a lot of people. He said, "Dude, how did you . . . you were living in your car and your energy, your attitude . . . nothing changed. You would think most people, if you're living in your car, something about them would change." He told me that nothing about me changed at all, which, like I said, I wasn't doing intentionally or unintentionally. I was just living. So I think for a lot of people, if you're living outside the box and you see all these things that you're "supposed" to be doing, don't put a value on them. Don't put negative energy onto yourself because of that. You're still a high-quality human being. You're still doing what you think you should be doing, which is, I think, the strongest thing you can do as a person.

CHAPTER 19: WE'RE NOT THE ONLY ONES

Well before I had the courage to reach out to Gabriel Mizrahi and ask him if he'd consider being interviewed for this project, I heard an episode of *The Jordan Harbinger Show* podcast (I'm an avid listener) that popped out to me as totally relevant to this book. Actually, there are many episodes that are relevant and topical to this book. Regardless, I took a shot and emailed Jordan, explaining the premise of the book and asked if he'd consider allowing me to reprint that specific "Feedback Friday" episode's question, along with his, and Gabriel's, replies. To my delight, he said "Yes."

What follows is a portion of the transcript, direct from the show's website, starting at forty-two minutes and sixteen seconds, of episode #696 of *The Jordan Harbinger Show*, graciously provided by the man himself, Jordan Harbinger.

Gabriel Mizrahi: Hey, Jordan and Gabe. I'm a guy who has good, common sense. I'm generally well-liked and I run a moderately successful small business with 20 people who work for me. But the thing is I constantly feel inferior. I'm 41, and I feel like I should be a millionaire or a multimillionaire. I'm extremely frugal. I drive a 2003 car with 219,000 miles on it. I live comfortably on $50,000 per year. My wife and three kids are wonderful and supportive and my extended family is supportive too. Regardless though, I can't help but feel like a dud of a firecracker. Partly, because I consume so many business books, case studies, podcasts, and pieces of advice from my network. In fact, I had to take a break from listening to your show for a while, because I couldn't take one more interview with a wildly successful person. How do I handle surrounding myself with successful people when they often cause me to feel completely inferior? Signed, Leveling Up Without Spiraling Down.

Jordan Harbinger: So I love this. This is a really brave email.

Gabriel Mizrahi: Yeah.

Jordan Harbinger: And I am so glad you shared it with us. I love this question because candidly, I often feel the exact same way that you do. This, whatever it is, affects a lot of people, including and maybe especially people who consider themselves medium-to-high performers or just are medium-to-high performers.

So I have a few thoughts here. First of all, as we know, comparing ourselves to other people is horrible for our mental health. That impulse is wired into our brains. It's in our conditioning, it's in our culture. So it is very normal and it is extremely hard to shake. You can't just not look around at the other Homo sapiens and wonder how you're measuring up, where you're falling short. This is a tribal thing with millions of years of evolution and thousands of years of culture behind it. Plus the Internet plus social media, plus advertising and media and all that toxic crap, like this podcast that magnifies our worst tendencies. Okay, this podcast doesn't magnify your worst tendencies, but still, so it's not a personal failing on your part if you succumb to it from time to time. Really don't beat yourself up for that. It's designed this type of media, social media, and the Internet it's designed to make you miserable on some level to hook your attention. And again, I have fallen into that more times than I can count. So that's the first thing.

And if you want to know why we compare ourselves to other people so much and how you can rewrite that pattern, I recommend checking out the deep dive Gabe and I did on that exact topic a few years ago. That was episode 22, going way back into the vault there. We'll link to that in the show notes. Also this whole feeling miserable when you see successful people think that is directly tied to hustle culture. Those ridiculous motivational videos on YouTube, those annoying Instagram posts about running eight miles at five in the morning, those blog posts that talk about, you know, "Crushing it 24/7, or you're never going to be truly successful." That's hustle culture. It is deeply toxic. I hate it. In fact, I hate it so much that Gabe and I did a whole deep dive on that too — why hustle culture makes you miserable, how to break out of it and how to find self-help sources, personal development sources that'll build you up instead of tearing you down. That was recent episode 682, and we'll link to that in the show notes as well.

The last thing I want to say is despite everything you said in your email, you are impressive, man. First of all, you sound like a solid human being, people like you, you have a good head on your shoulders. You run a successful business with 20 employees. You're down to earth. You're responsible. I mean, come on, you are doing great. I'm not trying to invalidate how you feel, because I know that this stuff is really insidious and it has a way of getting inside your head. But you have to balance that with a healthy understanding of who you really are and what you've accomplished. By the way, you're almost certainly a millionaire if you count the value of your business. I know that's not what you meant, but like, look, if you want to split hairs and get in a definition, that'll make you sleep easier at night, you almost for sure are at least a millionaire if not a multi-millionaire with twenty employees in your business.

Also, what matters to you, man? It's easy to look at some d-bag Internet market or checking his crypto wallet on a 747. By the way, that guy's crying right now. So don't worry about those guys right now. If you're listening to this and it's even remotely, the time that this episode was released, the crypto guys are the least of your concerns. The 747 crypto dudes, those guys flex online, all that crap is fake most of the time. I'm not even going to get into that. It's just really easy to look at that and then look at your life and go, "Man, I'm not on a plane. I must be behind. I'm not posting my monthly cash flow statements to Instagram or TikTok," but that's when you have to take a step back. And remember how you define success, not in some hokey, like you decide who, whatever, that kind of stuff. I don't know about you, but having an amazing, you got three awesome kids, a thriving company, a family that loves and supports you, in my book, you are successful. That's not even just like consolation prize. That is the whole point of life, level of success.

Gabriel Mizrahi: Yeah.

Jordan Harbinger: And I promise you that is the stuff that matters when sh*t hits the fan. And that's the stuff that people remember when you are gone. That's what they remember. And look, I'm not saying you can't want more out of life. I'm not saying don't strive for bigger and better things if that's what you. I'm just saying you can't fall into the trap of pegging yourself worth to other people or their ideas or to the values of a largely corrupt society. Be a millionaire. Go for it. I love it. Just don't do it because some jerk on the Internet told you to do it or worse made you feel bad if you didn't do it. And when you do go after your goals, remember that money is just one metric of success. And it's usually the least interesting metric of success. Who you are as a person, what you put out into the world to earn that money, that is the real value. Money is just a byproduct. I know it's easy to say but look at people who earn their money in a way that's kind of crappy.

Gabe. Let me ask you this.

Gabriel Mizrahi: Mmm.

Jordan Harbinger: Have you ever met anybody who made a bunch of money in porn?

Gabriel Mizrahi: Yes.

Jordan Harbinger: You have?

Gabriel Mizrahi: Mm-hmm.

Jordan Harbinger: Yeah. Were they forthright about it?

Gabriel Mizrahi: Not particularly.

Jordan Harbinger: Not really, right?

Gabriel Mizrahi: Mm-hmm.

Jordan Harbinger: No. And I guarantee you that most of you out there have met a bunch of people who've made their money in porn, but they didn't freaking tell you because they're shame attached to it. They're not proud of it. Or if they are other people are judging them for it. Nobody's looking at your business and going, "Oh man, shame on that guy. How dare he do it?" There's something to be said for that. And I know there's shameless scammers all over the Internet that seem to not care, but how well respected are those guys by the people that count? I'm not so sure, man, Internet seventeen-year-olds love them, but you know, are they really respected? Not a lot of the time.

So all that said. I know the comparison stuff is brutal. So I'm proud to announce that my next interview, it's with my friend's cousin, Chad. He lives in his Aunt Margaret's basement. He's currently between jobs. He's trying to become a pro-gamer. That should help put things in perspective, man. You can compare yourself to that guy.

CHAPTER 20: FINAL WORDS OF WISDOM

Is there anything I haven't asked you that you want to share or discuss that you feel is relevant and helpful to this conversation?

Brian

If I said it before, I apologize . . . I am a "jump-in-the-deep-end, then figure-it-out" person. I am a "Hey, you want to do that thing? Great. Let's figure out how to do that thing by starting to do the thing, not figuring out every little micro-beat leading up to it." Now, everybody operates on a different level. I'm a deep-end jumper. My husband is a tiptoe, shallow-ender . . . two different ends of the spectrum. But we balance each other so well because I make him . . . his friend said to us one time, "You make him live for today, but he makes you save for tomorrow," which is a very good assessment of our relationship. In the meantime, if it's something you want to do, do it, try it, attempt it. You're never going to realize the value of it if you don't even get off the ground. This is especially true in the world of performing. I have a really hard time when I ask someone, "What do you do?" and the reply is, "I'm an actor," and I'll say, "Oh, what's the last audition you went on?" "Oh, I haven't auditioned in ten years."

I'm not saying you have to be in a show to be an actor, but you have to actively be trying to be an actor to call yourself an actor. You wouldn't say, "Oh, I'm a businessman, if the last time you worked in a business was twenty years ago." That's something, especially in the entertainment world, that's always rubbed me the wrong way. Being an actor can mean a multitude of things to a multitude of different people. But if you are not actively trying to do that thing, don't say that that's what you do. You can be a waiter, you can be . . . whatever it is that you are actively doing at that time is what you are.

Lisa

Part of my journey is learning not to apologize for who I am, or how I feel, or what I think, or what I know. My biggest piece of advice is to have an open, loving heart, and be unapologetically yourself.

Sabrina

I was actually thinking about . . . I re-read what you sent me, your original email, asking if I'd be a part of this book, and you were talking about, "Is there company loyalty anymore? Is there job loyalty anymore?" I was thinking about that because I keep hearing that come up in the social conversations that we're having now that . . . let me rephrase. We were having them when you and I were in that field, growing up. But I like what you said about you and I being part of that small generation that doesn't really have a name. We're right before the Millennials, but right at the end of Generation X. We are the transition generation. I think about that all the time. We are that generation that saw all of this change happen. I can see where the Boomers are coming from, but I can also see where the Gen X-ers and the Millennials and the Gen Z-ers are coming from. I can see everybody's point of view on this.

I think we are technically Gen X based upon the dates.

I think so.

We're on the cusp.

I know, I feel like five or six years of our lifetime just got left off of that scale. Sometimes I'm called a Millennial, sometimes I'm called Gen X. I think that's the point. We're in this gray area of a generation of people who grew up watching the social transition happen right in front of our eyes. We are probably the most adaptable generation, I think. I believe that. We've lived through how many recessions . . . how many wars? We've watched society change, and the societal message that we give to people change. We've watched the growth of more acceptance, but also more hate. We've also learned how to navigate the economy in many different ways. We've learned how to navigate all of these jobs, which is the thing that brought me to the point of this . . . we were brought up by the generation that said you stay in a job, you earn your benefits, you get your 401(k), and then you retire. That's not the reality anymore. The work environment, ever since we started working . . . I've been working since I was thirteen . . . we've been working since we were very young . . . the work environment has changed. Jobs are not what they used to be. There's no such thing as company loyalty because that doesn't exist anymore. You don't get a job and stay there for twenty-five years anymore.

Employee loyalty is also not a thing.

Correct, it doesn't exist anymore. It goes both ways. I worked at Conifer for eleven and a half years, and I watched people come and go from that place, and then all of a sudden, out of nowhere, they shut us down, and everybody was out of a job because it was cheaper to do that. So when they talk about how nobody wants to work anymore, and there's no employee loyalty, I think "No, no, this is the capitalistic environment that we're trying to navigate right now. The job scene has changed and we have to adapt to it, which means employers have to adapt to it. If you want employee loyalty, you need to offer something more than you used to offer in the past." I think that's the message that keeps getting lost somehow. It's just very one-sided. It's not a sustainable way of living anymore, for people like us who are just trying to pay our bills.

I think the younger generation, to sound like an old lady for a minute, these kids already know that going into the work environment. They already know, because they grew up in it. They know what the work environment is. They have no loyalty going in because they're going to job hop, and job hop, until they find something that works for them. Technology has changed too, and the work environment has changed with technology. We are part of that generation that watched it happen. I think it's interesting you're writing this book now because we are that adaptable generation that learned how to navigate this market well before the kids did. And we're the ones that kind of taught them how to do it. They watched us do it. Now they're going into this environment that's been created for them. Our parents created this environment. Our grandparents created it. So we had to inherit it and figure out how to adapt to it so we could pass those lessons down. I rambled a bit. Does that make sense?

Yes. I think every generation is passing along something.

For sure they are, and the next generation is going to pass some information down that we didn't have. That's how it should be. We should be passing it down to make it better, one would think. But who knows what's going to happen in the next fifty years? So, as I said, I was reading that thing you wrote about company loyalty and I thought the answer is "No. Of course there's not, anymore, because there's no employee loyalty." I was at Conifer for eleven and a half years and it was just gone because it was cheaper to shut us down. Why would I stay loyal to that?'

How many movies have we seen with that same scenario?

Yeah, right. That's just the environment we live in and we have to be very realistic about it. What I'm loving about the shift in the working world right now, and that I'm loving watching happen, is it has now become more of an employee's market, where we have all the options to choose who we want to work for.

Employers have started to . . . not all of them . . . there's still a lot of resistance and there always will be. That, I think, is natural. It's human to resist change. But employers, companies as a whole, are starting to learn that they're going to have to offer more to keep good employees. A lot of employers are starting to catch on to the idea that you have to catch up to the times. You have to be more adaptable, technologically. You have to be more adaptable to a better working environment. You have to pay more. You can't expect things to be the way they were because the economy doesn't match the way things were, either. I hate the argument, "Oh, back in my day I was able to go to college, buy a house . . .." I think, "Back in your day, college cost five hundred dollars, and a house cost three thousand dollars, and the minimum wage hasn't increased in almost fifteen years." So, the argument has shifted to the worker. It's more of a workers' environment now, where the workers have a little bit more control than they used to have. I'm kind of enjoying watching it. I'm kind of enjoying wondering what's going to happen. Are these employers going to catch on, or are they going to go out of business because they can't keep the doors open? What's going to happen?

Chris

I have no idea how to answer that question, since my answer is that I'm still figuring that out. I think when it comes to careers, everybody does have their own path, and what defines success for one person is not going to be success for another. And that idea of success may change or may stay the same, but operates under different parameters, depending on the conditions. That's the thing . . . nothing in life stays the same, ever. And no two people are alike. So defining a career, success, and individual pathways is really difficult because as human beings . . . I am a person who's kind of all over the place, and have been my entire life. Then there's somebody else who goes in one direction, and then makes an abrupt career change, at a certain point in their life, and then continues on that new trajectory . . . or has that moment three times. I think it's interesting because you never know how the individual is going to shape the circumstances, or how the circumstances are going to shape the individual, because it goes both ways.

Daphne

Awwww, now this is interesting. You've got some good questions that make people go "hmmmm." I have to think about that. I like that. I don't think there's anything missing. I feel like you've touched on more than I anticipated in questions. I love that I didn't have the questions ahead of time because it allowed it to be, as you said, so organic, and just come from the heart and not thought through in advance.

And I actually did . . . earlier today, I looked back at what you sent me and have been thinking about it, but it wasn't about that. It was about answering the questions. And I liked that. I like that format of whatever you're asking, thinking about it at that moment, and letting it be . . . what comes forth then.

Thank you. I hope the readers will do that, too.

Heather

Hmmmm. Yeah. I would say if you're happy in your life, and where you're at, how do you double down and squeeze just a little more juice out of it? If you're unhappy, don't be afraid to make a move. But first, do some digging, do some journaling, do some documenting. Try to find the root of the unhappiness. Conversely, you can find the path to joy. Every single experience has led you up to this point. Wherever you want to take it from there, move forward with confidence, my friend, and don't ask for permission!

Donna

I'll just come back to the title of that best seller, *Do What You Love and the Money Will Follow*. I see so many kids getting out of college who are just about "What can I do to make the most money?" I even see people thinking about starting consulting practices later in their careers, who are so focused on "How much money can I make?" and I keep responding, "Well, what are you good at? What do you like to do, and how do you make a business out of that and make money at it? Because if you're not great at it, if you don't love it, how will you force yourself to work like a dog at it? If you don't love doing it, if you don't feel a sense of satisfaction at the end of the day doing it, why would you want to get up tomorrow and do it again?" It's the piece of advice that's so obvious, and yet most of them ignore it. That's why they fail. One of things I learned at the National Speakers Association was that if somebody asks for your advice, if somebody asks you to share your secrets to success that you've learned along the way, that you've learned the hard way, give it all away. Answer every question they have. Because the fact is, when they hear how hard it is to actually be successful, most of them won't do it, and a large percentage of the ones who try will fail, because they won't follow the advice, because it may not seem intuitive to them. They'll do what they want instead of heeding the advice, and they'll fail. So, you can afford to be magnanimous and give away all the secrets, because most of them will never get that far.

I have lived that because I've had that lunch conversation, and phone conversation, and Zoom conversation with so many people who are very knowledgeable, but they can't make it in business because they don't follow that flow. They don't do the right things that they should be doing, and they don't make it. To start a business today, especially a consulting business, is much more challenging than when I started thirty-plus years ago, when there were fewer people doing it. The competition is a whole lot fiercer. You have to know what distinguishes you from all the other ones out there. If you can't explain that in three sentences, you're in trouble.

Wei
I think . . . well, let's see. I think that in regard to our organic selves, yes, we have to stay true to our own nature. I think reinforcing what has been said to me a lot is that you should figure out what your path is, but definitely make sure that you find mentors along the way.

A lot of things that have been told to me, over the course of decades, have stuck with me. And they were all said by well-intentioned people that shared their life experiences and their wisdom, to help me off of ledges. I think back to one person that, when I was ready to quit being a government employee, because I went from being a system admin, somebody who actually turned the knobs on systems, to to being a PowerPoint Ranger, really helped me. I literally was about to resign when that mentor of mine said that the best was yet to come, and that I should have patience and see what opportunities were ahead of me. And I did. Rather than quitting six months into a job, I stuck it out and I've been a government civilian now for almost fourteen years, and it's been amazing. The things that I've been able to do have been incredible. Unfortunately, he's long since passed, but I can still hear him, clear as day, telling me to have patience. Here's the kicker . . .

come to find out, he was a civil rights leader, and if I Google search his name, I can find a photo of him being hosed down in California during the civil rights movement. In that iconic photo, he was one of the recipients of that fire hydrant hose.

Gabriel

As time has gone on, I think I've only seen myself succeed when I invite more of myself to the table. When I was directing that short film a few weekends ago, which was probably the most significant professional experience of my life, I was incredibly nervous . . . incredibly nervous. I wanted to do a good job. I'd never made a film before. I'd never directed before. I was working with people who are really good at what they do, from the crew to the actors to . . .. This project, in my mind, when I first set out to do it, was going to be simple and small. I knew it was going to be not great. It evolved into something . . . I just watched, for the first time, the footage last night and I thought, "Oh, this is a movie. This is a good movie," which I was not expecting. I was very, very nervous, and I had a moment, which might speak to your question . . . maybe three weeks before shooting . . . I'm not a particularly anxious person. I certainly have my moments, but I would say, in general, I probably get sad more than I get anxious. That's just the way I'm wired. But I was annnnn- xious. I couldn't sleep. I would fall asleep for an hour, wake up and be awake for half the night. I was having stress dreams. I think my heart rate was elevated for three weeks. And I just had this moment where I realized that between now and the shoot, I was not going to become a significantly better director. In fact, the only way I can become a better director at this point is by directing. So I needed to make peace with the fact that I was not going to be perfect. I was not going to know everything. I was not going to be great. I was going to make mistakes. Otherwise, I was going to miss this opportunity.

I was very lucky because I was surrounded by a lot of very experienced, talented people who just saved me and taught me. I had to ease into that. But basically, the corner I turned on that project was that you need to invite your ignorance and your fear into this process and not work so hard to cover them up. Now that doesn't mean that I need to go around the set telling everybody how incompetent I am and how afraid I am. That's a different thing. But there were many moments where I just turned to my producer and said, "I have no freaking idea. *What* did you just ask me? Can you . . . can you explain that?" And she would do that. Sometimes I even had to say, "I'm sorry. I think I understand eighty percent of it. Can you do it one more time?" And her reply was, "Sure. Here it is." There were moments when my actors would ask me a question, a really good question, and I would have to say, "Let me think about that for a moment. I don't know the answer to that. That's a really good question." And then two minutes later, I might say, "Okay, so here's what I think." Or I would say, "You know what? I don't know, but can we try it? Can we just try this take and let me see?" And it would be like that. For the first time in a very public setting . . . I wasn't just in my mind saying, "Okay, you're in touch with your nervousness". . . it's sort of like publicizing it to some degree, in a forum where there are sixty people on set and they're watching me do this job that I "should be good at." But I'm not. I'm not there *yet.* So it was extremely exposing, and I wouldn't call it pleasant, but in another way, it was kind of pleasant because I didn't have to cut off those parts of myself in order to do the job. Doing the job was getting in touch with those parts of myself and inviting them in.

I would say that in almost every respect, being in touch with my ignorance, and my fear, and my anxiety, and also my excitement, and my desire for it to go well, all of it, that's what makes the thing good. I think authenticity works, and absolutely is important. It's a little bit hard sometimes to know when to invite it out and how much. It doesn't mean you need to be on ten all the time with every thought and every feeling you have, but I think in general we only succeed . . . and I'm speaking now as a guy who was not in touch with this for a long time . . . we only succeed when we invite the most raw parts of our personalities to the table.

Steve

I don't know exactly how this applies, but one of the mottos, we kind of joke about it being a family motto, is "Anything worth doing is worth overdoing." It's kind of a tongue-in-cheek inside family joke . . . a little OCD and ADHD . . . "Anything worth doing is worth overdoing" is something that I do kind of keep in mind as I'm doing things. I don't know if it's a good thing or bad thing. Certainly, there are times where that's come in handy, and why I probably work as hard as I do on some projects that maybe I'm not getting as much out of as I would like. But I can't help it.

I appreciate having had this time with you because I truly feel a little bit . . . I don't know, a little bit better about myself and where I'm at. I tend to question myself even now. What do I want to do when I grow up? Again, I'm fifty five years old and I don't know what I want to do. I know I love what I do right now, but is this going to be all I do? I don't think so. I can't imagine that there isn't going to be another direction, or that I'm not going to do something else.

Don't be afraid to say screw it, and do what you want to do.

Victoria

This subject has been discussed with many others. Going out on a limb, I've expressed my point of view that your generation . . . yes, your's Matt . . . has it right. Why in the heck would anyone stay at a job or career longer than needed? Life is an experiment!

The way I look at it, you have, give or take, twenty more good years to explore what you want to do. An attorney, where I worked before, used the reference that the career choices at XYZ company were like a playground jungle gym . . . no clear path to get or do what you want to do. There are just so many opportunities available. You have the opportunity to go this way, or this way, or to learn this skill so you can get to here. I have told several people that have just started their careers at XYZ company, "Hey, if you're not where you want to be in three years, exit." Maybe I'm wrong in doing so, but that's my opinion.

When I'm asked my opinion, I'm going to give it.

I think that society today . . . think about the workforce, or anything in life, not just work. . . . your personal life . . . I think that people should be open to evolving into different human beings with different career paths. For instance, if people work for an organization that is a wonderful, wonderful organization . . . absolutely love it . . . their values and everything, they don't leave. They stay there for twenty-plus years. However, if you have a role that you're in and you want to advance to a different role, I think after a reasonable amount of time, if that doesn't happen, an individual should leave the organization and find a different career, or an opportunity to fulfill themselves.

We go to work, and we help them solve a problem, and they in turn give us a paycheck. But there's so much more than just a paycheck. It's peace of mind. It's for that individual's well-being, their happiness. And I'm not talking "ha ha" happy. I'm talking about fulfillment. I need to feel like I'm making you change as an individual. I need to feel like I'm solving problems. If you get to the point where you feel like you're not solving problems, and they're not helping you fulfill your own desires, and needs, then I think it's time to move on and find something that does fulfill you.

It was interesting . . . somebody at the company I came from talked about how traditionally, in the day, it was a career path. You started here. You got to this rung on a ladder, this rung on a ladder, this rung on a ladder . . . but I think if you look at it sort of like that jungle gym, it isn't so linear now. If I was a thirty-year-old and I was deficient in one area, there are so many opportunities now to learn, and opportunities to learn that skill that motivates me to the next thing. Before, it was, "Okay, my boss says I'm working really hard, so I'll continue to work really hard, and they're going to move me up." I don't think that's gone. It should be.

I absolutely love this book idea, and it *will* resonate with, again, your generation, as well as future generations . . . those people that are still just beginning in the workforce. They have an opportunity. Now, with that being said, I have a concern. I don't understand how the next generation, or the generation that decides to move every three years, is going to plan for the future. How do they do that? I don't know. I guess it's just ignorance on my part. My husband and I have been able to amass enough to be able to retire a little bit early, and to start an adventure. I'm just curious how that will happen for them. How will they take care of that, those golden years, those retirement years?

Jesus

As I said before, I'm a determinist. I don't know if you're familiar with what that philosophy is, but basically it's this idea that when the Big Bang happened, it set in motion everything that would happen . . . it all happened at once. So I try to explain it to Eric in this way: you and I talking now . . . we're actually dead. We're just in the present. When the big bang happened, the past, the present, and the future all happened at once.

It's kind of like when you look at a star, you're really looking at something that's already dead. That's just the light from that sun reaching us, but that's been dead a long time. When the ball starts rolling, it hits this thing, that then hits that thing, that then causes a chain reaction. Some philosophers and scientists believe that everything that happens in your life is predetermined. There isn't anything you could have done to change it . . . nothing. Whether it's a good thing or a bad thing, life doesn't care. It's not giving you an illness because it hates you. That's just how it happened. It's not giving you a million dollars because it likes you more. That's just how it happened. So even if I could go back, let's say even if the Big Bang happened all over again, it would still happen the same way. That is the theory that some scientists believe. It is just a theory. We don't know. So everything that happened was supposed to happen this way. We can't control it.

If tomorrow I find out a show I was cast in isn't happening anymore, that was going to happen whether I wanted it or didn't want it. We think that we have some kind of control. We think we have some kind of choice. It's debatable for me. I think we do have a certain amount of control, but not overall. That's how I see my life now, where whatever happens is going to happen. However, I'm a thinking person. I don't know what's going to happen, so I act as if I can control the outcome. I'm going to go to the audition, because if I don't go, how am I going to possibly get a part? I don't like to think about, "Oh, this turn in your life was . . ." or, "Had that not happened, your life wouldn't have been . . .." Maybe if I had gone to therapy when I was younger, my life would be way better than it is, or maybe it'd be way worse. I have no idea. But, there are things that happened that led me to where I am. You don't have control, so you might as well follow what's in front of you, and what your heart tells you to do, at the time.

Michael

This is going to sound really basic, but remember that it can be hard sometimes. You're not always going to be having fun. You're not always going to love what you have to do. But I like to think that in the end, everything is always going to work out the way you want it to, if you just do the right things, and you do what you feel you should be doing. If you want to use golf as an example, when you're just learning how to golf, you're probably going to hate it a lot in the early stages, because it's not that easy to learn. But, eventually, if you keep putting in the work and doing what you feel you should be doing, you'll pick it up and you'll start enjoying it a lot more.

That could obviously be used as an example for anything in life. If you're learning a new skill, or if you want to go get a degree in something, or if you want to get a new job . . . any of that. I think it applies to all. If you just do what your heart thinks is the right thing to do, I like to think the world rewards you for that.

EPILOGUE

So what, exactly, is the point of sharing these stories? Yes, I did actually have a point when I started this project. At the end of our first of two interviews, Victoria turned the tables on me and said, "Let me ask you this . . . just because I want to be clear, that's all. It's just for clarity on my part. What problem are you solving with this book?"

"I don't know."

She replied, "What is it you want to accomplish with this? I'm not challenging you like, "Oh, my God, that sounds horrible," but I really would love to know a bit because I may want to gift the book to somebody . . . maybe somebody graduating from college."

I replied that I thought there were a lot of answers to this, and at the time of our interview, I told her that it was off the record. Now that I'm at the point of wrapping up this project I guess I'll put it out there. How can I not show a slight bit of myself after the wonderful interviewees, who participated in this project, did? This is what I said to her . . .

Part of it was simply to share my experiences. I don't know if it was to be a cathartic outlet or what. I think that was kind of the impetus as I've had a very nontraditional, non-linear career path, and have often found myself comparing myself to other people, often my parents, at certain benchmarks, or ages, in life. I certainly felt nowhere near where they were, in many regards. Now that I'm older, what's important is more along the lines of "Am I doing something worthwhile?" How many times have we heard the story of someone who is burnt out after five years on Wall Street, or working for a hedge fund, or whatever? Whether it be a true story, in a movie, on a T.V. show, in a book, or whatever, the question is "Why?" Why do that? You can still be successful, however you identify or describe that, without a traditionally-celebrated job, and actually be happy. I think if more people were not disgruntled employees, we'd all be happier. I don't

299

want to sound all kumbaya saying that the world would be a better place, but it would. I'm a capitalist. I'm all about capitalism. Great. But you should still be happy with what you're doing.

Victoria agreed.

I think another big part of writing this book is the timing. Coming out of this pandemic has been a challenge for the workforce. Why is it so challenging to find people to do work? Is it actually because people are lazy, or because they're still living on pandemic financial aid, or is it something else? So, as you're re-entering the workforce, think about doing something that you're good at which also makes you happy, because happiness will only help you do your job better.

Look, this book was originally going to be about my personal experiences, and at some point, I realized that there are so many other people who have nontraditional paths, whose stories are worth reading and from which others, including me, might learn. Maybe their experiences will spark something in readers, or provide an "aha" moment.

That's the short answer I gave Victoria.

I'll conclude with a number of thoughts on life from individuals far more insightful, or at least well-known than I.

> "Your time is limited, so don't waste it living someone else's life. Don't be trapped by dogma - which is living with the results of other people's thinking." - Steve Jobs

> "Life is ten percent what happens to you and ninety percent how you respond to it." - Charles Swindoll

> "Life is what we make it, always has been, always will be."
> - Grandma Moses

"Too many of us are not living our dreams because we are living our fears." - Les Brown

"I believe every human has a finite number of heartbeats. I don't intend to waste any of mine."
- Neil Armstrong

"Live as if you were to die tomorrow. Learn as if you were to live forever." - Mahatma Gandhi

"Every moment is a fresh beginning." - T.S. Eliot

"The best way to predict your future is to create it."
- Abraham Lincoln

"There are no mistakes, only opportunities." - Tina Fey

"It's never too late - never too late to start over, never too late to be happy." - Jane Fonda

"Be where you are; otherwise you will miss your life."
- Buddha

"You cannot control everything that happens to you; you can only control the way you respond to what happens. In your response is your power." - Anonymous

And, finally, since our lives are so integrated into our mobile telephones, I thought it most fitting to end with a thought from the man who invented the telephone . . .

"When one door closes, another opens; but we often look so long and so regretfully upon the closed door that we do not see the one that has opened for us."
- Alexander Graham Bell

ABOUT THE AUTHOR

In 2009, Matt May founded Verve Central Productions to provide quality entertainment and services to its clients and audiences through special events & entertainment, theatrical production, creative & business consulting, and education.

After several years of producing and facilitating corporate team building programs, on a freelance basis, Matt recognized that there was an alternate way to provide individuals and corporations with engaging, interactive experiences. As a result, he created Premier Team Building & Interactive Experiences®, in 2017, delivering programs nation-wide, and abroad. As the company's president, he is responsible for the design & development of its team building and interactive experiences, overseeing the production and facilitation of these programs, customer support, and staff training.

In addition to having produced and facilitated hundreds of large and small-group team building experiences, in his career, May has served as a producer, director, manager, administrator, educator, and consultant for various event and live entertainment, theatrical, and educational organizations.

A sought-after speaker and published author, Matt excitedly shares his passions and experiences with his books and presentations.

Matt is the co-author/producer of the award-winning theatrical musical comedy *Diego & Drew Say I Do*. He holds a Bachelor of Arts degree with a double major in Theatre Arts and Arts Administration, and a Master of Science degree in Interdisciplinary Arts.

Made in the USA
Columbia, SC
10 December 2023

27368788R00173